Analysing sociolinguistic variation

The study of how language varies in social context, and how it can be analysed and accounted for, are the two key goals of sociolinguistics. Until now, however, the actual tools and methods have been largely passed on through 'word of mouth' rather than being formally documented. This is the first comprehensive, 'how-to' guide to the formal analysis of sociolinguistic variation. It shows step-by-step how the analysis is carried out, leading the reader through every stage of a research project from start to finish. Topics covered include fieldwork, data organisation and management, analysis and interpretation, presenting research results and writing up a paper. Practical and informal, the book contains all the information needed to conduct a fully fledged sociolinguistic investigation, and includes exercises, checklists, references and insider tips. It is set to become an essential resource for students, researchers and fieldworkers embarking on research projects in sociolinguistics.

SALI A. TAGLIAMONTE is Associate Professor of Linguistics at the University of Toronto. Her research focuses on variation and change in the evolution of English. She is author of *African American English in the diaspora: tense and aspect* (with Shana Poplack, 2001).

KEY TOPICS IN SOCIOLINGUISTICS

Series editor:
Rajend Mesthrie, University of Cape Town.

This new series focuses on the main topics of study in sociolinguistics today. It consists of accessible yet challenging accounts of the most important issues to consider when examining the relationship between language and society. Some topics have been the subject of sociolinguistic study for many years, and are here re-examined in the light of new developments in the field; others are issues of growing importance that have not so far been given a sustained treatment. Written by leading experts, the books in the series are designed to be used on courses and in seminars, and include useful suggestions for further reading and a helpful glossary.

Already published in the series:
Politeness by Richard J. Watts
Language Policy by Bernard Spolsky
Discourse by Jan Blommaert

Forthcoming titles:
World Englishes by Rakesh Bhatt and Raj Mesthrie
Language and Ethnicity by Carmen Fought
Bilingual Talk by Peter Auer

Analysing Sociolinguistic Variation

SALI A. TAGLIAMONTE

CAMBRIDGE UNIVERSITY PRESS
Cambridge, New York, Melbourne, Madrid, Cape Town,
Singapore, São Paulo, Delhi, Tokyo, Mexico City

Cambridge University Press
The Edinburgh Building, Cambridge CB2 8RU, UK

Published in the United States of America by Cambridge University Press, New York

www.cambridge.org
Information on this title: www.cambridge.org/9780521778183

First published 2006
Third printing 2009

A catalogue record for this publication is available from the British Library

ISBN 978-0-521-77115-3 Hardback
ISBN 978-0-521-77818-3 Paperback

For Tara, Shaman, Freya and Dazzian
Love
Mom

Contents

Preface

The variationist approach to sociolinguistics began during the 1960s, when Labov, working with Uriel Weinreich, developed a theory of language change (Weinreich et al. 1968). Thereafter, Labov continued to advance the method and analysis of language variation and change, which today is often referred to as variation theory (e.g. Labov 1963, 1966/1982).

In the 1970s, one of Labov's graduate students at the University of Pennsylvania was Shana Poplack. In 1981, Shana became a professor of Sociolinguistics at the University of Ottawa's Department of Linguistics, the same year I entered the MA programme. I was fortunate to be Shana's student until I completed my Ph.D. dissertation in 1991. Everything you will read in this book has come directly from what has been passed on from this lineage – training, techniques, insights, knowledge, and sheer passion for the field. The entire period from 1981 to 1995 was an invaluable apprenticeship through my studies with Shana and our many collaborations (e.g. Tagliamonte and Poplack 1988, Poplack and Tagliamonte 1989, 1991). I also benefited tremendously from the influence of David Sankoff, whose input to my questions of method and analysis was innumerable.

Most knowledge and learning in variation theory has been acquired like this, passed on through word of mouth, from one researcher to the next (see also Guy 1988: 124). In fact, it has often been noted that the practical details of how to actually do variation analysis are arcane, largely unwritten and, for the most part, undocumented (but see Paolillo 2002). This is precisely why this book was conceived and has now been written. The method needed to be recorded, systematically, thoroughly and straightforwardly.

I had originally intended this book to be completed by the mid-1990s, but academic life is unforgiving for time and relentless for energy. The advantage is that I have had that many more years of experience. Between 1995 and 2005, I have trained some of the next generation of variationist sociolinguists and, as has always been the case, the students have helped the teacher learn a lot more than what she thought she already knew. Yet there is always room for improvement.

In completing this book, I requested 'no-holds-barred' comments from the best methodologists of my colleagues and students. I am indebted to Alex D'Arcy, Ann Taylor, Jennifer Smith and James Walker, who came through with the best feedback one could hope for – an intense amount of red ink. Through the Herculean efforts of my assistant Sonja Molfenter, who took on the unenviable role of 'book bulldog' during the revision process, I have taken all their comments into account, and then some. My own method has evolved in just this way, incrementally changing from one research project to the next, one student to the next, in my perpetual efforts to do things more usefully, more efficiently and more transparently. At the same time, the basics endure. The original ideas enshrined in Weinreich et al. (1968), built upon and elaborated by William Labov (Labov 1966/ 1982) herein are fundamental and pervasive. In sum, this book is simply one user's tried-and-true manual of best practice.

Notes on codes and abbreviations

Codes in parentheses refer to the community from which the data come (see abbreviations), followed by a single character speaker code which identifies the individual speaker in each community. In some cases additional information may appear, e.g. the audio-tape number. Abbreviations for communities are: BCK = Buckie; CLB = Cullybackey, Northern Ireland; CMK = Cumnock, Scotland; DVN = Devon, Southeast England; ESR = Ex-Slave Recordings; GYE = Guysborough Enclave; GYV = Guysborough Village, Nova Scotia; KID = a corpus of child language acquisition, England; MPT = Maryport, England; NPR = North Preston, Nova Scotia; OTT = Ottawa; ROP2–4 = data collected in Toronto, Canada, in the years 2002–2004 through the Research Opportunities Programs at the University of Toronto; PVG = Portavogie; ROO = Roots Corpus, data collected in remote communities in Northern Ireland, Lowland Scotland and Northwest England; SAM = Samaná, Dominican Republic; TIV = Tiverton, England; TOR = Toronto, Canada; WHL = Wheatley Hill, England; YRK = York, England. Abbreviations for additional corpora include ST1, ST2 and ST3 – all narrative data sets of Canadian English.

1 Introduction

This book is about *doing* variation analysis. My goal is to give you a step-by-step guide which will take you through a variationist analysis from beginning to end. Although I will cover the major issues, I will not attempt a full treatment of the theoretical issues nor of the statistical underpinnings. Instead, you will be directed to references where the relevant points are treated fully and in detail. In later chapters, explicit discussion will be made as to how different types of analysis either challenge, contribute to or advance the basic theoretical issues. This is important for demonstrating (and encouraging) evolution in the field and for providing a sense of its ongoing development. Such a synthetic perspective is also critical for evolving our research in the most interesting direction(s). In other words, this book is meant to be a learning resource which can stimulate methodological developments, curriculum development as well as advancements in teaching and transmission of knowledge in variation analysis.

WHAT IS VARIATION ANALYSIS?

Variation analysis combines techniques from linguistics, anthropology and statistics to investigate language use and structure (Poplack 1993: 251). For example, a seven-year-old boy answers a teacher's question by saying, 'I don't know nothing about that!' A middle-aged woman asks another, 'You got a big family?' Are these utterances instances of dialect, slang, or simply performance errors, mistakes? Where on the planet were they spoken, why, by people of what background and character, in which sociocultural setting, under what conditions? How might such utterances be contextualised in the history of the language and with respect to its use in society? This book provides an explicit account of a method that can answer these questions, a step-by-step 'user's guide' for the investigation of language use and structure as it is manifested in situ.

1

At the outset, however, I would like to put variationist sociolinguistics in perspective. First, what is the difference between sociolinguistics and linguistics? Further, how does the variationist tradition fit in with the field of sociolinguistics as a whole?

LINGUISTICS

The enterprise of linguistics is to determine the properties of natural language. Here, the aim is to examine individual languages with the intention of explaining why the whole set of languages are the way they are. This is the search for a theory of universal grammar. In this process, the analyst aims to construct a device, a grammar, which can specify the grammatical strings of one language, say English or Japanese, but which is also relevant for the grammar of any natural language. In this way, linguistics puts its focus on determining what the component parts and inner mechanism of languages are. The goal is to work out 'the rules of language X' – whether that language is English, Welsh, Igbo, Inuktitut, Niuean, or any other human language on the planet.

The type of question a linguist might ask is: 'How do you say X?' For example, if a linguist was studying Welsh, she would try to find a native speaker of Welsh and then she would ask that person, How do you say 'dog' in Welsh? How do you say 'The child calls the dog', 'The dog plays with the children', etc. This type of research has been highly successful in discovering, explaining and accounting for the complex and subtle aspects of linguistic structure. However, in accomplishing this, modern theoretical models of language have had to exclude certain things, consigning them to the lexical, semantic or pragmatic components of languages, or even outside of language altogether. For example, in a recent syntactic account of grammatical change, Roberts and Rousseau (2003: 11) state:

> Of course, many social, historical and cultural factors influence speech communities, and hence the transmission of changes (see Labov 1972c, 1994). From the perspective of linguistic theory, though, we abstract away from these factors and attempt, as far [sic] the historical record permits, to focus on change purely as a relation between grammatical systems.

In this way, linguistic theory focuses on the structure of the language. It does not concern itself with the context in which the language is learned and, more importantly, it does not concern itself with the way the language is used. Only in more recent forays have researchers begun to make the link between variation theory and syntactic theory (e.g. Beals et al. 1994, Meechan and Foley 1994, Cornips and Corrigan 2005).

SOCIOLINGUISTICS

Sociolinguistics argues that language exists in context, dependent on the speaker who is using it, and dependent on where it is being used and why. Speakers mark their personal history and identity in their speech as well as their sociocultural, economic and geographical coordinates in time and space. Indeed, some researchers would argue that, since speech is obviously social, to study it without reference to society would be like studying courtship behaviour without relating the behaviour of one partner to that of the other. Two important arguments support this view. First, you cannot take the notion of language X for granted since this in itself is a social notion in so far as it is defined in terms of a group of people who speak X. Therefore, if you want to define the English language you have to define it based on the group of people who speak it. Second, speech has a social function, both as a means of communication and also as a way of identifying social groups.

Standard definitions of sociolinguistics read something like this:

> the study of language in its social contexts and the study of social life through linguistics (Coupland and Jaworski 1997: 1)

> the relationship between language and society (Trudgill 2000: 21)

> the correlation of dependent linguistic variables with independent social variables (Chambers 2003: ix)

However, the many different ways that society can impinge on language make the field of reference extremely broad. Studies of the various ways in which social structure and linguistic structure come together include personal, stylistic, social, sociocultural and sociological aspects. Depending on the purposes of the research, the different orientations of sociolinguistic research have traditionally been subsumed by one of two umbrella terms: 'sociolinguistics' and 'the sociology of language'. A further division could also be made between qualitative (ethnography of communication, discourse analysis, etc.) and quantitative (language variation and change) approaches. Sociolinguistics tends to put emphasis on *language* in social context, whereas the sociology of language emphasises the *social* interpretation of language. Variation analysis is embedded in sociolinguistics, the area of linguistics which takes as a starting point the rules of grammar and then studies the points at which these rules make contact with society. But then the question becomes: How and to what extent? Methods of analyses, and focus on linguistics or sociology, are what differentiate the strands of sociolinguistics. From this perspective, variation analysis is inherently linguistic, analytic and quantitative.

VARIATIONIST SOCIOLINGUISTICS

Variationist sociolinguistics has evolved over the last nearly four decades as a discipline that integrates social and linguistic aspects of language. Perhaps the foremost motivation for the development of this approach was to present a model of language which could accommodate the paradoxes of language change. Formal theories of language were attempting to determine the structure of language as a fixed set of rules or principles, but at the same time language changes perpetually, so structure must be fluid. How does this happen? The idea that language is structurally sound is difficult to resolve with the fact that languages change over time.

> structural theories of language, so fruitful in synchronic
> investigation, have saddled historical linguistics with a cluster of
> paradoxes, which have not been fully overcome. (Weinreich et al.
> 1968: 98)

Unfortunately, because it is such a expansive field of research, sociolinguistics often comes across as either too restricting to social categories such as class, sex, style, geography (the external factors), or too restricting to linguistic categories such as systems, constraints and rate of change (the structural factors). In fact, when sociolinguistic research using variationist methods has shown a focus on the linguistic system, as opposed to the social aspects of the individual and context, it has garnered considerable criticism (e.g. Cameron 1990, Rickford 1999, Eckert 2000). More than anything this highlights the bi-partite underpinnings of the field (Milroy and Gordon 2003: 8). When attempting to synthesise both internal and external aspects of language, the challenge will always be to fully explore both. While this will likely always be tempered by researchers' own predilections, it is also the case that the research questions, data and findings may naturally lead to a focus on one domain over the other. Having said all this, the variationist enterprise is essentially, and foremost, the study of the interplay between variation, social meaning and the evolution and development of the linguistic system itself.

Indeed, as Weinreich et al. (1968: 188) so well described in their foundational work,

> Explanations of language which are confined to one or the other aspect – linguistic or social – no matter how well constructed, will fail to account for the rich body of regularities that can be observed in empirical studies of language behaviour . . .

This 'duality of focus' has been fondly described more recently by Guy (1993: 223) as follows:

> One of the attractions – and one of the challenges – of dialect research is the Janus-like point-of-view it takes on the problems of human language, looking one way at the organisation of linguistic forms, while simultaneously gazing the other way at their social significance.

In my view, variationist sociolinguistics is most aptly described as the branch of linguistics which studies the foremost characteristics of language in balance with each other – linguistic structure and social structure; grammatical meaning and social meaning – those properties of language which require reference to both external (social) and internal (systemic) factors in their explanation.

Therefore, instead of asking the question: 'How do you say X?' as a linguist might, a sociolinguist is more likely not to ask a question at all. The sociolinguist will just let you talk about whatever you want to talk about and listen for all the ways you say X.

Note

There is a distinct 'occupational hazard' to being a sociolinguist. You will be in the middle of a conversation with someone and you will notice something interesting about the *way* he or she is saying it. You will make note of the form. You will wonder about the context. You may notice a pattern. All of a sudden you will hear that person saying to you, 'Are you listening to me?' and you will have to say, 'I was listening so intently to how you were saying it that I didn't hear what you said!'

The essence of variationist sociolinguistics depends on three facts about language that are often ignored in the field of linguistics. First, the notion of 'orderly heterogeneity' (Weinreich et al. 1968: 100), or what Labov (1982: 17) refers to as 'normal' heterogeneity; second, the fact that language changes perpetually; and third, that language conveys more than simply the meaning of its words. It also communicates abundant non-linguistic information. Let us consider each of these in turn.

ORDERLY HETEROGENEITY

Heterogeneity is essentially the observation that language varies. Speakers have more than one way to say more or less the same thing. Variation can be viewed across whole languages, e.g. French, English, Spanish, etc. In this case, variation would be in the choice of one language or the other by bilingual or multilingual speakers. However, linguistic variation also encompasses an entire continuum of choices ranging from the choice between English or French, for example, to the choice between different constructions, different morphological affixes, right down to the minute microlinguistic level where there are subtle differences in the pronunciation of individual vowels and consonants. Importantly, this is the normal state of affairs:

> The key to a rational conception of language change – indeed, of
> language itself – is the possibility of describing orderly differentiation
> in a language serving a community . . . It is *absence* of structural
> heterogeneity that would be dysfunctional. (Weinreich et al. 1968:
> 100–1)

Furthermore, heterogeneity is not random, but patterned. It reflects order and structure within the grammar. Variation analysis aims to characterise the nature of this complex system.

LANGUAGE CHANGE

Language is always in flux. The English language today is not the same as it was 100 years ago, or 400 years ago. Things have changed. For example, *ain't* used to be the normal way of doing negation in English, but now it is stigmatised. Another good example is *not*. It used to be placed after the verb, e.g. *I know not*. Now it is placed before the verb, along with a supporting word, *do*, as in *I do not know*. Double negation, e.g. *I don't know nothing*, is ill-regarded in contemporary English. Not so in earlier times. Similarly, use of the ending *-th* for simple present was once the favoured form, e.g. *doth*, not *do*, and pre-verbal periphrastic *do*, e.g. *I do know*, and use of the comparative ending *-er*, e.g. *honester*, not *more honest*, used to be much more frequent. Such examples are easily found in historical corpora such as the Corpus of Early English Correspondence (Nevalainen and Raumolin-Brunberg 2003).

Variation analysis aims to put linguistic features such as these in the context of where each one has come from and where it is going – how and why.

SOCIAL IDENTITY

Language serves a critical purpose for its users that is just as important as the obvious one. Language is used for transmitting information from one person to another, but at the same time a speaker is using language to make statements about who she is, what her group loyalties are, how she perceives her relationship to her hearers, and what sort of speech event she considers herself to be engaged in. The only way all these things can be carried out at the same time is precisely because language varies. The choices speakers make among alternative linguistic means to communicate the same information often conveys important extralinguistic information. While you can inevitably identify a person's sex from a fragment of their speech, it is often nearly as easy to localise her age and sometimes even her socioeconomic class. Further, depending on one's familiarity with the variety, it can be relatively straightforward to identify nationality, locality, community, etc. For example, is the following excerpt from a young person or an old person?

> I don't know, it's jus' stuff that really annoys me. And I jus' like stare at him and jus' go … like, "huh". (YRK98/S014c)

How about the following? Male or female? Old or young?

> It was sort-of just grass steps down and where I dare say it had been flower beds and goodness-knows-what … (YRK/v)

I am willing to bet it was relatively easy to make these decisions and to do so correctly. The first is a young woman, aged eighteen. The second is a female, aged seventy-nine.

KEY CHARACTERISTICS OF VARIATIONIST SOCIOLINGUISTICS

Given these three aspects of language – inherent variation, constant change and pervasive social meaning – variationist sociolinguistics rests its method and analysis on a number of key concepts.

THE 'VERNACULAR'

A specific goal of variationist methodology is to gain access to what is referred to as the 'vernacular'. The vernacular has had many definitions in the field. It was first defined as 'the style in which the minimum attention is given to the monitoring of speech' (Labov 1972c: 208). Later discussions of the vernacular reaffirmed that the ideal target of investigation for variation analysis is 'every day speech' (Sankoff 1974, 1980: 54), 'real language in use' (Milroy 1992: 66) and 'spontaneous speech reserved for intimate or casual situations' (Poplack 1993: 252) – what can simply be described as informal speech.

Access to the vernacular is critical because it is thought to be the most systematic form of speech. Why? First, because it is assumed to be the variety that was acquired first. Second, because it is the variety of speech most free from hypercorrection or style-shifting, both of which are considered to be later overlays on the original linguistic system. Third, the vernacular is the style from which every other style must be calibrated (Labov 1984: 29). As Labov originally argued (1972c: 208), the vernacular provides the 'fundamental relations which determine the course of linguistic evolution'.

The vernacular is positioned maximally distant from the idealised norm (Milroy 1992: 66, Poplack 1993: 252). Once the vernacular baseline is established, the multi-dimensional nature of speech behaviour can be revealed. For example, Bell (1999: 526) argues that performance styles are defined by normative use. Thus, the unmonitored speech behaviour of the vernacular enables us to tap in to the broader dimensions of the speech community. In other words, the vernacular is the foundation from which every other speech behaviour can be understood.

Note

Many of my students report that their room-mates switch into their vernacular when talking to their mother on the phone. However you will notice it shine through whenever a person is emotionally involved, e.g. excited, scared, angry, moderately drunk, etc. Listen out for it!

THE SPEECH COMMUNITY

In order to 'tap the vernacular' (Sankoff 1988b: 157), a vital component of variation analysis requires that the analyst immerse herself in the speech community, entering it both as an observer and a participant. In this way, the analyst may record language use in its sociocultural setting (e.g. Labov et al. 1968, Trudgill 1974, Milroy 1987, Poplack 1993: 252). Due to its focus on unmonitored speech behaviour, this methodology has succeeded in overcoming many of the analytical difficulties associated with intuitive judgements and anecdotal reporting used in other paradigms (Sankoff 1988b). This is crucial in the study of non-standard varieties, as well as ethnic, rural, informal and other less highly regarded forms of language, where normative pressure typically inhibits the use of vernacular forms.

For example, when you hear people use utterances such as (i) 'I ain't gotta tell you anything', certain social judgements will surely arise. Whatever judgements come to mind are based on hypotheses that arise from interpreting the various linguistic features within these utterances. What are those features? Most people, when asked why someone sounds different, will appeal to their 'accent', their 'tone of voice' or their 'way of emphasising words'. However, innumerable linguistic features of language provoke social judgements.

One way to explore this is to contemplate the various ways the utterance in (i) could have been spoken, as in (1). Each possible utterance has its own social value, ranging from the highly vernacular to standard. Notice, too, how each feature of language varies in particular ways. *Ain't* appears to vary with *haven't* and possibly *don't*. *Gotta* appears to vary with *have to* as well as *got to*. *Nothing* varies with *anything*. In this way, each item alternates with a specific set – different ways of saying the same thing.

(1)
a. I ain't gotta tell you nothing/anything
b. I haven't gotta tell you nothing/anything
c. I don't have to tell you nothing/anything

The linguistic items which vary amongst themselves with the same referential meaning are the 'variables' which are the substance of variation analysis. But the next question becomes: How do you determine what *truly* varies with what?

FORM/FUNCTION ASYMMETRY

The identification of 'variables' in language use rests on a fundamental view in variation analysis – the possibility of multiple forms for the same function. Do all the sentences in (1) mean the same thing? Some linguists might assume that different forms can never have identical function. In variation analysis, however, it is argued that different forms such as these can indeed be used for the same function, particularly in the case of ongoing linguistic change. In other words, there is a basic recognition of instability in linguistic form/function relationships (Poplack 1993: 252) and, further, that differences amongst competing forms may be neutralised in discourse (Sankoff 1988b: 153). Where functional differences are neutralised is always an empirical question. It must first be established what varies with what and how. Notice that you can't say *I ain't haven't to tell you nothing*. Why? The goal of variation analysis is to pinpoint the form/function overlap and explain how this overlap exists and why.

LINGUISTIC VARIABLES

Different ways of saying more or less the same thing may occur at every level of grammar in a language, in every variety of a language, in every style, dialect and register of a language, in every speaker, often even in the same sentence in the same discourse. In fact, variation is everywhere, all the time. Consider the examples in (2) to (10), all of which are taken from the York English Corpus (YRK), which represents the variety spoken in the city of York in north England (Tagliamonte 1998).

Phonology/morphology, variable (t,d):

(2)
I did a college course when I **lefØ** school actually, but I **left** it because it was business studies. (YRK/h)

Phonology/morphology, variable (ing):

(3)
We were **having** a good time out in what we were **doin'**. (YRK/E)

Morphology, variable (ly):

(4)
You go to Leeds and Castleford, they take it so much more **seriously** ... They really are, they take it so **seriousØ**. (YRK/T)

Tense/aspect, variable future temporal reference forms:

(5)
... I think she'**s gonna** be pretty cheeky. I think she'**ll be** cheeky. (YRK/O)

Modal auxiliary system, deontic modality:

(6)
'I'**ve got to** cycle all the way back and then this afternoon I'll be cycling back up again!' ... You **have to** keep those thoughts err thoughts to yourself. (YRK/X)

Intensifiers:

(7)
I gave him a **right** dirty look ... and I gave him a **really** dirty look. (YRK/O)

Syntax/semantics, variable stative possessive meaning:

(8)
He'**s got** bad-breath; he **has** smelly feet. (YRK/i)

Syntax, agreement:

(9)
She **were** a good worker. She **was** a helluva good worker. (YRK/¥)

Discourse/pragmatics, quotative use:

(10)
He just **said** 'Fine, go.'
It **was like** 'It 's gonna cost me a fortune!'
I **thought** 'Ah,' and that was it. (YRK/d)

How can such variability become interpretable? It is necessary to refer to more than just social meaning. Such variation might be explained by external pragmatic factors; however, it is more often the case that variation such as this has complex social, linguistic and historical implications. In the case of variable (ly), stative possessive *have got*, the modal auxiliary system, intensifiers and others, variation amongst forms can be traced back to longitudinal change in the history of the English language. In the case of adverb placement and variable agreement, synchronic patterns may address issues pertaining to the configuration of phrase structure, feature checking and other issues of theoretical importance. Indeed, much of the work on historical syntax has highlighted the complexity of how linguistic structures evolve in the process of grammatical change (e.g. Kroch 1989, Warner 1993, Taylor 1994, Pintzuk 1995).

THE QUANTITATIVE METHOD

Perhaps the most important aspect of variation analysis that sets it apart from most other areas of linguistics, and even sociolinguistics, is its quantitative approach. The combination of techniques employed in variation analysis forms part of the 'descriptive-interpretative' strand of modern linguistic research (Sankoff 1988b: 142–3). Studies employing this methodology are based on the observation that speakers make choices when they use language and that these choices are discrete alternatives with the same referential value or grammatical function. Furthermore, these choices vary in a systematic way and as such they can be quantitatively modelled (Labov 1969a, Cedergren and Sankoff 1974; see also more recent re-statements in Young and Bayley 1996: 254, Poplack and Tagliamonte 2001: 88). This is perhaps most candidly put by Sankoff (1988b: 151):

> whenever a choice can be perceived as having been made in the course of linguistic performance, and where this choice may have been influenced by factors such as the nature of the grammatical context, discursive function of the utterance, topic, style, interactional context or personal or sociodemographic characteristics of the speaker or other participants, then it is difficult to avoid invoking notions and methods of statistical inference, if only as a heuristic tool to attempt to grasp the interaction of the various components in a complex situation.

The advantage of the quantitative approach lies in its ability to model the simultaneous, multi-dimensional factors impacting on speaker choices, to identify even subtle grammatical tendencies and regularities in the data, and to assess their relative strength and significance. These measures provide the basis for comparative linguistic research. However, such sophisticated techniques are only as good as the analytic procedures upon which they are based:

> The ultimate goal of any quantitative study ... is not to produce numbers (i.e. summary statistics), but to identify and explain linguistic phenomena. (Guy 1993: 235)

THE PRINCIPLE OF ACCOUNTABILITY

According to Labov (1972c: 72), 'the most important step in sociolinguistic investigation is the correct analysis of the linguistic variable'. 'Correct' in this case means 'accountable' to the data. In variation analysis, accountability is defined by the 'principle of accountability', which holds that every variant that is part of the variable context, whether the variants are realised or unrealised elements in the system, must be taken into account. In other words, you cannot simply study the variant forms that are new, interesting, unusual or non-standard – *ain't*, for example, or *got*. You must also study the forms with which such features vary in all the contexts in which either of them would have been possible. In the case of *ain't*, this would mean all the cases where *ain't* is used as well as all other negation variants with the same referential value as *ain't*, e.g. I <u>*haven't*</u> *got nothing* or perhaps even I <u>*don't*</u> *got nothing* – whatever occurs in the same context. By definition, an accountable analysis demands of the analyst an exhaustive report for every case in which a variable element occurs out of the total number of environments where the variable element could have occurred, but did not. In Labov's (1972c: 72) words, 'report values for every case where the variable element occurs in the relevant environments as we have defined them'. 'As we have defined them' is the important point here. What does this mean?

CIRCUMSCRIBING THE VARIABLE CONTEXT

How does the analyst determine the variants of a variable and the contexts in which they vary? This procedure is most accurately characterised as a 'long series of exploratory manoeuvres' (Labov 1969a: 728–9):

1. Identify the total population of utterances in which the feature varies. Exclude contexts where one variant is categorical.
2. Decide on how many variants can be reliably identified. Set aside contexts that are indeterminate, neutralised, etc.

These manoeuvres accentuate that variation analysis is not interested in individual occurrences of linguistic features, but requires systematic study of the recurrent choices an individual makes (Poplack and Tagliamonte 2001: 89). Analysis of these recurrent choices enables the analyst to 'tap in' to an individual's use of the targeted forms. In this case, a 'pattern' refers to 'a series of parallel occurrences (established according to structural and/or functional criteria) occurring at a non-negligible rate in a corpus of language use' (Poplack and Meechan 1998: 129). So, now the question is: How do you find the patterns?

TESTING HYPOTHESES

Labov's (1969a: 729) third exploratory manoeuvre is to 'identify all the sub-categories which would reasonably be relevant in determining the frequency' of forms. These are the underlying patterns, the internal linguistic contexts that are hypothesised to influence the choice of one variant over another. How does one find them? Sometimes these are discovered by scouring the literature, both synchronic and diachronic. Sometimes they 'emerge from the ongoing analysis as a result of various suspicions, inspections, and analogies' (Labov 1969a: 729). Sometimes they are stumbled upon by chance in the midst of analysis and a 'Eureka!' experience unfolds. More often, the very worst days of variation analysis come when you are in the midst of reams of statistical analyses and data and numbers, and you just can't see the forest for the trees! As long as one's practice has been 'carried out with a degree of accuracy and linguistic insight', Labov promises that 'the end result is a set of regular constraints which operate upon every group and almost every individual' (Labov 1969a: 729). Indeed, it never ceases to amaze me what patterns underlie linguistic variables that one has no inkling of in the beginning.

Note

While I was writing my dissertation, I came to a particularly impassable dead end in my analysis. I could not see any patterns! In desperation, I wailed at one of my mentors, 'There are just no patterns at all.' The response was empathetic, but firm: 'Take it from an old variationist like me – there will be patterns. Keep looking.' And, of course, there were.

Once it can be established that a variable exists in a body of materials, the variationist sociolinguist will embark on the long process of studying the feature: circumscribing the variable context, extracting the relevant data from corpora, coding the material according to reasoned hypotheses gleaned from the diachronic and synchronic literature, and then analysing and interpreting the results in situ.

The question inevitably arises: Why use variation analysis? My answer is this. It is an area of the discipline that involves 'real' language as it is being used, so it is inherently hands-on and practical; it employs a methodology that is replicable and 'accountable' to the data; it provides you with the 'tools' to analyse language, not simply on an item-by-item basis, but at the level of the underlying system. Finally, variation analysis puts language in context, socially, linguistically, synchronically and diachronically. In the end, by conducting a variation analysis you get closer to knowing what language is and what human beings are all about.

ORGANISATION AND LOGIC OF THIS BOOK

The book is organised so that the chapters take the reader from the first stages of research right through to the last ones. The chapters build from simple observations, to basic conceptual initiatives, to training procedures. I then move to general research problems and issues and gradually turn to explaining how to resolve complex data handling, computational and linguistic problems. In the final chapters, the focus turns to performing analytic techniques and developing interpretation skills. Examples from my own research demonstrate problem-solving at each stage in the research process. This presents you not only with the techniques of variation analysis, but also with the *process* through which it unfolds. Each chapter ends with an exercise highlighting the topic just covered.

Most of the examples come from two linguistic variables which are the most well known and the most extensively studied in the field – variable (t,d) and variable (ing).

In order to tap into the structured heterogeneity that is rich in living language, it is necessary to gain access to language in use, whether it is in the literature, in the media or, as is most typical of the variationist approach, in the street. For the latter undertaking, it is necessary to go out of the office, beyond the anecdotal, and into the speech community. Fieldwork and data collection will be described in Chapter 2.

Exercise 1: Becoming aware of linguistic variation

The purpose of this exercise is to develop your ability to observe linguistic variability. In the process you will begin to develop a sociolinguist's ear and eye.

Find some language material. Any data will do, e.g. an audio-tape, a video, a TV show, a newspaper, a novel, an email message, an MSN conversational history. Then examine it – carefully.

Consider features from different areas of grammar (e.g. phonology, morphology, syntax, discourse). Notice morphological, syntactic or discursive alternations, e.g. zero plurals, zero possessives, missing prepositions, articles, discourse markers, variation in quotative use, syntactic structure, etc. Provide an inventory of different variants that occur in the data. Illustrate intra-speaker alternation of forms, as in (i):

(i) I mean I was **_real_** small and everything you-know **_really_** tiny built ... (YRK/O)

Summarise the nature of the features you have identified. Are there any features that are unfamiliar to you? Are there features that are typical of older rather than younger speakers? Male more than female, or vice versa? Standard vs non-standard, etc.? Do they vary across your sample? Is one variant predisposed to certain sectors of the population over the other? How? Also make note of the types of contexts in which each variant occurs. Can you spot any trends?

When you make a linguistic observation from a data set, always back it up with an example. Further, ensure that the example is referenced to the location in the original data sample (i.e. speaker number and line number), audio-tape (counter number) or whatever is suitable for the data you are examining.

Note

I will typically take the front page of the newspaper from the day I present this topic to a class and use it to illustrate how normal variation in language really is. There are usually some good examples. Try it!

2 Data collection

How do you collect data? This chapter will outline tried-and-true data collection techniques.

The most fundamental challenge for sociolinguistic research is how to obtain appropriate linguistic data to analyse. But how do you actually do it? The best exemplars that exist – Labov (1972a), Milroy (1987) and Sankoff (1973, 1974) – were written in the 1960s and 1970s. Detailed individual accounts are rarely published, except in dissertation methodology chapters. Some of most memorable fieldwork tips I ever received were from chatting to sociolinguists at conferences (see also Feagin 2002: 37). In fact, fieldwork methods may be the best-kept secret of sociolinguistics. In this chapter, you will learn everything I know about how to collect data.

THE BASICS

The very first task is to design a sample that addresses 'the relationship between research design and research objectives' (Milroy 1987: 18, Milroy and Gordon 2003: 24). At the outset, a sociolinguistic project must have (at least) two parts: 1) a (socio)linguistic problem and 2) appropriate data to address it.

Perhaps the consensus on good practice in this regard is to base one's sampling procedure on 'specifiable and defensible principles' (Chambers 2003: 46). The question is: What are these, and how to apply them?

DATA COLLECTION

According to Sankoff, the need for good data imposes three different kinds of decisions about data collection on the researcher: a) choosing what data to collect; b) stratifying the sample; and c) deciding on how much data to collect from how many speakers.

> 'Good' data is defined as language materials of sufficient type and quantity, as well as materials which take into account the social context in which the language data is gathered. This is referred to as defining the sampling universe. (Sankoff 1974: 21–2)

However, how will the data 'universe' be circumscribed? Perhaps the best answer is, 'it depends':

> the objectives of a piece of research to a very large extent dictate methods of speaker selection. (Milroy 1987: 28)

> The hypothesis that motivates the project will influence how to go about collecting the data. (Feagin 2002: 20)

The boundaries of a data set may be geographic, social, or otherwise; however, it is particularly important to decide what is going to be contained in your corpus. Depending on the nature of the data and the nature of the research question under investigation, different factors will be important. Who are you going to study, and why? What are the boundaries of the group or community? If location in space is important, where is it? If location in time is important, how will this be accomplished?

SAMPLING STRATEGIES

A number of different sampling strategies have been employed in variation analysis; however, over the years the sociological model of representative sampling and earlier dialectological survey techniques have become modified to suit sociolinguistic research. To contextualise these developments, let us first review the main strategies from which contemporary sampling strategies have developed.

RANDOM SAMPLING

Originally, sociolinguists based their methodology on sociological methods, attempting to achieve 'representativeness' in their data collection practices by constructing a random sample of their targeted group. When the targeted group was a city, as was the case in early research (e.g. New York, Detroit, Washington), there had to be a way to ensure that the sample truly represented the city. However, in order for a sample to qualify as 'random', a strict sampling criterion must be maintained:

> Each person in the total population sampled must have an equal chance of being selected for the sample. (Shuy et al. 1968: 229)

> anyone within the sample frame has an equal chance of being selected. (Milroy and Gordon 2003: 25)

This modus operandi was linked to the objectives of these early studies. The goal of the Detroit language study (Shuy et al. 1968: 228) was 'to provide a cross-section of [all] the people of Detroit'. Defining the universe of the sample as such a large group of people meant that sampling procedures had to be as random as possible. With this type of research goal, you cannot simply interview your own group of friends and acquaintances, or anyone else's, because such a selection would not be 'representative'. If you talked to people you knew, either directly or indirectly, you would get a very different view than if you had selected people randomly. When the goals of a study are to give a scale model of variation in a city as a whole, random sampling is the ideal.

Researchers have gone to great lengths to achieve random sampling in order to minimise the effect of bias on the selection of speakers. In so doing they aimed to avoid the following difficulties (Milroy 1987: 24):

(a) selection influenced consciously or unconsciously by human choice
(b) inadequate coverage of the population
(c) inability to find certain sections of the population
(d) lack of cooperation by certain subsections

Random sampling means that the fieldworkers do not know the individuals they are talking to. In fact, interviewer and interviewee are usually strangers to one another and, since most data collection endeavours only interview a speaker once, the interaction is limited and represents a 'one-off'. Such a situation can work against the ideal of tapping into the most casual form of speech behaviour. Indeed, familiarity, including the rapport that interacting individuals develop, greatly influences language style in sociolinguistic interview situations (e.g. Paradis 1996, Cukor-Avila and Bailey 2001). The study of language in its social context cannot achieve its goal of 'tapping the vernacular' by employing this sampling strategy.

THE ETHNOGRAPHIC APPROACH

Antithetic to the large-scale survey approach, a tradition of participant observation is also fundamental to variation analysis. Beginning with Labov et al's (1968) research in New York City and Martha's Vineyard (Labov 1972c), numerous techniques have evolved for 'reducing formality in face-to-face interviews and obtaining data on a wide range of styles' (Labov 1984: 28). Participant observation, evolving from anthropological linguistic studies, is when the analyst integrates themselves within the community under investigation, either by engagement in local affairs and/or developing personal associations with members. Participant observation has been successfully combined with survey techniques, beginning with Labov's studies of South Harlem (Labov et al. 1968). Thereafter, many projects in variation analysis which grew out of Labov's early research methodology have used a combination of participant observation and survey techniques to collect their data. Indeed, a well-developed ethnographic approach has become a component to any research studying 'language in its social context'.

Ethnography requires that the analyst engage in research in situ. This unique position is consistent with the methodology of the variationist framework, which aims at the analysis of the vernacular. An ethnographic approach 'consists of the intensive involvement of the researcher in a given social setting in order to describe and identify, through the use of a variety of complementary research techniques, the cultural patterns and regularities that structure and perpetuate a society' (Poplack 1979: 60). In other words, the ethnographic approach puts the sociolinguist in touch with the cultural context of the speech community so that the linguistic reflections of that community can be interpreted and explained. Further, knowledge of the cultural context can also provide lucid indications of what is important to analyse:

> while survey fieldwork focuses on filling in a sample, ethnographic fieldwork focuses on finding out what is worth sampling. (Eckert 2000: 69)

Ethnographically informed fieldwork may consist of any number of strategies that give the analyst insights into the dynamics of the speech community. The most ubiquitous of these is participant observation.

Perhaps the most famous participant observation study is Eckert's long-term ethnographic research in a Detroit high school (Eckert 2000). Another longitudinal participant observation research project is Wolfram's research on Ocracoke Island in North Carolina (Wolfram and Schilling-Estes 1995 inter alia). Wolfram and his associates have been collecting data from the community since 1992 and in the process have organised and implemented numerous schemas for communicating their linguistic findings to members. Cukor-Avila's (1995) research in the town of Springville in the southern United States is similar. She began collecting data in 1988 and due to her intimate relationships with members of the speech community has continued to collect materials, often from the same individuals at successive intervals of time, up to the present day. The rich natural data that come from such studies give the analyst incredible insights into some of the most important questions in the study of language variation. Indeed, studies that have involved long-term, ongoing participation within the speech community have demonstrated how important it is for sociolinguists to become partners with the community concomitant with their academic research.

SOCIAL NETWORKS

Another approach to data collection is founded on the concept of social networks (Milroy 1980). The chief characteristic of a network approach to data collection is that the unit of study is some pre-existing social group, not the individual as the representative of a more abstract social category. As with participant observation, the main practical advantage of this approach is that the researcher is able to attach herself to a group and, by making use of the group dynamics which influence patterns of language use, obtain large amounts of spontaneous speech (Milroy 1987).

The 'friend of a friend'

An interesting component of the social network approach is the 'friend of a friend'. These are people who play an intermediary role in the community. It is the 'friend of a friend' who helps you to get the things you want, 'who helps to obtain goods at cost price, to mediate in a brush with the authorities, or to secure the services of a handyman' (Milroy 1980: 47). When it comes to fieldwork, intermediaries help you get things done here, too.

In the social network method the investigator must find a means of approaching a group to which the investigator (typically) may have no pre-existing personal ties. Techniques that can be used for a circle of personal friends are too limited. This is when the 'friend of a friend' becomes most useful. These are people with a status that is neither that of an insider nor that of outsider, but something of both. With a 'friend of a friend' you do not go into a situation cold. You have some 'in' into the situation. Naming yourself a 'friend' means that you have an entry into the relationships of the network you have attached yourself to. Such an 'in' cannot be underestimated. The usefulness of the 'friend of a friend' approach has been invaluable in many studies, including my own.

Using the 'friend of a friend' approach also means that the researcher becomes enmeshed in exchange and obligation relationships as well. In other words, the fieldworker becomes part of the community – an observer who is also a participant.

Tip

When making contacts in a speech community or social network, avoid anyone who has official status, e.g. priests, teachers and community leaders. This is important, because if you enter a community through such a person you will inevitably end up with speakers within that contact's social networks. This, in turn, would produce a sample with a bias toward the relatively standard speech styles typical of such members of a population, which, in turn, will not be representative of the whole.

PROBLEMS WITH RANDOM SAMPLING

Many problems arise in applying strict random sampling methodology to sociolinguistic studies. Perhaps the most important of these is the often extreme difficulty in finding the subsection of the population that you wish to study, whether this is due to socioeconomic, ethnic or other demographic reasons. As is typical, such subgroups in a multiplex urban context will be 'geographically and socially distributed amongst the population in a non-random way' (Milroy 1987: 24). If the population you are looking for is of this type, then random selection of participants with uniform probability over the entire population is, in fact, not very useful.

Moreover, as more and more projects were undertaken, it was discovered that sampling methods for studies in the speech community did not actually require traditional random sampling. First, it was discovered that even so-called random sampling used in linguistic surveys was not 'random' in the strict sociological sense anyway.

Second, ongoing work in sociolinguistics found that relatively small samples – samples too small to be technically representative – were sufficient to account for language variation in large cities.

> Speech communities tend to consist of many varieties spoken by groups containing very different numbers of individuals, so that uniform sampling leads to redundancy for some groups and risks missing others entirely. (Sankoff 1988a: 900)

Therefore, sampling methods in variation analysis were modified to embrace the most relevant strategies of random sampling alongside more anthropological approaches.

STRATIFIED RANDOM SAMPLING

Stratified random sampling (also known as quasi-random or judgement sampling) modifies the random sampling methodology along lines more amenable to the data required for variation analysis. First, a more useful notion of representativeness was developed, requiring:

> not that the sample be a miniature version of the population, but only that we have the possibility of making inferences about the population based on the sample. (Sankoff 1988a: 900)

This type of representativeness is accomplished by stratifying the sample according to secondary variables which are suspected to be correlated with some aspect or other of linguistic variation, e.g. age, sex, place of birth, etc. Each of these must be represented as fully as possible in the sample. This sampling method is defined by two fundamental practices: the researcher 1) identifies in advance the types of speakers to be studied; and 2) seeks out a quota of speakers who fit the specified categories. For example, in Trudgill's (1974: 20–30) study of Norwich, England, he selected four wards from the voter registration lists which had the same social and economic characteristics as the city as a whole. Then he chose names from the voter lists randomly.

A minimum requirement for any sample is that it have a degree of representativeness on the bases of age, sex, and (some way of determining) social class, education level, or both. This ensures that as much as possible of the linguistic diversity in the targeted community is represented in the sample (Sankoff 1988a: 902). In other words, stratified random sampling requires extralinguistic justification for its selection criteria, whether sociological, demographic or otherwise. In the case that the composition and characteristics of the population to be surveyed is unknown, objectively specifiable dimensions can be sought in census data, community reports and sociological surveys. Once a target population has been defined, however, it is a good idea to observe principles of random selection as strictly as possible in order to ensure reasonable representativeness across the sample.

I refer the reader to large-scale projects from the 1970s, which set the standards for research (e.g. Sankoff and Sankoff 1973, Payne 1976). Poplack's (1989) Ottawa-Hull French project, based on the sampling schema of the Montreal French Project, is an exemplary standard for research. An excellent summary of sampling strategies can be found in Milroy and Gordon (2003: 49–87). In each data collection context, the objectives of the study, the target data or population and the support documentation and ethnographic research combine to create a well-defined data set.

Note

Each decision you make about what you want to study (sociolinguistic issue) and the data that will elucidate it (the linguistic variable) sends you in a specific direction. Everything falls out from these initial decisions.

Here is a checklist for data collection:

* Identify the target population.
* Determine where they are likely to be found.
* Engage in extensive background reading, demographic and archival research.
* Circumscribe the location of the speech community.
* Determine its boundaries.
* Devise appropriate means to 'enter the community'.

African Nova Scotian English project

The African Nova Scotian English project (Poplack and Tagliamonte 1991) targeted a little-known population in Canada – people descended from African Americans who immigrated to Nova Scotia in the late eighteenth and early nineteenth centuries. Because the two African Nova Scotian communities sampled were chosen specifically on the basis of 1) their relatively homogeneous racial and socio-economic characteristics, 2) their presumed isolation from speakers of surrounding white varieties, and 3) the likelihood that their speakers could provide samples of vernacular speech, a sociologically stratified speaker sample was neither feasible nor necessary. In this case, it was more important that the data be representative than the speakers. Thus, no attempt was made to stratify the speakers for purposes of sample constitution either by socioeconomic class, age or any of the other standard sociological indicators. On the contrary, we employed a 'friend of a friend' approach, entering the community through ethnographic means and selecting speakers through social networking. We targeted relatively insular older informants who had been born and raised in the community for the following reasons: 1) during the time these informants were acquiring their language (1915–40), schools were primarily segregated; 2) elderly informants are less likely to be participating in ongoing linguistic change initiated by the younger generation; 3) our research goals dictated that the sample be comparable to other corpora that were comprised of older speakers.

This strategy produced a sample, as in (1) (Poplack and Tagliamonte 1991: 314). The male/female disproportion is expected given our emphasis on social network methodology. The uneven distribution by age is, of course, a natural selection bias.

(1)

African Nova Scotian English Corpus (primary sample)

Speaker age	North Preston		Guysborough	
	Male	Female	Male	Female
53–64	3	9	8	8
65–74	3	5	6	3
75+	4	5	3	10
Total	10	19	17	21

The 'friend of a friend' method was also critical for the success of this project. The summer of 1991 was a less than ideal time for fieldwork in the African Nova Scotian communities in Nova Scotia. Race riots had broken out in Halifax, the capital city, and racial tension was high. It was critical for me to be able to get 'in' to the communities themselves – but how? An initial reconnaissance trip into North Preston (the community on the outskirts of Halifax) revealed that a 'cold call' approach was unacceptable. Through a 'friend of a friend' I made a contact with someone from the community. This man was the turning point of the entire fieldwork enterprise. Through contacts he put me in touch with, I was able to make further contacts in the community, thereby initiating the fieldwork phase of the project.

Tip

It may be fruitful to use your own personal background to 'authenticate' as well as assist fieldwork. For example, given the racial climate in Nova Scotia in 1991, you might expect that an outsider, particularly a white 'in-lander' (from the interior of Canada) was not going to be regarded entirely favourably. I can still remember sitting across from my contact as he made a phone call to another person from the African Nova Scotian community and told him about the project. I could tell that the person on the other end of the line was sceptical. At one point, my contact paused, listening for a moment. Then, he confidently said, 'No, no. She's not white. She's Italian!' I have never been so appreciative of my mixed ethnic background.

Despite the utility of these methods, fieldwork is not easy. The personal stamina required to 'stick it out' is often high. However, the difficulties are usually due to the uncomfortable circumstances, both physical and emotional, and the frustrations of waiting on interviewers and/or informants, rather than the challenges of data collection itself.

Tip

Every fieldworker likely has fieldwork stories to tell. I recommend judicious use of an interview module somewhat along the lines of 'fieldwork adventures'. It may prove invaluable for engaging in small talk with sociolinguists, if you ever happen to run into one at a conference party and do not know what to talk about.

One of the most difficult aspects of doing fieldwork in small, insular, tight-knit communities is to gain access to the everyday speech of their inhabitants, i.e. the vernacular (see also Poplack and Tagliamonte 1991). In most, if not all, such communities, outsiders of any kind are unlikely to be viewed or treated on an equal footing, let alone as interlocutors with whom one engages in informal banter. As I mentioned earlier, common personal associations (ethnicity, religion, nationality, place of origin, etc.) are often critical, not only for being able to enter these communities successfully, but also for mitigating the 'observer's paradox'. Shared background can make or break the temper of the interview situation.

Note

Fieldworkers experience many difficulties, calamities and 'hilarities' in their pursuit of the right data. You might wonder why you do not hear more about these escapades. The fact of the matter is that sociolinguists are indebted to their interviewers, informants and innumerable 'friends of friends'. This makes them very protective of them. Sociolinguists are reluctant to say anything that might offend their field contacts in any way whatsoever. Indeed, for many of us, the personal contacts we have made from our fieldwork experiences are quite close to our hearts.

SUMMARY

The major methods for data collection in the variationist tradition each have their advantages. Random sampling provides for broad sociological representation of the speech community. Ethnographic methods and the social network approach provide for selective sampling of certain members of the speech community. While the former makes sure a full spectrum of a target population is contained in the study, the latter is more likely to provide the right type of data for analysis. Different research questions require different sampling techniques. For stylistic analysis and more qualitative approaches to variation, including identity markers and features of style, non-stratificational sample designs may be more useful. Similarly, in large-scale stratification studies, the onus is on the analyst to provide a socially embedded treatment and interpretation of stratificational data.

Virtually all sociolinguistic research projects since the early studies in New York, Washington and Detroit have exercised a weaker interpretation of representativeness. Indeed, according to Chambers (2003: 33), judgement sampling has become the 'consensus in the field'.

Despite a movement away from imposing traditional demographic classifications, it is still necessary to maintain some level of representativeness of the community, whatever that community is defined to be. This is also critical for the broader enterprise of comparing across varieties. Letting classifications emerge from ethnographic analysis alone, or network analysis alone, removes a study from being representative of the broader community, which any subgroup of the population must be viewed against (see Eckert 2000: 77).

In sum, a balance between random sampling and the social network approach via judgement sampling is undoubtedly the most common fieldwork technique. Whereas random survey methods ensure representativeness of the sample, a social network approach goes a long way towards mitigating the observer's paradox and reaching the right people. The critical component of this hybrid methodology for variation analysis is that the researchers decide which type of representativeness is sufficient – or attainable – depending on the focus of their study.

DESIGNING YOUR SAMPLE

When it comes to designing your own study, how will you proceed? First, think about a compelling sociolinguistic issue. Second, think about the speaker sample that will provide the ideal data to explore it. How will you find these speakers? For example, you might hypothesise a difference in the language of elderly people who have had children vs elderly people who have not had children. This is an interesting linguistic question, but how would you go about finding the sample? Certainly not using random sampling. Instead, it is necessary to let the research questions guide the fieldwork techniques. In this way, the point from which everything else falls out is this: What is the sociolinguistic issue under investigation? This decision will determine the type of data of relevance and, later on, it will influence how you will be able to get it.

THE SOCIOLINGUISTIC ISSUE

Sociolinguistic issues are as multi-dimensional as sociolinguistics itself. Consistent with the descriptive-interpretative strand of sociolinguistics, an issue inevitably involves external factors, although in this case there must also be a linguistic correlate. An external issue may be as enigmatic as the explanation for why the variety of English spoken by people of African descent in the United States is different; or as pervasive as why male and female speech is different; or as eternal as why younger people do not sound like older people. An issue may also involve tracking the origins and function of a given feature in a given dialect, evaluating the grammaticalisation of a form, or even to determine acquisition patterns. All that is required of an 'issue' is that there is an interesting question to investigate which justifies undertaking the research in the first place.

The ideal issue might involve conflicting claims in the literature, e.g. one researcher says 'X', the other says 'Y'. When such opposing claims can be found, they are ideal for sparking a variation analysis because this puts an analyst in an ideal position to contribute further evidence to the controversy or, at best, for determining which claim is right. Many of my own research papers begin with a controversy.

In a study of verbal -*s* in Samaná English and the Ex-Slave Recordings (two varieties construed to represent an earlier variety of African American Vernacular English) (Poplack and Tagliamonte 1989: 53), we identified four conflicting claims about the origin and function of verbal -*s*. Furthermore, depending on the function, verbal -*s* could be construed to have one source or another. This presented an excellent test situation both for assessing the function of verbal -*s* as well as for evaluating the ancestry of the varieties under investigation. A study of variation amongst relative pronouns in English (*that, who* and zero) (Tagliamonte et al. 2005) had its starting point with conflicting evidence. According to one researcher the relatives *who, which,* etc. had not permeated spoken British English. Yet another researcher explicitly states that they have. Who is right?

A more common point of departure for variation analysis is simply a claim or observation in the literature, as in (2)–(4):

(2)
Deontic modality
Have got to for the expression of necessity/obligation is one of the success stories in English grammar of the last 150 years (Krug 1998: 179, 187). This suggests that data representing different points over the last century should provide insights into the mechanism underlying these changes.

(3)
Negative vs auxiliary contraction in British English
The frequency of AUX contraction increases 'the further north one goes' (Trudgill 1978: 13). This observation is explicitly testable if you have access to corpora from different latitudes in Britain.

(4)
Zero subject relatives in subject function
This feature represents an area of 'notable difference between AAVE and other English vernaculars' (Martin and Wolfram 1998: 32). This observation could be tested through comparison of relevant varieties.

Whenever you are reading, highlight all the claims or observations that can be subjected to empirical testing.

SAMPLE DESIGN

Long before data collection begins, it is critical to have a plan. You might begin with a template that looks something like the schema in (5), adjusting the external criteria by what is relevant for your study. The stratification by age, the horizontal axis in (5), is often the most salient external factor for most studies. However, this categorisation could as easily be community, as in (6), or region, or some other external factor.

(5)

Template for sample design 1

Age	Male	Female	Total
20–30	4	4	8
30–50	4	4	8
50–70	4	4	8
70+	4	4	8
Total	16	16	32

(6)

Template for sample design 2

Community	Male	Female	Total
A	4	4	8
B	4	4	8
C	4	4	8
Total	12	12	24

Any number of stratification schemas could be constructed depending on the research question, the relevant data and any other practical constraints. When you are planning your study, get out a pencil and sketch out your sample design.

Depending on the sociolinguistic issue, different data is required. Select a sample that works. Suppose you define your population (sampling universe) as young people between the ages of 10 and 20 who are native speakers of English and who live in two different neighbourhoods representing two different socioeconomic classes. How would you create a stratified design?

First, you divide the speakers along some salient social dimension, e.g. sex, boys and girls, and within your targeted group, e.g. all those between 10 and 15, and all those between 16 and 20. Then, one cell might contain all girls between 10 and 15 in the middle class, as in (7). Then choose how many speakers are allotted to each cell. For example, in this hypothetical sample you might want to have 2 speakers per cell. Adding 1 speaker per cell would increase the sample size to 28; doubling it, 32; and so forth. How many per cell is enough? Some statisticians say 3, some say 5. Obviously, you want more than 1, otherwise you don't know if the behaviour of the individual is idiosyncratic or reflects their membership in the group. On the other hand, starting small and circumscribed is better than nothing.

(7)

	Working class		Middle class	
Age	Male	Female	Male	Female
10-15	2	2	2	2
16-20	2	2	2	2
Subtotal	4	4	4	4
Grand total		16		

A different sociolinguistic question might involve the investigation of different ethnic groups in the same neighbourhood in one city. A relevant social dimension would be length of time in the neighbourhood, e.g. first generation, second generation, third generation. A sample design might be constructed as in (8):

(8)

Ethnic background	British	Chinese	Italian	Greek
First generation	2	2	2	2
Second generation	2	2	2	2
Third generation	2	2	2	2
Subtotals	6	6	6	6
Grand total		24		

However, a male/female differences should probably be distinguished here too, i.e. one male and one female per cell. Alternatively, perhaps two of each per cell would be better? What about socioeconomic class, education, and any number of other important external characteristics? An important rubric to follow is to keep it well delineated. Ensure that if one dimension changes, the other dimensions stay constant; otherwise it will be impossible to disentangle the effects. The sample design must stop somewhere, while at the same time allowing for relevant external dimensions to be taken into account. On the practical side of things, you must also reflect on the following. How much time do you have? How much funding? How much energy? In the end, every sample design must be a balance between answering the research questions and getting the research done.

SAMPLE STRATIFICATION

Once the design has been constructed, the next step is to determine the broader characteristics of the sample that correlate with the variation targeted for investigation. This is where the specific research question(s) become important: 'the questions asked determine where the researchers look to answer them' (Milroy and Gordon 2003: 33). In other words, if your interest is in sociolinguistic reflexes of ethnicity, then it will be important to construct a sample design reflecting ethnic disparities in a given community, including the targeted group as well as the comparison group(s). If your interest is in regionally diffusing sound change, then it will be important to select locations at relevant geographic locations. If your interest is in active changes in progress, then it will be important to select representation of different age groups. Purposeful structuring of the sample according to relevant aspects of the research question under investigation is thus critical for making decisions about how to stratify your sample.

SAMPLE SIZE

Finally, the amount of data to be collected must be decided. How much data from each informant will be sufficient? Some advice from Feagin (2002: 21) is that 'a small amount of data is better than an unfinished grandiose project'. On the other hand, you do not want to be criticised for having too little data. In my experience this is something that sociolinguists are quick to point out.

Large-scale research projects conducted between 1968 and 1973 tended to sample large numbers of speakers – New York City, Lower East Side, 122 speakers (Labov et al. 1968); Montreal French, 120 (Sankoff and Cedergren 1972), etc. However, excessively large corpora require an immense outlay in research hours for data transcription and processing (Poplack 1989). In Shuy et al.'s (1968) study in Detroit, 702 interviews were conducted; however, the most detailed analysis of these materials (Wolfram 1969) used only 48 of these. For the York English Corpus (Tagliamonte 1998), we had enough funds to transcribe only one hour of interview per speaker, yet many of the interviews lasted two hours or more. In these cases, we transcribed only the second hour of data.

It is better to design your sample to be smaller and better circumscribed than to end up with lots of data but not enough funds (or energy) to use it. The size of the sample must necessarily be balanced with the available time and resources for data handling. Whatever strategy you use, make it defensible, logical and workable.

FIELDWORK ETHICS

Variation analysis often involves contemporary speech communities. It is incumbent on the researcher to follow ethical practices in dealing with the human beings who contribute the linguistic material for investigation. In earlier research, ethical guidelines were much more flexible than they have become in more recent times. Earlier sociolinguistic fieldwork did not require full disclosure of the goals and aims of the project. At present, at least in North America, researchers must adhere to stringent institutionalised ethical guidelines. For the African Nova Scotian English project in 1991, we explained the project in the context of the history and culture of the community. In contrast, for the Toronto English project in 2003 (Tagliamonte to appear b) we were required to explain the project in terms of our interest in language and even as far as to name the variables targeted for investigation.

The main ethical guidelines for collecting informal interviews remain constant: 1) consent for audio-recording; 2) guaranteed anonymity; 3) voluntary participation; and 4) access to researcher and research findings. On the companion website, in Appendix A, I have included as examples the approved Information Sheet and Informed Consent forms from the Toronto English project.

FIELDWORK TECHNIQUES AND STRATEGIES

Labov's (1972a) classic discussion of 'entering the speech community' offers the beginner fieldworker a set of principles to follow which are the 'tried-and-true' strategies from Labov's sociolinguistic research projects. Each of these strategies outlines a particular stance, or state of mind, which is most conducive to a positive fieldwork experience. In most cases, the foundation is one simple axiom – meet your speakers authentically and enthusiastically, in their own reality.

However, different social-cultural situations, different cities, different locations in a country (urban vs rural) challenge the fieldworker in a multitude of ways. Fieldwork practices from the 1960s and 1970s may not be as effective in the 2000s. In our recent fieldwork in Toronto we found that the most important strategies for success were much more practical, as in (9) (Tagliamonte et al. 2004):

(9)
a. work in pairs
b. time door-to-door sampling carefully: i.e. not after a long weekend, not on a rainy day, not between 2pm and 4pm, not after a big sports win, etc.
c. ring the doorbell *and* knock on the door
d. tell the prospective informant about the project
e. confirm that they fit the sampling criteria by asking: 'So, what part of Toronto were you born in?'
f. ideally, conduct an interview on the spot; if not, suggest a time and book it
g. call to remind the informant about the interview the night before

Tip

The best fieldwork advice I ever got was before I left on my fieldwork expedition to Nova Scotia in the spring of 1991. I met a famous, and coincidentally African American, sociolinguist at a conference and expressed my concern about being able to collect data from the African Nova Scotian communities in Canada. For me, it was a formidable task. Could I ever gain access to this secluded community, let alone gain access to their vernacular? The response was: 'Be honest; be interested. People will respond to that.'

SUMMARY

There is one general principle which holds true no matter what speech community you go into or how you are required to fulfil ethical guidelines. The finest sociolinguistic data comes from fieldworkers who are aware of their consultants' local interests, values and general social norms. This is perhaps best stated by Baugh (1980: 42):

you will probably have little success collecting colloquial speech through direct inquiries that are not framed in terms of the consultants' cultural perspectives.

In sum, the optimal situation for conducting fieldwork is in the fullest sociocultural awareness of your target community. Further, I cannot stress the importance of the 'friend of the friend' in your initial contact and subsequent dealings in the community. It is often the case that a single helpful individual can make or break a project.

Unfortunately, much of the ethnographic contributions of sociolinguistic fieldwork is not often published. As Feagin (2002: 36) points out, 'the more successful the fieldwork, the less noticeable it is in the final analysis'. Information about how sociolinguistic fieldwork is conducted is more properly found in its legends, the stuff of late-night gatherings in the conference hotel bars and other informal settings. On the other hand, there are occasional inklings of how poignant the impact of sociolinguistic research really is:

> The fieldwork experience made me feel good because of the laughter it brought me, because of the joy of discovery which it opened to me, because of the individual good it did me as well as my informants, and because of the general benefit which, perhaps presumptuously, but at least optimistically, I feel that it brought to the world in some small way. (Shuy 1983: 357)

In the next chapter, I will turn to methods and techniques for talking with members of your target population.

Exercise 2: Designing a study

The purpose of this exercise is to plan your study. Devise, with justification, a data sampling scheme that enables you to test your hypotheses about a (socio)linguistic issue of interest to you. Use the following guide:

The (socio)linguistic issue(s)

Introduce and describe the (socio)linguistic issues that you are targeting for study.

(a) What question(s) in the literature prompted your interest? The issue you target may relate to internal and/or external features of language variation and change.
(b) Detail the linguistic implications.
(c) Detail the social and cultural implications.
(d) Situate these within the literature.

(e) What is the specific linguistic feature you are targeting for investigation?

(f) Discuss the issues surrounding this particular feature.

(g) How will you approach the variable methodologically?

(h) Will your method involve extension, elaboration, deviation from tradition approaches to the same phenomena?

The data

Introduce and describe the data that will enable you to test hypotheses regarding the (socio)linguistic issues described in I above. If your selected sample can be defined spatially, locate it on a map. If it is defined more by its social boundaries, identify these. What are your targeted speakers' ages, incomes, occupational, residential, educational and other characteristics consistent with the sources you have consulted? How do these, or other, characteristics allow you to test your (working) hypotheses?

Construct a stratified design for your data sample. Illustrate it in a table.

Identify any inherent biases of your study. Indicate how they will be controlled. For example, are there individuals and/or areas that are of linguistic interest to your study that your sampling universe *excludes*? Why? Are there sectors of this sample that are typically not included in official counts? How would you go about obtaining information on them? Are there individuals and/or areas that your sampling strategy includes that are *not* of possible linguistic interest to your study? What are your reasons for excluding them?

For reference read the introductory sections in the following:

Godfrey, E. and Tagliamonte, S. (1999). **87-94**.

Tagliamonte, S. (1998). **153-6**.

Tagliamonte, S. and Hudson, R. (1999). **147-51**.

3   The sociolinguistic interview

How do you conduct a sociolinguistic interview? How do you talk to your targeted speakers? This chapter will discuss ways and means of mitigating *the observer's paradox*, enabling the analyst to obtain natural speech data.

In the last two chapters, I have focused on setting up a research project, entering the speech community, and fieldwork ethics. Now, I turn to the question of how to collect appropriate data.

THE 'INTERVIEW'

The basic tool for recording conversation in sociolinguistic variation is referred to as the 'sociolinguistic interview'. In fact, this is a misnomer; a sociolinguistic interview should be anything but an 'interview'.

MODULES

Labov (1984: 32) defines the sociolinguistic interview as 'a well-developed strategy' that is defined by a number of goals. The most important of these is to record one to two hours of speech and a full range of demographic data for each speaker within one's sample design. In Labov's (1984: 33–4) early formulation of the sociolinguistic interview, it was defined as a series of hierarchically structured sets of questions, what he refers to as conversational modules or 'resources' (Labov 1973).

A typical module is shown in (1). In this case, the topic is school.

(1)
School
Do [Did] you go to one of the schools in this neighbourhood?
  How far is it from your house?
Do [Did] you have any teachers that are really tough?
  What would they yell at a kid for?
  What was the worst thing you ever saw a teacher do to a kid?
  Or a kid do to a teacher?
Did you ever get blamed [punished] for something you didn't do?
Did you ever have a teacher that was really unfair? That you liked?
Did you ever pass notes in school?
  Did a teacher ever catch you passing notes?
  What happened?
What kind of group did you have in your school?
  Do [Did] you have jocks? Nerds? Goths? Thugs?
  What is/was your group like?
  What sorts of clothes do they wear? Haircuts? Earrings?
  Could a guy [girl] from one group go out with a girl [guy] from another?

Notice that the questions within the module are not ordered randomly. Within the full set, referred to as the 'interview schedule', the modules are not ordered randomly, either. In both instances, the underlying aim is to progress from general, impersonal, non-specific topics/questions to more specific, personal ones.

Labov was very specific in describing optimal techniques for the sociolinguistic interview. 'Optimal' means those questions which elicit 'narratives of personal experience', stories that people tell you about their lives. Certain questions, such as the by-now-famous 'danger of death' question, or the one above, 'Did you ever get blamed for something you didn't do?', are highly effective for putting speakers into storytelling mode. Once engaged in this type of discussion speakers tend to produce vivid recollections rich in vernacular features (Labov 1984: 34).

The most useful questions for elicitation of the vernacular depend on the age of the speaker and on the type of community. Questions which ask a speaker where they were, or what they were doing, at a momentous time in history are excellent at tapping personal stories, as in (2).

(2)
a. In Nova Scotia, Canada
   Do you remember the Halifax Explosion? (1917)
   The sinking of the *Titanic*? (1912)
   Did you ever get caught out in a storm? (fishing stories)
b. In York, England
   Where were you the night the Minster [York Minster Cathedral] burned?
   (1984)
   Do you remember the York blitz? (World War II)

> c. In Toronto, Canada
> Where were you when the lights went out? (blackout, 2003)
> Do you remember Hurricane Hazel? (major hurricane, 1957)

A general observation is that questions which implicate the speaker in extraordinary events in which they participated are crucial for tapping the vernacular.

The ideal structure of a sociolinguistic interview is to begin with questions relating to demography, community, neighbourhood, etc. and progress into more personal modules such as Dating, Dreams and Fear. If you are going to be including a module on Language, always put it at the very end of the interview when your informant has exhausted all the more personal topics.

With any module, begin with exploratory queries. This enables you to assess whether the interviewee is interested and/or willing to talk about a particular subject. If the informant shows an interest in the topic, continue to the more detailed questions. If not, go on to the next module until you find something that the informant enjoys talking about. If the existing modules do not stimulate an informant's interest, improvise! It perhaps goes without saying that a sociolinguistic interview should have no rigid insistence upon a pre-set order of topics (see Eckert 2000: 80).

Ideally, the interviewer plays a part in the conversation which approaches that of any other participant in an informal exchange: 1) volunteer experience, 2) respond to new issues and 3) follow the subject's main interests and ideas wherever they go. But it is important not to talk too much! The sociolinguistic interview is considered a failure if the speaker does no more than answer questions.

Labov's test of a good interview

Fast-forward an audio-record of an interview.
Listen. Who do you hear? The interviewee? If so, good.
If you hear the interviewer, go forward another five minutes into the interview.
Listen. Who do you hear? The interviewee? Great.
If you hear the interviewer, go forward another five minutes.
Listen. Who do you hear? The interviewee? Wonderful!
If all you hear is the interviewer using this technique, the interview is not so good.

On the companion website I have included in Appendix B, the Interview Schedule I am currently using. It is based on Labov's original interview schedule (Labov 1973); however, this one has been revised and adapted through several large-scale sociolinguistic projects (e.g. Poplack and Tagliamonte 1991) and now represents probably the fourth generation of questions that were first developed by Labov. Many of the original questions have been updated and/or modified to suit different times and different populations, while other questions are entirely new. However, some questions have been so useful, they endure from the prototype.

ADAPTING THE SOCIOLINGUISTIC INTERVIEW

Some questions apply across just about all speech communities, as in (3).

(3)
a. Did you ever have a dream that really scared you?
b. Were you ever in a situation where you thought, 'This is it'?
c. Did you ever get blamed for something you never did?

Other questions will be community-specific. These must be modified to suit the particular community under investigation.

Most communities will have particular sensitivities that require you to pose questions in specific ways, as in (4)–(6). Indeed, every research project requires modifications to the sociolinguistic interview along social and cultural lines.

QUESTIONING TECHNIQUES

(4)
The Turkish community
One of my favourite things . . . is the Nasreddin Hoca stories. Do you know any of them? Tell me one?

(5)
The York community
Have you ever seen anyone do Morris dancing? Do you do it? (local customs)
Have you ever done the Micklegate Run? (pub crawl)

(6)
The Hindi community
What were you told about flying kites on the roofs of houses? What happened when you first 'cut' another kite?

You may even want to tailor your style to suit your interviewee, as in (7).

(7)
a. A teenager in 2003
   So, like have you ever had like a really freaky experience?
b. A senior citizen in 2003
   Can you remember a significant story from your life?

Note

If you modify your language in an interview, it must sound natural! For example, an 80-year-old interviewer would sound silly asking a question as in (7a). The ideal interview speech style is your own vernacular or one you are eminently familiar with.

WORDING QUESTIONS

Avoid yes/no questions. Instead, try those in (8).

(8)
a. *Interviewer:* Tell me about where you were born. (YRK/a)
b. *Interviewer:* What's been your best holiday? (YRK/D)
c. *Interviewer:* What do you like best about living in York? (YRK/D)

Of course, yes/no questions are often unavoidable, so back them up with a follow-up tag of some sort, e.g. 'Did you ever get blamed for something you never did? *What happened?*'

Many questions can be reworded to become much more successful.

Instead of asking questions directly, use indirect means. For example, instead of saying, 'Is it true that . . .', it's better to say, 'I've heard that . . . Some people say that . . . I've noticed that . . .', etc. Instead of saying, 'Do you like/hate X?', it's better to say, 'What do you like/hate about X?' Ask people how they felt about things, what they thought about things. Ask them to give an example or tell you about one time they did something, heard about something, etc.

Two good examples are the way you might ask someone's age and their education. When you ask someone their age, it is much more tactful to ask what year they were born. If they feel positive about their age, they will tell you themselves how old they are. If they do not, do not ask. You will be able to calculate their age later. When you ask some-one about their education, it is better to acknowledge that some people have not had much opportunity to go to school. In such cases, it is more tactful to say, 'Did you have a chance to go to school?' than to say, 'How much education did you get?' or 'How far did you get in school?'

Often people respond far better to questions that are worded in terms of *other* people and do not specifically implicate them. For example, instead of saying, 'Were your schooldays the best years of your life? (which is also a yes/no question), it is often better to say something like, 'A lot of people say that their schooldays were the best years of their lives. What do you think? Was it like that for you?'

Neutralise any questions that impose a value-judgement. This means avoiding questions that begin with 'Do you believe in X?' Instead, it is better to say, 'A lot of people I know believe in X. What do you think?' or 'A lot of people around here have experienced X. How about you?', 'I knew someone one who X. Have you ever heard about something like that?', etc. Wording questions in this way gives your informant 'the OK' to provide their opinion, recount their experience, etc.

Another valuable technique in wording questions is to ask them in the context of providing an example. This type of questioning has the added advantage of 'jogging' your informant's memory, as in (9).

(9)
a. You know that game you play where someone counts and everyone else hides? How'd you play that?
b. You know that game with the rhyme 'Eeny, meeny ...'. How does it go?

At the same time avoid questions that are vague. Ask a specific question or prompt the informant by giving an example. Some other examples are shown in (10).

(10)
a. *Interviewer*: What sort of adventures did you used to have like, in the fields ...? (YRK/a)
b. *Interviewer*: You-know, people often say, 'Oh schooldays are the best days of your life.' (YRK/a)

In the same vein, try to pick up on local culture to provide an example in your questions, as in (11).

(11)
Wartime in York
a. *Interviewer*: A lot of people have said that after the- after the end of the war a lot of the community spirit got lost in York ... (YRK/2)
Walking
b. *Interviewer*: I saw that you had the, um, James Herriot Yorkshire book ... (YRK/L)

SELECT APPROPRIATE QUESTIONS

Some question types, e.g. those dealing with work, business, human rights, will tend to elicit speech in the formal range. Although political, philosophical, opinion-oriented modules contain questions that might be posed in a normal interview situation, they are not right for the sociolinguistic data gathering situation.

Remember to include the 'tried-and-true' questions from earlier studies, i.e. questions like 'Did you ever get blamed for something you never did?', the 'danger of death' question, etc. These questions have a long history of working well and are important to include in your interviews (Labov 1984: 33).

Keep in mind that you are not asking questions to get information; you are asking questions that reach the 'real' sentiments of your speakers and which elicit natural, spontaneous speech. The more culture-specific, familiar and personalised the questions are (without being overly imposing), the better. Perhaps the most famous interview in my collection is a two-hour narration by an elderly man about how to breed slugs! Listen to what your informants say, then phrase questions that tap in to what they are visibly interested in, as in (12).

(12)
a. *Interviewer*: So have you always had dogs in your family? (YRK/Z)
b. But, I thought the Beatles were wonderful. *Interviewer*: Right, did you ever go and see them in concert? (YRK/t)

Some questions are too personal. It is best not to ask questions like, 'What was your first sexual experience like?' or 'How much money do you make?' If this information is offered, OK; but such prying questions about money and someone's personal affairs are not appropriate. As a general rule do not ask questions dealing with serious violence, rape, incest, etc. You may get into something you do not have the training to handle. Leave this for the social workers and psychiatrists.

Nevertheless, sensitive subjects inevitably arise spontaneously in the interview situation. In my experience, the way to handle this type of situation is to do what any good listener would do: be empathetic and listen.

GOOD QUESTIONS

The so-called 'danger of death' question is said to be the one of the best questions for eliciting narratives of personal experience (Labov

1984: 33). However, depending on your subjects, other questions can work just as well, as in (13).

(13)
a. What kind of memories do you have about being taught to ride a bike or learning to swim?
b. Have you ever had one of those nights that seemed totally bizarre the next day? What happened?

ORGANISE

Organise your questions so that one question leads naturally to the next. As discussed earlier, a topic should start out with a general question and then proceed to more detailed, specific questions. This type of hierarchical array will enhance your ability to retrieve questions by memory – a valuable thing in the middle of an interview when you run out of questions.

Another level of question organisation is the way in which you sequence questions *within* a module. Always structure the order of your questions in this way, i.e. moving towards question types that will elicit a personal experience or personal memory, as in (14).

(14)
In a question set on Family:
How would you describe your upbringing?
What were your parents like when you were young?
    Could you talk to them? Did they have expectations of you? What kind?
Were there strict table rules? Curfews? Bedtimes?
What happened when someone stepped out of line?
Ever get blamed for something you didn't do?

Aim to begin with a non-specific, broad question and progress to a more personal one. A critical questioning technique is to use add-ons to questions, as in (15). Another is to make judicious use of follow-up questions, as in (16).

(15)
a. Really? What
   happened?
b. Tell me about it . . .

(16)
a. *Interviewer*: Lovely couple, aren't they? [026] Yes. *Interviewer*: **How'd they meet each other?** (YRK/z)

> b. I wasn't there the night York was blitzed, cos it wasn't far from the station. Um. That was very traumatic. *Interviewer: Tell me about that night.* (YRK/£)

Always be aware of the information your informant supplies. This can help you in at least two ways. First, it will enable you to ask relevant questions about their experience during the interview, as in (17).

> (17)
> [018] ... the scrapes she got into was just nobody's business. *Interviewer: **Can you tell us any of them?*** (YRK/r)

Second, if someone tells you a story in one interview, you can use it to elicit informal speech in a subsequent interview, as in (18).

> (18)
> *Interviewer:* ... one time, didn't you get taken to the police station in your curlers or something? You had your s – slippers on. [002] Oh yes, oh yes. *Interviewer: **Are you going to tell us about that?*** (YRK/a)

An added benefit of this line of questioning is that such in-group information is rapport-building and it marks you as an accepted participant/observer in the community or social group. In general, always follow the second most important Sociolinguistic Interview Rule – Be observant!

All these techniques will elicit personal life experiences rather than philosophical ideas or generalities. Also, keep in mind that these are general comments. In a real live interview situation you must always follow the foremost Sociolinguistic Interview Rule – Keep it natural!

RETAIN YOUR AUTHORITY

It is appropriate when interviewing to maintain a level of professionalism when it comes to technical aspects of recording. You must take on an air of authority in telling people where to sit so you can get the best sound. If you encounter the interviewee outside, suggest moving indoors. Make suggestions about the place to sit, i.e. away from windows. Insist on turning off televisions, electric fans, etc. Move away from a noisy motor. Whatever you do, do not interview someone beside the fridge, mantle clock or aquarium. If at all possible, make sure you are sitting in a room with carpeting. In fact, the ideal room in the house for interviewing is the living room.

INTERVIEW TECHNIQUES

Within the context of the sociolinguistic interview a number of more general techniques have evolved over the years which lead to optimal results, i.e. informal, spontaneous, natural dialogue. These techniques permit neutralisation, or at least mitigation, of the natural obstacles inherent in the interview situation.

LET THE INFORMANT TALK!

The first technique is perhaps the most obvious – let the informant talk. This means if you ask a question and the person talks on and on *and* off topic, let them. The whole idea of getting beyond the observer's paradox is to have data that is spontaneous. One of the worst things an interviewer can do is interrupt the informant. Note the inappropriateness of the interviewer's question at the end of the excerpt in (19). It would have been better to simply say, 'Really, tell me more about that!'.

(19)
[070] That's where he shot, right in that rock there. Uncle John. George Ashe shot him there. *Interviewer*: *Royce, what's the name of your children?*

The effectiveness of the sociolinguistic interview should not be underestimated. People love to talk about their own personal experiences in life. A sociolinguistic interview can be an extremely cathartic experience for the interviewee. It can also be quite an eye-opener for the interviewer, especially if you are interviewing someone you already know. You may find out things you never knew before.

Tip

Practise sociolinguistic interviewing technique at family gatherings. Sit beside an elderly relative and start a conversation. Ask them what it was like growing up in their day; and be interested in whatever they tell you. Ask another question. See if you can get them to tell you a story about their life. I'll bet you will hear some highly interesting linguistic variables!

APPROXIMATE THE VERNACULAR

Another technique involves approximating the vernacular of the informant. Labov calls this 'colloquial format' (1984: 33). Inexperienced interviewers tend to act like they are traditional interviewers. They will formulate questions very formally with standard (or formal) grammar and intonation. This, of course, causes the interviewee to act in the same way – exactly what you do not want. If you can, naturally and appropriately approximate the vernacular used by the informant. If you are relaxed and speaking informally, the informant is likely to, as well.

ASK SHORT QUESTIONS

Another technique is simply to ask short questions. Questions formulated without preparation tend to be quite long, with many restarts. Labov (1984: 34) suggests that each question should take less than five seconds to deliver, and in many cases, less than one second, as in (20).

(20)
a. *Interviewer*: What did he do? (YRK/f)
b. *Interviewer*: What was it like? (YRK/7)

TAKE AN INSIDER'S POINT OF VIEW

Pay particular attention to how you formulate questions (see Labov 1982: 34). Here the idea is to show that you understand the critical issues of the community/neighbourhood or group. Make reference to something you know about the community, as in (21).

(21)
a. Hey, did you see that accident last night?
b. What was Mr X doing on the roof yesterday?

Let the informant know that you can ask questions that point at real problems of concern to the people. In this way, the conversation takes on life.

BE THE LEARNER

Labov says that the basic counter-strategy of the sociolinguistic interview is to emphasise the position of the interviewer as a learner.

However, this can lead to some interesting interviewing moments, as in (22), where you can observe that Labov's strategy had worked far better than I (the interviewer) had imagined.

(22)
[104] And in the morning you had skim that, and there was churning to do. And there was the old dash then.
Interviewer: What's that?
[104] Churn the butter *(laughter)*. ***Oh-god, you're stupid!*** *(GYV/104)*

WISDOM OF INFORMANTS

In the end, the data that you will collect by using these strategies will be more remarkable than you can imagine. I never cease to be amazed at how poignant sociolinguistic interviews can be. In fact, some of the wisdom, sayings and thoughts of people whose words I have analysed have been etched in my memory for ever, as in (23).

(23)
a. If you can do the right things, you do the right thing. Sometimes you do the right thing, it's the wrong thing. So, I mean, life is a big risk. (GYE/Ô)
b. Money- money doesn't mean a thing, love. As long as you've enough to pay your bills, that's all you want. You don't want money in the bank, you just want to get through. (YRK/b)

SUMMARY

Sociolinguistic interviews are highly variable and depend on the personality of the interlocutors (both interviewer and interviewee) and the rapport they build together during the course of their time together. Nevertheless, the techniques I have outlined in this chapter will go a long way towards making each of your interviews as successful as possible. In my own experience the sociolinguistic interview is one of those uncommon situations in which you end up learning a lot more than you could have thought possible. As you collect data, continue to refine your interview technique along the general lines discussed in this chapter. As you progress, note modules and individual questions that are successful, and reuse them. Add new modules. The key is to be responsive. The ultimate reward is the quality of the data you collect.

Exercise 3: Adapting the sociolinguistic interview

Based on what you have already learned about your target data (group) from completing Exercise 2, prepare a preliminary version of an Interview Schedule for your target population.

Using the model Interview Schedule in Appendix B on the companion website, adapt the questions so as to be compatible with your particular group and situation. Find ways to reword questions so that they are appropriate to the group and/or neighbourhood you plan to work with. Add or remove modules where appropriate. Add or revise questions and examples that are relevant and interesting to your prospective informants. Make plenty of references to issues and/or problems current in the community/group. To the best of your ability, use in-group knowledge and terminology in creating your questions. Use wording that feels comfortable and natural to you.

Your interview schedule should be organised into topics/modules, and should include at least one section dealing specifically with the neighbourhood/group in question.

Try out the interview schedule on a friend. Keep track of problems as well as successes. Make sure you are familiar with all the questions.

4 Data, data and more data

What do you do with your data once you have collected it? This chapter will elucidate the procedures for handling a large body of natural speech.

Chapters 1 to 3 have focused on methods for collecting optimal data for analysis. Now it is time to learn what to do with data once you have it. This chapter focuses on data handling and, in particular, techniques for representing speech data in writing.

When faced with a collection of dozens upon dozens of audio-tapes, minidisks or sound files, what do you do next? How can you make the invaluable data contained within maximally accessible and useful?

In this chapter, I focus on tried-and-true procedures from my own experience. I build on the foundations of earlier corpus-building projects (Poplack 1989, Poplack and Tagliamonte 1991). However, I also focus on data arising from fieldwork conducted in the British Isles between 1995 and 2001 (e.g. Tagliamonte 1998, Tagliamonte et al. 2005).

THE CORPUS

The components of a corpus, at least in my own research, are listed in (1):

Components of a corpus

(1)
a. recording media, audio-tapes (analogue, digital) or other
b. interview reports (hard copies) and signed consent forms
c. transcription files (ASCII, Word, txt)
d. a transcription protocol (hard copy and soft)
e. a database of information (FileMaker, Excel, etc.)
f. analysis files (Goldvarb files, token, cel, cnd and res)

The basic substance of a language corpus is the data. Most of my corpora have been collected on audio-tapes and represent one to two hours of conversation between a single interviewer and an informant. These audio-tapes are catalogued (minimally) by number, date and name of the speaker. Each audio-tape has a corresponding 'interview report', a document which provides anthropological information and observations about the speaker and the interview context. More recently, due to ethical guidelines, every interview must have a signed consent form from the interviewee. Transcription files refer to the soft-copy computer files in which these conversations have been transcribed. The transcription protocol documents the method by which the conversations have been transcribed. The database of information is a relational database in which all kinds of information about the corpus is accounted for, including information from the interview reports, speaker codes and numbers, etc. as well as ongoing information about the linguistic studies. Finally, the analysis files. These are the hundreds of different computer files that are produced when a particular linguistic feature is subjected to a fully fledged study (see Chapters 8–10).

Perhaps the most important strategy for corpus-building is to have a strict procedure in place for identifying the components of a corpus and linking them together and, further, for making it all maximally usable. However, the most onerous and time-consuming task of all is transcribing the data. The analyst must be able to assess the materials easily and efficiently – in other words, data at your fingertips.

LABELLING

First of all, how are all the bits going to fit together? The audio record must exhibit a link with everything else that was produced from that record – interview reports, transcription files, etc. In order to connect all the relevant information you must provide each informant or speaker in your corpus with a pseudonym. Pseudonyms can be assigned by various means. A search through a local telephone directory will locate numerous appropriate local surnames. Attach these randomly to the speakers in the corpus or use a method known only to yourself. In all my British projects I simply utilised the speakers' own initials but filled in new ethnically consistent names, as in (2).

(2)
a. Katy Webster   = Katherine Walters
b. Bobby Hamilton = Barry Hatfield

Note

When I taught my first course in sociolinguistic research methods, the students' audio-tapes came back with names like 'Mickey Mouse', 'King Henry VIII', 'Baby Spice' and the like. While amusing, such names obscure the origins and nature of the data.

Each member of a corpus is also provided with an informant number and, critically, a single-character speaker identification code for use in coding data for analysis (see Chapter 6). Each audio record, interview report, as well as the computer transcriptions, is labelled with this information, the corpus or community, the informant pseudonym, informant number, tape number and speaker identification code. This information for a speaker from the York English Corpus, E. Burritt, is shown in (3).

Protocol for identification ▬▬▬▬▬▬▬▬▬▬▬▬▬▬▬▬▬▬▬▬

(3)
Corpus/Community, e.g. York [YRK]
Informant pseudonym, Elise Burritt [EB]
Tape number, 003
Informant number, 002
Speaker identification code, b

The unique numbering for each speaker across all the components of each corpus enables the data associated with that speaker to be permanently traceable back to its original source.

An identifying string with much of the same information is placed at the beginning of the transcription file, as in (4).

(4)
Protocol for labelling transcription files
[York, Elise Burritt, 82, EB 002, Clare 1, Angela 2, Tape 003]

Here, as well, are indicators of speaker age, 82, the interviewer(s) who conducted the interview, e.g. Clare and/or Angela, and the identifier numbers that have been assigned to them, 1 and 2 respectively. Information about other participants in the interview is provided as well. In addition, the transcriptions record information about the number of the audio-tape, as well as the side of the audio-tape, if applicable (e.g. Side A or B).

Data manipulation

Concurrent with the corpus construction phase, create a place to store information about your speakers. Once contained in such a database, this information is available in many different ways. For example, at any given time, the corpora in my archive can be searched for, say, males aged 70–75. How many are there? Who are they? What are their other characteristics, such as education level, occupation, etc. When I search for such individuals in my York English Corpus, I get the results in the table in (5). This type of information is always at my fingertips using the search engine within this program.

(5)

Table 1: Automated retrieval of speaker information and characteristics

Speaker #	Pseudonym	Speaker ID	Sex	Age	Birth place	Education
018, 019	Hugh Phillips	j	M	72	York, UK	Up to age 14
030, 031	David Wallis	q	M	72	York, UK	Up to age 14
032, 033	Walter Evans	r	M	72	York, UK	Up to age 15
113, 114	Harry Peerson	≠	M	75	York, UK	Up to age 14

Some programs can also produce tape labels, informant lists and data analysis information. I also record additional information we discover during transcription, e.g. additional demographic information, familial relationships across the corpus, etc. In this way the informant database becomes a critical add-on to the data files.

DATA TRANSCRIPTION

One of the major problems in transcribing conversational data is that the spoken language is not at all like written language, yet translation from one medium to the other is required. In fact, recorded conversations of 'real' language present many very tricky challenges. How do you end up with a corpus that provides a maximally usable rendition of the spoken language in an affordable amount of time? A crucial first step is to determine the form the transcription will take.

Practically speaking even a one-hour interview might require an investment of anywhere from a day's worth of work to an entire week or more. A standard estimate for a first transcription following the procedures detailed below is that one hour of recorded data equals four hours of transcribing. However, this estimate varies widely depending on the sound quality, the number of speakers in the recording and the transcriber's familiarity with the dialect represented on the audio record. Given the time and financial constraints of any project, keep this practical constraint in mind when balancing between detail of transcription and time it takes to complete.

In the first place, it is critical to understand that there are inherent and unavoidable limits to any type of transcription. You will not ever come close to recreating the sound recording. The audio record will at all times, and every instance, remain the primary documentation of your data.

In light of these considerations, you might think that the most complete, the most detailed transcription would be the best (Macaulay 1991: 282). In fact, this is not the case. If you had to represent even some phonetic and phonological variation of natural speech in writing, it would take an interminable time to transcribe. In early corpus construction projects, up to six tiers of transcription, all representing a different level of the grammar, were attempted. However, it soon became clear that such a transcription was overly complicated, requiring years of research expenditure in time and funding. The transcription process is all about deciding, carefully, about what to represent and what not to represent so as to facilitate future research.

A first step in this direction is to decide the purpose of the transcription, i.e. to ask what the research goals are. Discussing the Ottawa-Hull project, one of the largest computerised corpora in the world (3.5 million words), Poplack (1989: 430) notes that 'there's a major trade-off between size of the data base and level of detail of the transcription'. The goal of a transcription can be encapsulated as in (6):

Transcription goals

(6)
∗ detailed enough to retain enough information to conduct linguistic analyses in an efficient way
∗ simple enough to be easily readable and relatively easily transcribed

Maintaining a workable balance between these two goals is the key component of any corpus construction endeavour.

THE TRANSCRIPTION PROTOCOL

The major challenge for making a corpus machine-readable is to ensure that the recorded speech data be represented faithfully and consistently. This means transcribing exactly what the person said regardless of whether it follows the so-called 'rules' of the standard language. In other words, you should not edit or otherwise modify the language in your audio record in any way. Syntax, lexical choice, omissions, additions and neologisms of all sorts should be scrupulously respected.

In order to keep track of precisely how you do this, you need a 'transcription protocol'. The transcription protocol is a reference document of transcription practice. It is a permanent record that ensures consistent representation of words, phrases, features of natural discourse, and features particular to the data within and across all the transcriptions in a corpus. On the companion website, in Appendix C, I have included as an example my current transcription protocol.

ORTHOGRAPHIC CONVENTIONS

The first rule of transcribing is authentic representation of the data (see Poplack 1989: 434), including lack of subject–verb agreement, lack of number agreement, zero subjects, definite articles and complementisers, unusual verb forms, and a large number of other constructions not sanctioned by prescriptive grammarians, as in (7).

(7)
Behind house, we'd come down there, you never seed a paper, you never seed a van of no description. We were down there weeks and weeks over end and never seed a soul. And this like weather like this in summer-time, well there was a few come walking round, but er, in winter-time you could go two months and never see a soul. (YRK/¥)

Use of standard orthography and standard punctuation are critical for readability and ease of transcription (Preston 1985, 2000). First, transcribe the word the way it is normally spelled (unless you have just cause to include a different rendition of a word). Second, use standard punctuation, i.e. full stops, question marks, commas, etc. as you would normally use them in writing.

Transcription conventions ▰▰▰▰▰▰▰▰▰▰▰▰▰▰▰▰▰▰▰▰▰▰

However, because speech is replete with false starts, interrupted words, hesitations and rephrasing, etc., these must be represented in the text in a consistent and readable way as well. The flow of conversation from one speaker to the next must also be indicated.

As mentioned earlier, each speaker in the corpus is assigned a numeric code. This numeric code is then placed before each utterance of that speaker in the data. In the data excerpt in (8), participants in the interview are 1 and 2 and 001. These numbers appear in square brackets. Interviewers are assigned single-digit numbers, e.g. '1', '2' or '3', and informants two- or three-digit numbers, e.g. '01' or '001', depending on the total number of speakers in the corpus. Additional participants are also assigned single-digit numbers, e.g. '4' or higher.

(8)
[1] What year was that? [001] Well it would be in the fifties. [1] Yeah? [2] What did you think of them? [001] Well I can't really remember now ... (YRK/a)

Orthographic conventions

False starts are represented with single hyphens, as in (9).

False starts

(9)
a. And it's *a-* I've got it in shed anyway. It's er, *a-* a ball ... (YRK/W)
b. [046] And I just *didn't-* I didn't want to be rotten. (YRK/T)

Partial words are represented with double hyphens, as in (10).

Partial words

(10)
a. [001] And she *love- -* loved that job, it was lovely. (YRK/a)
b. [002] So you had to *unlo- -* unload your bull (YRK/b)

Audible pauses in the discourse are marked with three dots, as in (11).

Pauses/silence

(11)
a. [001] I got to um ... when I were about fifteen, we went to Cayton-Bay. (YRK/a)
b. [002] And er ... I can't tell you exactly what happened. (YRK/b)

Like the use of standard punctuation, these markers guide the reader through the words in the data, thus facilitating readability of the transcription.

Hyphenation

Another useful strategy for transcribing data is the prudent use of hyphenation. The hyphen can be used as a linking device to associate words with each other so that they are treated together in data processing.

For example, an informant might have an overwhelming number of forms such as 'is that right?', 'you don't say', 'oh my gosh' spotted throughout his or her discourse. What is the function of these chunks? Do the words that make it up have equal function status to those same words used in other contexts? If not, then the entire chunk is a good candidate for being a discourse marker of some sort. If so, then it may be more usefully treated as a single item. I will also typically hyphenate tags, as in (12), as well as exclamations and fixed expressions, as in (13). This procedure ensures that these forms will also be treated uniquely for later retrieval and analysis. It also keeps these constructions separate from other more grammatical uses of the same words.

Tags

(12)
a. you-know
b. I-mean

Expressions

(13)
a. as-I-say
b. oh-my-God

I also hyphenate names of people, places, songs and games, as in (14):

People, places, songs, games

(14)
a. Bootham-Bar
b. Piggy-in-the-Middle

Numerals are represented orthographically, as in (15), since numerals are always reserved to indicate speaker/informant interchanges.

(15) There's **_a-hundred-and-forty_** in North-Yorkshire. (YRK/¢)

Paralinguistic intervention, such as *huh, er, uh, mm,* etc. are also indicated in standardised orthography. However, do not overly complicate the transcription protocol with innumerable spellings for these types of things. This will significantly complicate the transcription process as transcribers attempt to judge which spelling to employ every time they hear a different one. I have typically opted to represent the *major* forms of the dialect and abstract away from the innumerable details (Tagliamonte to appear a).

In British English we ended up with forms such as *er*, *mm* and *um*, as in (16).

> (16)
> a. [1] Was that Maureen? [002] **Er** yes, Maureen was the eldest. (YRK/b)
> b. [002] Oh that's lovely, **mm**. (YRK/b)
> c. [046] The blimmin **um**, what-you-call-it. (YRK/T)

Laughter, as in (17a), other noises, and contextual information which aids in interpreting the text, as in (17b), are marked off from the text with parentheses.

> (17)
> a. [002] The man never moved so fast in his life! *(laughter)* (YRK/b)
> b. [046] *(knocking)*. Hello? Well it's late. (YRK/T)

Inevitably, some parts of natural speech data are entirely incomprehensible. Sometimes this is due to the quality of the recording, sometimes to interference from other noise on the recording, sometimes simply because the transcriber has not familiarised themselves sufficiently with the phonology of the dialect. Discourse that is not understood by the transcriber is transcribed with '(inc)', as in (18).

> (18)
> a. [046] You haven 't given me my *(inc)*. (YRK/b)
> b. [002] Before I *(inc)* it will do no good. (YRK/T)

Another aspect of natural speech data is that conversations are inherently overlapping. What is to be done with simultaneous speech by two or more interlocutors? A two-tiered transcription significantly complicates the transcription. My practice is to record what the first person says, then the second, as in (19), even though many interchanges overlap.

> (19)
> [007] Oh aye, aye, I seen that old boy. (laughter) [1] You're laching, you're la- - [007] I'm no laching, I'm jo- - I'm telling you. [1] You've seen it? [007] Scared the life out o me. [1] Tell us [009] Yeah, tell her about it [1] Tell us about it? [007] I was coming- I'm very pally wi a feller called Jim-Steele ... (PVG/007)

These procedures for transcription are easily maintained with the transcription protocol in ready proximity for reference.

The next problem is to determine the level of linguistic detail you will represent in your transcription.

Which linguistic phenomena to represent?

The trickiest aspect of transcription is that spoken language contains all kinds of natural linguistic processes, including vowel reduction, consonant elision, etc. At the same time, there are literally hundreds of variable processes happening at all levels of the grammar – inherent variation.

Each word may have a number of different pronunciations in the same discourse and these different pronunciations can be represented in a number of different ways, as in (20):

(20)
a. 'just'   *just*, *jus'*
b. 'going to'   *going to*, *goin' to*, *gonna*, *gon*
c. 'because'   *'cause*, *'cos*, *beca'*, etc.
d. 'my'   *my*, *mi*

It is necessary to decide which of these variants are meaningful to your ongoing research interests and which are not. Every distinction you decide to represent will complicate the transcription process in terms of having to listen to and distinguish these items phonologically while transcribing. Further, it will complicate the readability of the end product.

Beware of inconsistency in transcription, i.e. representing a word like 'and' in two or more different orthographies, e.g. *and, an' an,* etc. There are innumerable comparable examples. If you represented *all* of them orthographically, just think how many different entries you would have for each form. They would be worth differentiating if any of them were meaningful distinctions for future analysis. Think of the transcription protocol as a blueprint which balances the complexity of transcription with the requirements of the analyses that will follow.

Phonological processes

Phonological processes are typically not represented in a transcription. This means no commas to indicate dropping of 'g's, 't,d' deletion, or the like. No abbreviations of things like 'lemme' for 'let me', 'wanna' for 'want to' and untold others. Representing any or even some of these creates a transcription that is difficult to read, understand and work with, and has few returns linguistically. As I mentioned earlier, any analysis of phonological variation is going to require relistening to the audio record anyway. Moreover, if the transcription is orthographic, then this will assist you later on when you are engaged in extraction and coding phonological variables. If words have been consistently rendered in the transcription, regardless of pronunciation, then you can search for and highlight all the strings in which the variable may be present in the transcription file before you start listening to it. For example, extracting variable (ing) becomes much simpler if you can 'see' the tokens (all word-final 'ing' highlighted in yellow, for example), coming up as you listen to the sound file.

In sum, my overarching strategy for transcription is to represent variation resulting from the operation of phonological processes in standard orthography regardless of the actual pronunciation of the form.

Morphological processes

Representing morphological variation in your transcription is more likely to be useful, particularly if you want to analyse morphological variability. If variant pronunciations of forms affect the entire morpheme, representing the variants orthographically ensures that the linguistic process responsible for the variants could be extracted from the data automatically. However, every orthographic anomaly will detract from the readability of your transcription. For example, variable plural marking produces forms such as two *miles* and two *mile*. In order to represent the latter variant and distinguish it from singular forms, a unique orthography is required. Ideally, the form you chose to represent the word should remain as close to the standard as possible, e.g. *mileø*. Notice how this immediately compromises readability. This is why you should avoid adopting ad hoc, idiosyncratic or arbitrary symbols such as capitalisation, or strange symbols which will complicate your transcription even further. Remember that one of the prime objectives is to keep your transcription as simple and readable as possible.

There will be many features which you will want to distinguish by orthographic means. When this is called for, how do you decide on a variant of standard orthography? Use common sense and the principle of simplicity. Do not place a great deal of emphasis on creating new spellings of variant pronunciations. Complicating your transcription protocol in this way is only justifiable when it can be linguistically motivated.

For example, why bother to create a distinct form 'buy't' to represent 'buy it' in the sentence *I can **buy't** here*. This unnecessarily obscures the transcription in that: 1) it creates a distinct form for a phonological reduction process; and 2) it puts two distinct morphemes with distinct functions together, i.e. *buy* and *it*. If you can motivate a distinct orthographic representation, then OK, but keep in mind that the most sensible objective is to keep like forms together.

Moreover, once you decide to represent a particular feature in a certain way, this must be done every single time. If not, the transcription will be unreliable. The problem is that more often than not these decisions are not transparent and require additional linguistic interpretation. The transcriber must interpret the function of each form before transcribing it. This is the danger of creating variant forms. It adds to the complexity of the transcription process and can lead to errors.

In fact, pre-deciding the way forms will be transcribed is a particularly thorny issue. Most critical is that the function of non-standard forms is often unknown a priori. In most cases, analysis is required to determine what the actual function of a non-standard form is. Furthermore, some forms, as with *like*, are in the process of rapid change. Transcribers in one age bracket might not have the same grammaticality judgements as project directors in another age bracket. Inconsistencies and errors arising from this type of practical problem can have a major impact on future work on a corpus. In the end, it is often better to opt for the most conservative decision – transcribe like forms in like manner – and leave the analysis of their (potential) different functions for a later stage in the research process.

The best practice for data analysis using machine-readable corpora is to combine automated extraction with the exacting methodological procedures that arise from the principle of accountability and circumscribing of the variable context (see Labov 1970, 1971, Sankoff 1974, Sankoff and Thibault 1980, Wolfram 1993; see also Chapters 1 and 5).

Words that don't exist in dictionaries

Another challenge for the transcription process is to record the words people use in speech. Many words and expressions are not found in standard dictionaries. Other words may appear in dialect dictionaries, but have several different orthographies. A decision must be made about which spelling to use. The transcription protocol is the place to keep a record of each decision you make.

Dialect words

Most corpora will inevitably have dialect features which will require a unique representation. For example, in York the form *nowt* and *owt* are used for *nothing* and *anything* respectively, as in (21a). When you find the same forms elsewhere, e.g. in Maryport, as in (21b), apply the same spelling.

(21)
Nowt/owt
a. Never got any nasties or **_owt_** like that. (YRK/&)
b. And he got **_nowt_**. Not a penny. (MPT/!)

Negative constructions are often quite different from Standard English in northern British dialects. We decided on the spelling *nae* for contexts such as (22) and *no* for contexts as in (23).

(22)
There was **_nae_** problem wi her. (PVG/a)

(23)
It's **_no_** very long. (PVG/a)

Dialect pronunciations of mundane words can be quite distinct. You may opt to transcribe idiosyncratic pronunciations of common words in order to give a certain amount of 'flavour' to the data, e.g. *snaw* for 'snow', *drap* for 'drop'.

All these forms are entered into the transcription protocol for reference so that they are consistently represented across all corpora. The standard procedure for deciding which dialect spellings to use is simple. First, consult the literature, i.e. existing dialect dictionaries, online dictionaries and other corpora, and establish form, function and spelling conventions. When different orthographic choices exist, choose the most frequently used one. In the rare case that a word cannot be found, make a reasoned choice at its spelling and record it in the transcription protocol for future reference.

Non-standard verbal morphology

Verb forms are notoriously varied in dialect data. Given a research goal to target morphosyntactic features, you may want to represent these unique forms, as in (24).

(24)
a. There were a lump **riz** on it. (CLB/q)
b. And eh, he used to **gie** you a hiding with stick. (MPT/a)

Slang, local terminology and expressions

Every variety will have its own swear words, local terminology and expressions, as in (25). Once documented in the transcription protocol consistent representation is possible.

(25)
a. blimmin'
b. crack = talk, gossip
c. roch-and-ready

There are many grey areas when it comes to making transcription decisions. For example, what does the analyst do with phonologically variable pronunciations of 'going to' when it is used as a future temporal reference marker? These can be represented orthographically as *going to, gointa, goina, gonna, onna*, etc. depending on the pronunciation. Should these be rendered by identical orthography and, if so, which one? Alternatively, should they be differentiated and, if so, to what level of detail? An important linguistic factor is that in ongoing grammatical change of *going to* as a future temporal reference marker, phonological coalescence of form is an important concomitant of the grammaticalisation process (see Poplack and Tagliamonte 2001). Thus, different phonological forms may be implicated in ongoing change. Is this worth representing in a data transcription? The only way to answer this question is to determine how important the distinctions will be for future research. Do you want to invest the time and attention during the transcription phase or later on?

These are the types of things that you have to be aware of and sensitive to in the transcription phase. If the variation is not going to form part of future research, it is wiser not to represent it orthographically. Put your energy into transcribing linguistic variation which is meaningful, interesting, wild and exciting – to you. Remember the prime directive – distinguish forms which represent potential linguistic processes which are likely to become part of the analytic phase of your research.

DATA PROCESSING

Once a corpus has been transcribed, it becomes machine-readable. The transcriptions can be processed automatically in any number of ways. A simple, straightforward concordance program for Macintosh is Concorder (Rand and Patera 1992). Others are available on the Internet, both for Macintosh and PCs. As long as your text files are simply ASCII files, they can be imported into most programs. Concorder, for example, enables you to produce word lists, indexes and concordances of your data files.

Because each individual in your data files has been identified by number and this appears before each of that speaker's utterances, you can select to process every word uttered by that speaker. Words or other parts of the transcription that have been enclosed in parentheses, such as incomprehensible sections, laughter and other commentary, can be ignored. These details are part of the Concorder requirements. Other programs will have similar stipulations so that the informant's words can be isolated for analysis.

INDEX

An index is an alphabetical listing of all the words in a given transcription file. Perhaps the most useful information in the index is the number of words of each type and the total number of words uttered by the speaker. This information is ideal for providing an overview of the general frequency of a form in the corpus. For example, if a feature such as discourse *like* occurs, what is its proportion of occurrence? In Toronto English in 2003, it represents 4 per cent of the total number of words in speakers aged 10–19. In English dialects in the British Isles in 1997, it represents 0.09 per cent of the total number of words in speakers aged 60 and upwards. This tells us quite a bit about the use of this feature in these different situations and amongst very different people.

The table in (26) shows an excerpt of the index entries from *than* to *three* for EB, speaker 002 in the York English Corpus. Notice that, even with this small excerpt, definite patterns of linguistic behaviour are notable. Function words are very frequent compared to lexical words. Compare *the* to *thermal* or *thing*, for example. Notice the different frequencies of certain pronouns, such as *that* [N = 134] vs *this* [N = 42] or *these* [N = 8] vs *those* [N = 17], or the distribution of tense forms in the same lexical verb 'think', i.e. *think* = 27 vs *thought* = 8.

(26)

Excerpt of an index using Concorder.

than	3	things	11
that	134	think	27
the	294	thinking	1
their	7	thirty	5
them	44	this	42
then	58	those	17
there	80	thought	8
thermal	1	thousand	1
these	8	thousands	1
they	126	threatened	2
thing	5	three	10

Such overall distribution patterns can point to likely linguistic features for investigation. In fact, a quick check of the index can reveal startling research results. For example, in my current research in Toronto, one of the first things I do after a transcription is finalised is to produce an index for the speaker. Then, I check the ratio of the word *like* to the words *and* and *the*. Remarkably, for many younger speakers, use of the word *like* is far more frequent than these two most common words in the English language! Compare the index entries in (27) for EB, female age 82, in York to CF, female age 16, in Toronto. Such findings, while preliminary, provide fruitful starting points for ongoing investigations.

(27)

	EB (YRK/b)	CF (TOR/a)
and	518	480
the	294	229
like	19	**1186**

Tip

One of my favourite ways to look for new research targets is to compile an index of every informant in a corpus to see which forms are being used frequently vis-à-vis others. Remember that one of the identifiers for grammatical change is a rise in frequency.

AUTOMATED EXTRACTION

Perhaps an even more useful function available to you with a computerised corpus is the ability to automatically extract selected forms in
the contexts in which they occur. For example, in (28), some of the
instances of non-standard *them* and standard *those* from EB have been
extracted from her interview.

```
(28)

THOSE/THEM variation in EB (YRK/b)
THOSE
1.40,82    because it was horses in THOSE days.
1.46,6     yards THOSE days, with a few pigs in, hens,
1.47,67    And in THOSE days, if you to go for a

THEM
1.49,24    In THEM days, you didn't care, but
1.131,31   And all THEM things, and the things
1.274,40   Ron, er it wasn't worth a lot of money THEM days,
```

The process of extracting all the instances of these forms took
seconds. This format provides two noteworthy advantages over simple word counts. First, the patterns in the data become visible. The
most obvious observation is that standard form is much more frequent than the non-standard form. Notice the preponderance of
certain lexical items, e.g. *day*. How likely is it that *day* will receive
the non-standard form? In the total data, there are fourteen instances of *day*. Of these, three are non-standard (20 per cent). This correlation can be calculated precisely, very easily, revealing that there
is no particular propensity for the non-standard form to appear on
this frequent lexical item. Second, the data are already in a format
which makes them (practically) ready to import into the variable
rule program (see Chapter 8) for coding and subsequent statistical
analysis.

Of course, automated extraction procedures like this can only be
fruitfully implemented for variants which are overt in the transcription. The search for zero tokens is the 'bugaboo' of orthographic
transcription practices. This is why many researchers opt to 'tag'
a corpus for other relevant linguistic information such as the
function of forms in the grammar (e.g. Taylor to appear). Again, your
decision about whether or not to do this will depend on how much
time you wish to invest in the corpus construction phase of your
research.

CONCORDANCE

A concordance processes the transcription files similarly but creates a formatted listing of all the words in the file alphabetically in the context in which they occurred in the discourse. The data files which are produced using this method are immense. For example, for EB's interview we recorded approximately one hour of audio-tape. This produced twenty-four pages of transcription, which takes up 72K of disk space. The concordance, however, takes up 992Ks of computer space and is 294 pages long! A very small excerpt of the concordance is shown in (29).

(29)

Concordance for EB (YRK/b), part of page 192 of 294 pages

```
THOSE 17
1 . 4 0 : because it was horses in those days. [1] Uh-huh
1 . 4 6 : had all the um, pub yards those days, with a few pigs
1 . 4 7 : 1] Yeah. [002] And in those days, if you to go

THOUGHT 8
1 . 5 9 : my family history, and I thought you wanted York
1 . 1 0 7 : the table.' And I never thought Harry meant it,
1 . 1 1 4 : because he- they all thought he was Harry
```

Each key word is centred in context for easy viewing. Each context is also indexed with the line number in the transcription file so that it can be traced back to its original location in the discourse.

DIGITAL DATA AND BEYOND

In recent years, the advent of digitisation has meant that audio-taped data can be easily transferred to computer. Using digital recording at the outset gives you a computerised corpus from the very beginning. Because technology has been changing so rapidly over the last few years, many different practices exist (e.g. Beal et al. to appear a). One thing is certain, tapes decay, hard drives crash and CDs may not be the ideal storage option. Whenever you invest time, energy and money into collecting speech materials, you should have some plan in place for long-term preservation of your priceless data.

SUMMARY

A machine-readable corpus is a boon for the analyst. One that has been transcribed consistently and comprehensibly is even better. One that also has easily accessible support materials and a simple way of seeking out and finding appropriate speakers and data will make you efficient and productive. Automated processing via indexing and concordancing is like the icing on the cake. Used judiciously, these procedures can provide you with a great deal of preliminary insights into your data, including word frequency information. More importantly, automated extraction will greatly facilitate the data extraction process. You will be able to accomplish a certain amount of initial coding, which can then be directly imported into the variable rule program. I will show you these techniques in the chapters that follow.

Exercise 4: Devising a transcription protocol

Representing speech data in writing in an accessible and usable way is a challenge and a skill. Try transcribing a sample of the data you are targeting for investigation. Take, for example, five minutes of a sociolinguistic interview and begin to type what you hear. Create an accompanying 'transcription protocol'.

Data transcription

Transcribe your data as consistently and faithfully as possible by following the rules for transcribing outlined in Chapter 4. Retain as many (linguistic) distinctions as you deem necessary, yet maintain the readability of your text. Represent choice morphological processes orthographically, decide on the spelling for idiosyncratic words and phrases. Apply hyphenation and standard punctuation conventions.

Notice the linguistic characteristics of your data that have implications for transcription. For example, understanding a community/group's distinctive phonology can help you understand their variety of English. Many words, not understood initially, can be decoded when you realise that a given speaker/group has a specific phonological process regulating the pronunciation of certain phonemes. In second language acquisition scenarios, this can sometimes be explained in terms of phonological and/or morphological transference from the first language. Deal with these distinctions in your transcription protocol. Whether you came up with the 'correct' way to represent these is not as important as the fact that you noticed them.

Using the model transcription protocol in Appendix C on the companion website, adapt it to be compatible with your data set and research interests.

5 The linguistic variable

How do you find a *linguistic variable*? This chapter will discuss the key construct in the variationist paradigm – the linguistic variable. It will detail the definition of a linguistic variable, describe what it is, how to identify it and how to circumscribe it.

DEFINING THE LINGUISTIC VARIABLE

> The definition of a linguistic variable is the first and also the last step in the analysis of variation. It begins with the simple act of noticing a variation – that there are two alternative ways of saying the same thing. (Labov to appear)

The most fundamental construct in variation analysis is the 'linguistic variable'. The quote above is the most recent one I could find from Labov himself; turning back to the original definition of the linguistic variable you find something a little more complicated. In 1966, Labov (1966/1982: 49) says the linguistic variable must be 'high in frequency, have a certain immunity from conscious suppression ... [be] integral units of larger structures, and ... be easily quantified on a linear scale'. Furthermore, the linguistic variable was required to be 'highly stratified' and to have 'an asymmetric distribution over a wide range of age levels or other ordered strata of the society' (Labov 1972c: 8). In this chapter, I shall 'unpack' what all this means. At the outset, however, the most straightforward and simple definition of the linguistic variable is simply 'two or more ways of saying the same thing' (Labov 1972c, Sankoff 1980: 55).

At the level of phonology, the linguistic variable is relatively straightforward. The alternates may simply differ by an extra phonological feature or two, such as the classic (t,d) and (ing) variables of English. Variable (t,d) involves word-final consonant clusters. Sometimes the cluster is realised; sometimes it is not, as in (1a). Variable (ing) involves word-final *-ing*. Sometimes it is realised as [ŋ]; sometimes as [n], as in (1b). Variable (t) involves the pronunciation of word-internal intervocalic [t]. Sometimes it is realised as [t], sometimes as [ɾ], as in (1c). In these cases, there is little contention of semantic equivalence, i.e. 'means the same thing', since the variant forms alternate within the same word.

(1)
a. I misse[t] the bus yesterday. vs I miss[Ø] the bus yesterday.
b. shoppi[ŋ] vs shoppi[n]
c. bu[t]r vs bu[ɾ]r

In morphosyntax, however, alternation of forms may involve variable inflections, alternate lexical items or elementary syntactic differences that arise in the course of sentence derivation, as in (2). Is the original definition of the linguistic variable as 'two ways of saying the same thing' viable?

(2)
a. go slow**Ø** vs go slow**ly**
b. the woman **who** ... vs the woman **that** ...
c. he **isn't** vs he**'s not**

The question becomes whether or not two different ways of saying the same thing ever happens in syntax and semantics. If it does, how is it to be recognised, interpreted and explained effectively? Crucial to these questions is the often difficult task of defining the context of meaning, which requires having some principled way of dealing with the problematic relationship between linguistic form and linguistic function. Indeed, one of the key preoccupations of variation analysis has been that different forms can have the same meaning. But how can this be? Shouldn't each form have a different meaning?

From the very beginning, linguistics and sociolinguistics have been opposed in their treatment of 'meaning':

> two different lexical items or structures can almost always have some usages or contexts in which they have different meanings, or functions, and it is even claimed by some that this difference, though it may be subtle, is always pertinent whenever one of the forms is used. (Sankoff 1988b: 153)

The first recognition of the form/function problem is found in Weiner and Labov (1983). They demonstrate that generalised active sentences, as in (3a), and agentless passives, as in (3b), are opposing choices of the same syntactic variable.

(3)
a. They broke into the liquor closet.
b. The liquor closet was broken into.

In order to include these two variants in one syntactic variable, the two forms must have the same referential meaning. Such a supposition calls into question the nature of equivalence.

This is where there has been heated debate in the field, which has, in turn, been responsible for an evolution in thinking about variables. Much of this development occurred when analysts started studying linguistic variables 'above and beyond phonology'. In effect, analysts had to become much more rigorous and explicit in how they treated the data.

In order to study the linguistic variable a two-step methodological process is required; first, identification of two or more variant expressions of a common underlying form; second, an accountable method for deciding all the possible variants and the contexts in which they occur; third, the source of the data must be accountable too, representing authentic data in a diversity of contexts.

A key principle underlying this method (see also Chapter 1) is 'the principle of accountability' (Labov 1982: 30). This principle is fundamental to variation analysis; it dictates that all occurrences of the target variable must be taken into account, not simply one variant or another. In other words,

> analysts should not select from a text those variants of a variable that tend to confirm their argument, and ignore others that do not. (Milroy and Gordon 2003: 137)

In other words, you must include all non-occurrences as well (Labov 1982: 30). Then, the occurrence of variants can be calculated out of the total number of contexts in which it could have occurred, but did not (proportional analysis; see Chapter 9). Similarly, statistical methods can be used to evaluate and compare different contextual effects as well as to detect and measure tendencies over time. Statistical techniques also permit correlations to be made among social and linguistic features. Still, a critical assumption underlies these procedures – the idea that the variants differ relatively little in terms of their function.

When the linguistic variable lies beyond phonology, the variants may not be similar at all. They may have entirely different lexical sources as well as different histories in the language. For example, the alternations between the *will* future and the *going to* future, as in (4), have distinct verbs as their source, Old English *willan* and the motion verb 'to go'. Alternation between *was* and *were*, as in (5), derives from two different verbs, present tense *beon* 'to exist' and past tense *wesan* 'to dwell'.

(4)
I think she's **gonna be** cheeky . . . I think she'**ll be** cheeky. (YRK/x)

(5)
There **was** always kids that **were** going missing. (YRK/h)

Such dissimilarities make it impossible to derive the variants from any meaning-preserving grammatical rule. Even the apparently mundane variation between *come* and *came*, as in (6), can be traced back to upheaval in the strong verbs of English in which varying vowel sounds within the verb stem produced different pronunciations of 'come'.

(6)
And Laura **come** in at five pound odd . . . I **came** in on the Friday . . . (YRK/J)

'Furthermore, the variant whose written form is *come* is much older than *came*. This highlights another issue – the variants may have entirely separate histories in the language not explicable on purely structural terms.

In the case of variables functioning at the level of discourse or pragmatics, the notion of semantic equivalence becomes even more problematic. For example, the variable constructions in (7), which include subject drop (7a), use of *like* (7b) and post-posing in (7c), may be considered semantically distinct.

(7)
a. *Ø* used to rent a house with er my mother's sister and cousins. Yeah, so **we** used to rent this big house . . . (YRK/w)
b. **Just like** little carriages, yes. Yes, **just** *Ø* little tiny things, yes. (YRK/9)
c. **I was** terrible, really . . . Very selfish, **I was!** (YRK/9)

Such cases are problematic for the original grammatical formalism of the variable rules as variants arising from a common underlying form, transformed by some rule of grammar.

In theory, no two forms can have identical meaning, but in practice two different forms can be used interchangeably in some contexts even though they may have distinct referential meanings in other contexts. In fact, you are dealing with at least two different levels of meaning: 1) comprehensive meaning, which takes into consideration every possible inference; and 2) meaning as it is used in the speech community.

While the first is subject to idiosyncratic interpretation and an infinite range of potential meanings, the second is by definition a consensus that is shared and relatively constant. The claim is that meaning in the latter sense should adhere to a narrower interpretation, and be restricted 'to designate the coupling of a given sentence with a given state of affairs' (Weiner and Labov 1983: 30). Indeed, the definition of the linguistic variable may be defined as the task of 'separating out the functionally equivalent from the inferentially possible' (Weiner and Labov 1983: 33). In other words, a foundational task in variation analysis is to 'circumscribe the variable context', the painstaking task which requires the analyst to 'ascertain which structures of forms may be considered variants of each other and in which contexts' (Sankoff 1982: 681).

RE-EXAMINING THE DEFINITION OF THE LINGUISTIC VARIABLE

When analysts first started analysing morphosyntactic variables, they borrowed the notion of semantic equivalence from the model of transformed and untransformed sentences in theories of grammar from the late 1960s (Weiner and Labov 1983). The problem of working out the common underlying grammatical basis for variants embroils the analyst in decisions about underlying and derived forms, which may differ depending on the theory of grammar, which, at the time when this first became an issue, was transformational-generative grammar. Variable rules beyond phonology did not work in this model for two main reasons. First, transformational rules were supposed to be meaning-preserving. However, with morphosyntactic variables this could not easily be defended in any theory of grammar, variationist or other. Second, forms which seemed to be equivalent to each other could often not be derived by the same transformational path.

However, these problems are not intrinsic to the nature of the linguistic variable itself, but are the result of the formalism in which they are embedded. As Sankoff and Thibault (1981) argued, the method of variation analysis obviates these problems. According to standard methodological procedures, the first step is the observation that two (or more) forms are distributed differentially across a community or within the discourse. In other words, the variationist method can only begin when the analyst is convinced that she is dealing with a bona fide variable. Indeed, the particular nature of the underlying form, or even its existence, is irrelevant (Sankoff and Thibault 1981).

You might ask, 'How can this be?' It comes back to the distributional facts of language. The advantage of variation analysis is working with real data, often from representative samples of communities, and from scrutiny of hundreds and perhaps thousands of instances of the linguistic variable. With this type of data on hand, the distributional facts about language use can be employed for understanding the nature of variation.

In the late 1970s and early 1980s studies of variation above and beyond phonology were breaking new ground. It is not surprising, then, that the operational definition of the linguistic variable was challenged (e.g. Lavandera 1978, 1982). The analytic method needed to be extended, revised and documented.

Sankoff and Thibault's study of weak complementarity demonstrated that the linguistic variable need not be semantically equivalent. Instead, discourse equivalence, or functional equivalence, was found to be the relevant criterion. Indeed, they argue that in many cases 'the most we will be able to say is that the proposed variants can serve one, or more generally, similar discourse functions. We cannot even require that they be identical discourse functions' (Sankoff and Thibault 1981: 208).

So how is one to recognise a linguistic variable, then? Even once you think you have found one, how can you be sure it is a good one? I now turn to exemplifying this pursuit in practical terms.

RECOGNISING THE LINGUISTIC VARIABLE

The linguistic variable can exist at virtually any level of the grammar, ranging from phonetics to discourse, from phonology to syntax, as in (8) (Wolfram 1993: 195):

(8)
a structural category, e.g. the definite article, relativisers, complementisers
  a semantic category, e.g. genitive *-s* vs *of* genitive, periphrastic comparative *more* vs synthetic *-er*
  a particular morpheme category, e.g. third person singular present tense suffix, the *-ly* suffix on adverbs
  a phoneme, a systematic or classical definition of a unit, e.g. [θ] in English
  a natural class of units in a particular linguistic environment, e.g. final stop consonant clusters in word-final position, Canadian Raising the process by which the onsets of the diphthongs /ay/ and /aw/ raise to mid-vowels when they precede voiceless obstruents (the sounds /p/, /t/, /k/, /s/ and /f/)
  a syntactic relationship of some type, e.g. negative concord, passive vs active permutation or placement of items, e.g. adverb placement, particle placement
  a lexical item, e.g. *chesterfield* vs *couch* vs *settee*

In this way, the linguistic variable is an abstraction. The varying forms must exist in some linguistically meaningful subsystem of the grammar. The linguistic variable must also have another important characteristic. It must co-vary, i.e. correlate, with patterns of social and/or linguistic phenomena.

A linguistic variable is more than simply a synonym, and more complex than simply two ways of saying the same thing. It must also have qualities of system and distribution as well, as in (9), even if these are only revealed by analysis:

(9)
a. synonymy or near synonymy (weak complementarity)
b. structurally embedded, i.e. implicated in structural relations with other elements of the linguistic system, e.g. the phonemic inventory, phonological space, functional heads, grammatical subsystems, etc.
c. correlation with social and/or linguistic phenomena

The fact of the matter is that the onus is on the analyst to provide defensible arguments to demonstrate relevant social and linguistic correlations. In other words, the proof of whether or not a linguistic variable is a linguistic variable is in the pudding.

In sum, early controversy over the extent to which the linguistic variable could be applied to all levels of grammar was really a developmental phase in variation analysis when definitions were being refined and improvements to the methodology were ongoing. Lavandera (1978) correctly pointed out that the linguistic variable, as it had originally been defined, could not be extended to variables above and beyond phonology. However, the research paradigm quickly caught up. Weiner and Labov (1983), Sankoff (1973, 1980), Sankoff and Thibault (1981) and Laberge (1980) demonstrated through detailed methodological argumentation that the linguistic variable need not be confined to cases in which the variants necessarily mean precisely the same thing. Instead, the linguistic variable may have weak complementarity across the speech community, i.e. functional equivalence in discourse. This malleability implicates the role of the linguistic variable in linguistic change (Sankoff 1982: 681–5, 1988b: 153–5, Sankoff and Thibault 1981).

LINGUISTIC VARIABLES AS LANGUAGE CHANGE

How can a linguistic variable involve variants that have no structural relationship or one-to-one equivalence? The answer has to do with how language changes. Linguistic change does not always occur gradually from one closely related form to another. Instead, language change may proceed by cataclysmic means:

> by forcible juxtaposition of grammatically very different constructions whose only underlying property in common is their usage for similar discursive functions. (Sankoff and Thibault 1981: 207)

Consider a number of examples. *Going to* and *will* are variants of future temporal reference in contemporary English, despite different sources in separate lexical verbs. In earlier times (and perhaps even today) the simple present tense varied systematically with the progressive, e.g. *the kettle boils* vs *the kettle is boiling*, *I love it* vs *I'm loving it*, etc. The relativiser *that*, a complementiser, often varies with *who*, a pronoun.

If one form appears to be replacing the other, either in time or along some socioeconomic or demographic dimension in the community (Sankoff and Thibault 1981: 213), then this may be an indication of change in progress. For example, if a variant is correlated with age, this may be evidence of ongoing evolution of a subsystem of grammar.

The application of variation analysis to formal models of grammatical change was foreshadowed in research in the early 1980s, long before variation analysis was explicitly applied to grammaticalisation theory per se (e.g. Poplack and Tagliamonte 1998, 2001). Sankoff and Thibault (1981) argued that when discourse alternatives coexist over time we may expect this equivalence to eventually become grammaticalised, i.e. functional analogues will become syntactic analogues. They speculated that the criterion of weak complementarity could be used as a diagnostic for stages in the development of forms. The progression of such change might be outlined as follows:

1. An innovation is introduced, it takes on the form of a discourse marker having some attentional or accentuation purpose.
2. The form gradually loses some of its original emphatic qualities.
3. Semantic distinctions gradually become neutralised.
4. Forms grammaticalise and take on the conventional characteristics of a linguistic variable.

Such an approach makes important and testable predictions for grammatical change, as in (10).

(10)
Predictions for grammaticalisation

Early stage	Later stage
Semantic constraints	Neutralisation of semantic constraints

Much more work needs to be done in this area. The challenge is to find the right set of circumstances, a diagnostic variable, and then to test the hypotheses of change. Variation analysis is ripe for research of this kind, and it appears to be a welcoming new frontier for future research:

> a fuller integration of sociolinguistic and developmental research with research on grammaticalization still remains to be worked out. (Hopper and Traugott 1993: 30)

The next question is: How do you choose which variable to study?

SELECTING A LINGUISTIC VARIABLE FOR ANALYSIS

Beyond the motivation to study something that interests you, what are the qualities that you should be looking for when choosing a linguistic variable? Wolfram (1993: 209) notes that 'selecting linguistic variables for study involves considerations on different levels, ranging from descriptive linguistic concerns to practical concerns of reliable coding'. These may seem overwhelming at first, but as you get the hang of it these decisions keep the process vibrant and intriguing.

IDENTIFY POTENTIAL VARIABLES

The first task is to identify potential variables in language. Faced with your data, where do you start? Students often ask me, 'What do I look for?' This is an entirely practical issue. The place to start is to take a long, hard look at your data. As discussed earlier in Chapter 1, language materials, of any type (e.g. written, spoken or otherwise), offer you a wide range of variables for investigation. All you have to do is find them. In the first instance, simply listen, read or look. What is different? What is interesting? Take notes about the things you observe. In some cases they may be structures that are not 'standard' English, or perhaps structures that are different from what you are familiar with in your own variety of English. In fact, when linguistic variables involve dialectal, informal, or non-standard variants they are a lot easier to spot. You tend to notice things that are different from your own idiolect. In other cases, you will need to focus intently on the flow of forms and structures in the discourse because the variables will slip by without you even realising they are there. Many linguistic variables in contemporary varieties of English, for example, comprise variants which are more or less acceptable in the language, with little associated stigma or affect. Variation is everywhere; you just have to notice it. Sometimes it is right under our noses, as in (11).

> (11)
>
> You **got to** breathe and have some fun ... We **must** engage and rearrange.
> (Lenny Kravitz, 'Are you gonna go my way')

A corpus collected using standard sociolinguistic interviewing typically contains one to two hours of speech per individual, which translates to approximately fifty pages of double-spaced words. Such materials will typically be replete with potential variables. In (12), we have an excerpt from a transcription of Mel, a 40-year-old male in the York English Corpus who works as a computer software trainer. The interview is very relaxed and he presents himself as an easy-going ex-hippie. This excerpt tells the story of how he quit one of his previous jobs. It involves a dramatic exchange between himself and the boss. Bold, underline and italics represent variants of the linguistic variables I will discuss momentarily. Italics represent potential linguistic variables. What I mean by 'potential' is that variants occur that the analyst may infer will vary with other forms in the larger context.

> (12)
>
> York English Corpus, Male, age 40
> ... So ... *sort-of-like* **jus'** sat in Fibbers, **havin'** a **pint** and the phone rang, and it was my boss. ... Oh! Oh, it's- **tol'** everybody I'd gone t'*pub*, they knew where to find *me* if they wanted *me*, *you-know*. And er, so the phone rang and it was the boss, *you-know* and she said, 'If- w -- what are you **doing**?' So I said, 'Well I'm **havin'** a beer.' What do you think? 'Er, what about- ...' Can't think of the name of- *the* guy's name, 'What about *this* guy's manual?' You-see. So I said, 'Well I'll do what I normally do.' You-know, Said, 'I'll do it at '*ome* tonight. It'll *be sorted*.' You-know, I said, '*Have* I ever let you down ... before?' So she said, 'No.' So I said, 'Well, why are you **hasslin'** now?' So she said, 'Well, I want **something** on my desk by five-o-clock.' *You-see*, well, 'You'*ve got no* chance.' 'Well when can I see it?' So I said, 'Don't worry, there'll be **somethin'** on your desk by nine o'clock tomorrow.' Put the phone down. That night w -- was- a few of us from work ... **goin'** out for a drink, so we're all sat over in the Red-Lion and *like* all these horror stories start **comin'** about, about *you-know*, how Joanne's *treat[?]ed* **differen[?]** ones of them you-know, and *shit* on them *and what have you.* 'Cos *it was like*, there's two bits. There's a **recruitmen[?]** bit and the **training** bit. And *I-mean* I was *sort-of-like* **tucked[t]** away upstairs by *myself* so I didn't get to see much of what **wen[?]** on downstairs. And *they were like* all- we were all sat in the **pub[u]** and everybody's **bitchin'** about *this* woman, *you-know* and I thought, 'Well I don't want to work with someone like *this*.' You-know, and I **jus'** said so, I said, 'That's it, I'm **'anding** my notice in tomorrow.' And *you-know* they'*re* all **goin'** *like*, 'Nah,' *you-know*, 'you won't, you won't.' **Followin' mornin**', um, c-you-know *I-mean*

I'd **told**[d] 'em about w- - *this* phone call. *You-know* and then when she'd said *like*, everybody had said oh, I though, 'Well *'ang on a minute*, I've said there'd be **somethin'** on her desk by nine-o-clock tomorrow ***mornin'***, it will be *my* re - - be *my* notice.' You-know everybody's **goin'**, 'Oh you won't you won't.' ***Followin' mornin'*** I got *up*[ʊ], shirt and tie on, suit as normal, **tootled**[d] around the corner, **walked[t]** into the office, and I said 'Joanne, you wanted ***somethin'*** on your desk by nine-o-clock, there's *my* time sheet, I quit.' . . . And **walked[t]** out. And you could **jus'** see everybody's face like drop. It's like . . . he's done it!

Even in this small excerpt, approximately three minutes of a two-hour interview, there are many features that hold promise for investigation. A number of linguistic variables can be authenticated. What I mean by this is that the alternatives are both visible.

Variable (ing) and variable (t,d)

Two variables readily apparent in this excerpt are variable (ing) and variable (t,d). Note that this excerpt has been embellished from the transcription file, with an indication of the actual pronunciation of the forms for illustration purposes. In fact, these are two of the most widely studied variables in the history of variation analysis. Take a closer look at each of the instances of these variables. The words in which they occur have been bolded, italicised and underlined for easy visibility. I have also indicated which of the phonological variants was produced in each case. The words containing variable (ing) and (t,d) are listed in (13) and (14) respectively.

(13)
Variable (ing)
havin', doing, *havin'*, *hasslin'*, something, *somethin'*, *goin'*, *comin'*, training, *bitchin'*, *'anding*, *goin'*, *followin'*, *mornin'*, *somethin'*, *mornin'*, *goin'*, *followin'*, *mornin'*, *somethin'*

(14)
Variable (t,d)
jus', pint, *tol'*, different, recruitment, tucked, went, *jus'*, told, tootled, walked, walked, *jus'*

How many of each variant occur in each variable set? For (ing), notice that the standard variant [ŋ] occurs only four times. For variable (t,d), there are four examples of the non-standard, zero form. The semi-weak verb *told* (in line 2), and monomorpheme *just* (lines 1, 21, and 31) exhibit simplification of the consonant cluster. In other words, this speaker uses mostly non-standard [n], but standard [t,d] forms in his speech. In the full studies of both these variables, these idiolectal tendencies hold across the broader sample of York English

(Tagliamonte 2004, Tagliamonte and Temple 2005). Overall there is relatively frequent use of the standard variant of variable (t,d), i.e. realised clusters, compared to other varieties. In contrast, the standard variant of variable (ing), i.e. the velar variant, is quite rare.

A multitude of other interesting and potentially variable forms are evident – some phonological, (15), and others morphological and syntactic, (16). These have been italicised in the excerpt.

(15)

Phonological
a. definite article reduction	gone *t'*pub	line 2
b. variable (h), dropping	*'*ome	line 7
	*'*anding	line 21
	*'*ang	line 25
c. variable (t)	trea[?]ed	line 15
d. variable (U)	*pub* [pʊb]	line 19

(16)

Morphological and syntactic
a. *of* vs *'s* genitive	the name *of -the* guy's name	line 6
b. agreement	there*'s* two bits	line 16
c. subject drop	Ø put the phone down	line 12
d. zero definite article	*following mornin'*	line 23, 27
e. possessive *have got* vs *have*	you*'ve got no* chance	line 10

Many discourse/pragmatic features are evident as well, as in (17):

(17)

Discourse/pragmatic
a. extension particles	*and what have you*	line 16
b. quotatives	*said*	line 4, 6
	thought	line 20
	going . . .	line 22, 27
	it's like	line 31
c. discourse *like*	*it was like . . .*	line 16
	like drop	line 31
d. discourse markers	*you know*	line 3, 4, 7, 14, 15, 20, 21, 22, 23, 24, 26
	I mean	line 17, 23
	you see	line 6, 10
e. discourse *so*	*so the phone rang*	line 3
	so I said	line 6
	so we're all sat	line 13

Of course, in such a small excerpt of material most of these potential variables cannot be authenticated. In other words, only one variant is actually present. You cannot be sure that the linguistic feature in question is variable in the data from the available evidence. However, if you know these variants participate in alternation with other forms, then the presence of even one of the variants is a good indication that the other may be present as well. Further examination of a greater portion of the data for this speaker would confirm which are variable and which are not. Nevertheless, the sheer number of possible features for study is quite remarkable.

Other features of note are morphosyntactic and lexical features that stand out nationally, regionally and locally, as in (18).

(18)

a. *we're sat* ...	vs	we're sitting
b. *it'll be sorted* ...	vs	it'll be fixed/worked out, etc.
c. *tootled around* ...	vs	walked
d. *hasslin'* ...	vs	bothering/bugging, etc.

Faced with such a data set, the analyst must decide which variable to tackle for a fully fledged analysis. Which one would you choose?

Notice in (12) that variable (ing) is quite frequent, occurring nearly once per line, for a total of 20 times. Variable (t,d) occurs 11 times. It is not surprising that these two variables have been so often studied in the literature. They are easy to spot and easy to find. Both characteristics are ideal criteria for selecting a linguistic variable.

In fact, some linguistic variables are better candidates for variation analysis than others. Variable items which lack systemic, linguistic foundations such as variable realisations of words like 'yes', (19a), 'because', (19b), or performance anomalies, (19c–d), may not be ideal for variation analysis.

(19)
a. ***Yes*** it has, very tiny. ... ***Yeah*** they're not- they're not that big. (YRK/™)
b. ***'Cos*** the atmosphere up there's different as well ***because*** um everyone's doing exams. (YRK/U)
c. We ***just go-*** really ***we'd um-*** we'd just go out ... (YRK/™)
d. The ***b--*** the ***boys*** from Brigg were um- ten of their team were- (YRK/U)

A number of criteria can guide the analyst in choosing a 'good' linguistic variable for analysis. Ideally, you want to select a variable that is interesting and relevant, both to you and within the field. But, in practice, this goal must inevitably be balanced on practical grounds.

Frequency

Linguistic features that are rare, either because of the relative infrequency of the structure or because of conscious suppression in an interview, may not be good candidates for analysis. They may be interesting linguistically, dialectally fascinating and critical for a comprehensive descriptive profile, but if they do not occur with sufficient numbers they can hardly be tabulated in a study of variation. Phonological variables are usually more frequent, while grammatical structures are rarer. Discourse features may be remarkably frequent or virtually absent depending on the variety under investigation, age of the speaker, etc.

Sometimes features occur extremely frequently, but cannot be ideal variables because the context of variation is questionable. This arises most obviously in the case of discourse-pragmatic features, where only one variant is overt in the discourse. But what is its alternative? Where *can* it occur, but did not? In contemporary English, features of this type are plentiful, including *like, anyway, so,* etc. My students always want to study these features. What they do not realise is the study of these forms using variation analysis is a very complex and difficult enterprise. Defining the variable context requires painstaking treatment of the data and advanced knowledge of syntax because the feature must be defined structurally in order to assess its function in the phrase structure (see D'Arcy 2005).

It is possible to structure interview schedule/questions to elicit specific types of constructions. For example, talking about past time will enhance the occurrence of past tense forms; talking about habitual activities will enhance the occurrence of habitual tense/aspect forms; and getting informants to tell you stories will enhance your ability to get quotatives. However, you may not know in advance which feature(s) you want to study, or which features may become important to you later on. In sum, not all goals can be achieved in every interview situation. The frequency of different types of variables depends greatly on the type of discourse situation and innumerable other, often uncontrollable, factors.

Tip

One of my strategies for finding a good linguistic variable is to compile an index of my interviews and look closely at the words in the data that occur most frequently (see Chapter 4). Another strategy is to read prescriptive grammars and find cases where alternate forms are mentioned. Another is to simply observe what linguistic variables researchers are talking about and check to see what is happening with those variables in your own data. If it is frequent enough, and the variation is robust enough, it is a good candidate for further investigation.

Robustness

Frequency is not necessarily the choice criterion for selecting a linguistic variable. A further requirement is that there is adequate variation between forms. Linguistic variables which are frequent but have minimal variation are less viable for investigation by this method. Although the structures themselves may be interesting, if the data at your disposal is near categorical (either 100 per cent or 0 per cent), then there is little room for quantitative investigation. If variability hovers at very low or very high levels, differences between variants in independent contexts may be too small to achieve statistical significance. In this case, you may rely on the constraint ranking of factors for comparative purposes (Poplack and Tagliamonte 2001); however, near categorical variables may not have sufficient numbers for even constraint ranking to be informative. In such cases, one of the possible variants may have such marginal status in the data that the variable itself will be unrevealing. If it is a change in progress, it may also be possible that the variable has either 'gone to completion' or is perhaps still so incipient, or so marginal in the data, that it cannot be reliably modelled using statistical methods.

Sometimes very low-frequency items, by their very characteristic of limited status in a variety, can be extremely important. Indeed, Trudgill (1999) argues that 'embryonic' variants may sometimes blossom into rampant change. Something of this nature has occurred in the contemporary English quotative system where a new form, *be like* as in (20), represented only 13 per cent of all quotative verbs in Canadian English in 1995 (Tagliamonte and Hudson 1999).

(20)
I'm like, 'You're kidding? Wow, that's really cool.'
She *says*, 'What do you think of him?'
I said, 'Well, yeah, he's cute.' (OTT/c)

Yet in the early 2000s it has risen to become the dominant quotative, 65 per cent – as in (21) (Tagliamonte 2005) – a four-and-a-half-fold increase in less than eight years.

(21)
She*'s like*, 'Have you taken accounting?'
I'm like, 'No.'
She*'s like*, 'Have you taken business?' (TOR/I/@)

A low-frequency variable which was well worth investigating was pre-verbal *do* in Somerset English, as in (22) (Jones and Tagliamonte 2004).

> (22)
> We ***did have*** an outside toilet, just a brick type of thing, you know.
> We ***did have*** a flush toilet there. (TIV/e)

Minimal presence of periphrastic *do* amongst the oldest generation and virtual absence amongst the youngest generation meant that this feature was finally dying out of the variety. This study likely represents the last opportunity to discover the grammar of this feature before it disappears for good. Therefore, despite the highly infrequent status of the feature, we decided to study it anyway.

Unfortunately, some obsolescent features in contemporary English are so far gone that they cannot be studied quantitatively at all. This was the case for the *for to* complementiser in British dialects, as in (23). While we attempted to tabulate its frequency and distribution in our data, in the end it was too rare for substantive patterns of use to be revealed in the data (e.g. Tagliamonte et al. to appear).

> (23)
> a. So the roads were crowded when it was time ***for to*** start. (MPT/v)
> b. He'd light a furnace ***for to*** wash the clothes. (TIV/a)

In sum, there may be extenuating circumstances for selecting a linguistic variable where one of the variants has very low frequency. Under most circumstances, however, variation analysis is best suited for a linguistic variable where at least some of the variants occur robustly. This permits a richer, more complex and informative analysis.

Implications for (socio)linguistic issues

Your choice of a linguistic variable should also be dictated by the extent to which it has the capacity to answer timely and relevant questions. For example, linguistic variables that are undergoing change are excellent targets for analysis since they give insights into the process of change itself. Those that implicate grammatical structures reveal details of the syntactic component of grammar. Those that differentiate dialects highlight parametric differences and so on.

Once you have decided which variable you will study, what next? It is time to extract all instances of the variable from your data according to the principle of accountability.

CIRCUMSCRIPTION OF THE VARIABLE CONTEXT

Deciding on precisely how and where in the grammatical system a particular linguistic variable occurs is referred to as 'circumscribing the variable context' (e.g. Poplack and Tagliamonte 1989: 60). This refers to the multitude of little decisions that need to be made in order to fine-tune precisely where alternates of a linguistic variable are possible.

The procedure for inclusion and exclusion of items must be set forth explicitly so that your analysis is replicable. If you do not provide this information, you violate the researcher's obligation to provide enough information for your study to be repeated with reasonable accuracy and hence comparability.

First, you must identify the contexts in which the variants occur. Do each of the variants occur with all speakers? Do certain subgroups use more than others? These questions lead the analyst in identifying the envelope of variation (Labov 1972c). The tricky part is that you must count the number of *actual* occurrences of a particular structure *as well as* all those cases where the form might have occurred but did not. In other words, you have to know 'what is varying with what' (Weiner and Labov 1983: 33). In fact, you must know what the alternative variants are, even when one of the variants is nothing at all. But if one of the variants is zero, as is often the case, how do you spot them?

This is where the task of circumscribing the variable context can present special difficulties. Moreover, depending on the linguistic variable, there will be confounding factors that necessitate the exclusion of some instances, or tokens, of the variable.

CATEGORICAL, NEAR CATEGORICAL AND VARIABLE CONTEXTS

There may be a particular context in which one or the other variant never occurs. This is called a 'categorical context', which means that the variable is realised either 0 per cent or 100 per cent of the time. Such a case must necessarily be excluded from variable rule analysis for the simple reason that it is invariant. This is not to say that categorical contexts are not important. They are. In fact, the contrast between categorical variable contexts are diagnostic of structural differences in the grammar.

However, if the categorical environments were included in the variable rule analysis:

1) the frequency of application of the rule would appear much lower than it actually is,
2) a number of important constraints on the variable contexts would be obscured, since they would appear to apply to only a small portion of the cases, and
3) the important distinction between variable and categorical behaviour would be lost (Labov 1969a, 1972c: 82).

For example, consider variation in the presence of periphrastic *do* in negative declarative sentences in a northern Scots variety, as in (24) (Smith 2001).

(24)
a. I *dinna* mine fa taen it. (BCK/a)
b. I *na* mine fa come in. (BCK/a)

Smith demonstrated that there were two types of contexts: 1) those that never (or rarely) had *do* absence, third person; and 2) those that were variable, first and second person. While the (near) categorical contexts could be explained on syntactic grounds, the variable contexts were conditioned by lexical, frequency and processing constraints. The divide between these two types of contexts showed the importance of the categorical/variable distinction in the grammar.

How do you circumscribe the *variable* contexts? If the context is 95 per cent or over, 5 per cent or under, these are also transparent candidates for exclusion from the variation analysis (Guy 1988). However, in most analyses there will be a wide range of frequencies across factors. The analyst must be aware of where the variation exhibits extremes at one end of the scale or the other, as these contexts will be critical for explaining the variation.

In other words, the questions to ask yourself as you define the envelope of linguistic variation are these: Does this token behave exceptionally? Does it behave like other tokens of the variable? The major part of circumscribing the variable context is to 'specify where the variable occurs and where it does not' (Weiner and Labov 1983: 36). In so doing, you must provide an explicit account of which contexts are *not* part of the variable context.

The decisions that go into circumscribing the variable context affect the results in very important ways. Be sure to make principled decisions at each step in the process. Even the most sophisticated quantitative manipulations will not be able to save the analysis if you do not do this first (Labov 1969a: 728). In the next section I turn to some practical examples.

Tip

Don't be afraid to falsify your own procedures! Circumscribing the linguistic variable is a process that unfolds as you go and is continually revised nearly right up to the end of the extraction process. I don't know how many times I've had to go back and include a token type because I found later that it was variable. I've also had to go back and exclude tokens that were later found to be invariable. This is all part of the discovery process. But remember to document everything!

EXCEPTIONAL DISTRIBUTIONS

One of the first things to attend to when circumscribing the variable context is whether or not there are contexts in the data that are exceptional in some way. Exceptional behaviour often becomes obvious only as research evolves. Certain exceptional behaviours are part of the knowledge base existing in the literature. It is the responsibility of the analyst to know what idiosyncratic behaviour has been noted in earlier research and to pay particularly good attention to how the variants of a variable are distributed in the data set under investigation. Are the co-varying nouns, verbs, adjectives, etc. behaving comparably? Are different structures, sentence types and discourse contexts the same, or different? Exceptional distributions may occur for any number of reasons and these will differ depending on the variable and depending on what is going on in a data set. This is undoubtedly part of what Labov meant by 'exploratory manoeuvres' (Labov 1969a: 728).

Asymmetrical contexts

It is critical that each linguistic variable be scrutinised for asymmetrical distribution patterns. For example, in a study of verbal -s in Early African American English (Poplack and Tagliamonte 1989), we knew that one of its salient characteristics was its use with non-finite constructions (Labov et al. 1968: 165). For this reason, we were looking for cases of verbal -s in these constructions in our data. When we did not find any, it was readily apparent we were dealing with a different situation. Similarly, we knew from earlier research that verbal -s tended to appear on certain verbs only. Once again, this was a red flag to us to pay attention to the distribution of variants by lexical verb.

Another good illustration of exceptional behaviour that must be taken into account comes from the study of relative markers in English, as illustrated in (25) from a single speaker in the York English Corpus. At the outset, it is extremely important to isolate the restrictive relative clauses. Why? Because in contemporary varieties of English, non-restrictive relative clauses differ on a number of counts from restrictive relatives, and thus cannot be treated in the same analysis. First, non-restrictive relative clauses occur primarily with *which* and *who*, but hardly ever with *that* and zero; second, their semantic function differs; third, non-restrictives are marked off prosodically (as indicated by commas in (25)). Given these characteristics, if non-restrictive relatives were included in a sample of data which included restrictive relative markers, as in the embedded clause in (25), the effect would be to raise the percentage of *which/who* forms and lower the percentage of the others (*that* and zero). Further, the results would not be comparable with other data where only restrictive relative clauses were studied.

(25)

Albert, **who** was one of the guys **that** I knew from the Bayhorse, got him to do his physics homework for him. (YRK/Σ)

In other words, because non-restrictive relative clauses are nearly categorically marked with 'wh' forms, they are exceptional when it comes to the presence of relative markers, and should not be included in the same analysis as restrictive relatives (see also Ball 1996).

Somewhat the same modus operandi led to numerous exclusions in my study of dual form adverbs (see Tagliamonte and Ito 2002: 246–8). The variation was restricted to adverbs that could take either -*ly* or -*Ø*, without a difference in function. Numerous adverbs had to be excluded which did not permit -*ly*, e.g. *high*, or whose adjectival form (i.e. the zero form) was not semantically related to the -*ly* counterparts, e.g. *shortly*. For example, *directly* in (26a) was excluded because it means 'immediately' in this context. However, the token in (26b) was included because *direct* in this context can alternate with *directly*, meaning 'in a direct way without deviation'.

(26)
a. He drove home **directly** after arriving (= 'immediately').
b. 'Cos in those days as well you used to get er milk **direct** from a - a- dairy on a morning. (YRK/?)

Sometimes you will not know a priori which contexts are variable and which are not. This is particularly true when you have targeted a variable which is undergoing change. Your own intuitions may not match what is happening in the speech community. For example, also in my study of dual form adverbs, I adopted a strategy of examining the data itself for evidence of a particular item's variability. This is because the literature and my own intuitions often failed to make the appropriate judgements about potential variability for the adverb (Tagliamonte and Ito 2002: 247). Indeed, a reviewer of the study criticised us for including certain types, as in (27), which he or she claimed were not variable. In the rewrite we had to demonstrate that they were, in fact, variable and, further, that they were non-negligible in number and diffused across a reasonable proportion of our speakers. We used these distributional facts to justify their inclusion in the analysis.

(27)
a. I was an angel, **_absolute_**. (YRK/?)
b. I had years of utter misery, **_absolutely_**. (YRK/?)

A variable must be investigated in tremendous detail in order to determine which contexts permit variation and which do not. Those that do not must be listed, and reasons for their exclusion explained.

Formulaic utterances

Typical constructions which exhibit exceptional behaviour for linguistic variables are those that have been learned by rote such as songs, psalms or sayings, as in (28a). In addition, metalinguistic commentary, as in (28b), is a context for exclusion since these constructions may be imitative. Therefore, neither (28a) nor (28b) were included in our study of plural -s (Poplack and Tagliamonte 1994).

(28)
a. I look up to the _hills_ where cometh my help. (SAM/J)
b. And then they say, you know, '_potatoes_'. They say '_potatoes_'. (NPR/008)

Exceptional distributions also occur in expressions where the individual lexical items have become part of a larger 'chunk'. In the study of verbal -s, contexts such as _I mean, you know, I see_ were excluded, as they were invariant (Godfrey and Tagliamonte 1999: 99–100). This is, of course, because they are functioning as discourse markers, not verbs, as in (29a–b). Similarly, in a study of past tense _be_ (variable _was/were_), contexts such as in (29c) were excluded (Tagliamonte and Smith 2000: 160).

(29)
a. We'd seen the roses, *you see*. (YRK/d)
b. Should have made it a bigger thing, *I think* (YRK/d)
c. So, I had friends, *as it were*, from my own environment. (YRK/8)

When the variable under investigation occurs in a context which is anomalous with respect to the variation of forms within it, these are typically removed from the analysis.

Neutralisation

Neutralisation contexts are tokens in which independent processes exist which make the reliable identification of the variant under investigation difficult (or near impossible). In other words, unambiguous identification of the variant is compromised. The simplest case of neutralisation comes from variables which are phonologically conditioned. For example, the juxtaposition of a noun or verb ending in [s,z] and a following word beginning with [s,z], as in (30), precludes being able to identify the segment accurately as the final suffix on the noun/verb or the initial segment of the following word (Wolfram 1993, Poplack and Tagliamonte 1994).

(30)
a. Pop wa[s] [s]at there rubbing her arm. (YRK/c)
b. You get[s] [s]ick of them if you had too many. (DVN/1/253)

Similarly, in studies of (t,d) deletion, juxtaposition of a word ending in [t,d] and a following word beginning with [t,d], as in (31), makes it impossible to determine whether the final (t,d) or the initial (t,d) of the following word has been removed.

(31)
We were suppose[d] [t]o land on the shore. (YRK/K)

Ambiguity

When a linguistic variable involves a grammatical feature whose varying forms implicate different semantic interpretations, the issue of circumscribing the variable context becomes more difficult. Word-final suffixes such as verbal -s or past tense -ed involve independent processes of consonant cluster simplification which render the surface forms of regular (weak) present and past tense verbs indistinguishable, as in (32):

(32)
She *liveØ* right up yonder. (SAM/E)

Verbs in past temporal reference contexts with no marker are ambiguous. They could be instances of uninflected present tense forms or past tense forms with phonologically deleted [t,d]. Including them will obviously skew the proportions of -s presence one way or another. Only forms for which past reference can be firmly established should be included. Past tense readings can often be inferred, for example, from adverbial or other temporal disambiguating constructions, as in (33a), as well as other indicators, as in (33b).

(33)
a. He *live∅* with mama thirty, thirty-two years... (ESR/ Î)
b. There was a pal *live∅* there. (YRK/®)

Other processes may also render the function of a variant indistinguishable from another. For example, in (34) it is impossible to determine whether the sibilant consonant represents the plural suffix followed by a deleted copula, or a zero plural followed by a contracted copula.

(34)
Them *thing[z]* a bad thing. (NPR/4)

Some contexts may be inherently ambiguous. For example, in a study of past tense expression, verbs with identical present and past tense forms such as 'put, set, beat' would not be included because there is no variation one way or the other, as in (35).

(35)
a. past tense
   That was before Tang-Hall was built you-see, they *put* in sewerage drain from Heworth, the top water and then they *put* in- then they got started building. (YRK/¥)
b. present tense
   ... things what you *put* your tea in. (YRK/¥)

Another source of ambiguity is when nothing in the context permits an unambiguous interpretation of the form's function. For example, in (36) you cannot tell whether the noun is plural or singular. Therefore, neither of these tokens should be included in an analysis of plural nouns.

(36)
a. Just behind the *tree*. (SAM/B)
b. I ain't gonna tell no *lie*. (ESR/Y)

In sum, many contexts may seem to be part of the variable context but are not. Sometimes you may not know they present a problem until much later. This does not matter. It is more important to include things than not include them, because it is way easier to include more tokens while you are extracting the data than to have to go back and get the ones you missed later on. In fact, excluding certain types of tokens from the data file is simple, as long as they have been treated uniquely in the coding system. I will tell you more about this in Chapters 8 and 10.

Ensuring functional equivalence

With morphosyntactic variables, following the criterion of 'functional equivalence' is often not straightforward. You must be particularly mindful that each variant is an instance of the same function.

The study of tense–aspect features in variation analysis has been particularly helpful in outlining procedures for excluding contexts which do not meet the criterion of functional equivalence. Tense-aspect features are often involved in longitudinal layering of forms in the grammar, in which only a particular subset may be implicated in variation of the linguistic variable under investigation. For example, the study of future temporal reference involves variation in the forms *will* and *going to*. However, different forms of *will* (e.g. *won't*, *'d* and *'ll*) may also denote other (non-future) temporal, modal and/or aspectual meanings. Therefore, any study of future time must restrict the variable context to include cases of *will* that make predictions about states or events transpiring after speech time. This involves identifying and excluding all forms that involve other semantic readings: 1) forms having a modal rather than temporal interpretation, as in (37a); 2) counterfactual conditions that are hypothetical not temporal, as in (37b); or 3) forms denoting habitual action in the present or past, as in (37c).

(37)
a. And today, I *wouldn't do* that for the queen ... (GYE/<)
b. If it *was* up to me, I'd have fish on Sunday. (NPR/a)
c. And we *would go* hitting each other brothers and then we *would fight*. (NPR/f)

By strictly circumscribing the contexts to those that are temporal and that make reference to future time, the variants included in the analysis are pertinent to the study of grammatical change in the future temporal reference system.

Repetitions

Tokens which occur directly after another in sequence as false starts or performance errors are typically not included in a variation analysis.

For example, in (38), only the first of the repeated tokens was included in the data file for these variables. Inclusion of repeated tokens would add a disproportionate number of instances of the same form.

(38)
a. And then *funny* enough, *funny* enough, I think in one year four of us got married. (YRK/?)
b. So they'd *played* one short- they'd *played* one short. (YRK/π)

Natural speech anomalies

As with all naturally occurring speech, accurate interpretation of any part of the discourse may on occasion be impossible. Intrinsic characteristics of oral discourse like false starts, hesitations, ellipsis and reformulations, as in (39), often lead to difficulty in interpretation. Any unclear or ambiguous contexts should be excluded from the analysis.

(39)
a. And there's another new one in this week *who*- (CMK/t)
b. And um, it *was* very- (YRK/c)

IMPOSING AN ANALYSIS

In circumscribing any variable context, you must be aware that your decision-making process may impose an analysis on the data from the outset. A good example of this comes from the study of variable (t,d) in African American Vernacular English (e.g. Labov et al. 1968, Wolfram 1969, Fasold 1972) and then, later, in Guyanese Creole (Bickerton 1975). Part of the variable context involves suffixal (t,d) alternating with bare verbs (i.e. no suffix) in contexts of past temporal reference, as in (40a). Another part involves past marking of strong verbs, alternating with their base forms, also in contexts of past temporal reference, as in (40b).

(40)
a. That's got how many years since they *kill∅* Papita? Yes, since they *kilt* him. (SAM/F)
b. I don't know where they *came* from, but anyhow they *came* there, they *begin* to work. (SAM/J)

Bickerton criticised early studies by suggesting that, if those studies had considered creole categories, such as distinctions of aspect, it would be revealed that the zero-marked verbs resulted, not from deletion of English morphemes, but from a pattern of overt and zero marking peculiar to creoles. In these grammatical systems the zero form actually encodes a different function, a particular aspectual reading.

One way to handle this type of pitfall is to configure your data to allow for different possibilities of analysis. For example, in Tagliamonte and Poplack (1993) we set up the coding system to test for both a creole and an English underlying grammar. No one analysis can claim to be the most accurate; however, a defensible and replicable analysis provides a sound foundation for future research.

THE TYPE-TOKEN QUESTION

The type-token question is whether to include frequently occurring items every single time they occur, or include only some (Wolfram 1969: 58). Such a strategy is particularly relevant for phonological variation where the inclusion of frequently occurring words with exceptional distribution patterns may distort the results. The best example I can think of is a recent study of dialect acquisition in young children (Tagliamonte and Molfenter 2005). The focus of investigation is variable (t) with variation amongst [t], [d] and [ʔ]. In the data, the children, aged 2–5, used the lexical item *little* extremely frequently, as in (41).

(41)
Mum, but we need- *little* holes. Why do we need *little* holes in it? Can I put *little* holes in it? Shaman can I put *little* *little* holes in? (KID/1)

A standard approach to such a situation is to restrict the number of tokens per speaker, e.g. five tokens per hour of recording per child. However, in the study of acquisition, frequency of forms is critical. In order to model this effect on acquisition it would be necessary to include *all* the forms. In this study we opted for an all-or-nothing strategy by devising a coding schema (see Chapter 6) that enables us to include only five tokens per hour per child or all of them. Time will tell which method supplies a better explanation for the data.

The type-token question may have varying implications depending on the level of grammar under investigation and/or the particular variable targeted. While restricting the number of lexical items in a phonological analysis of variation may be defensible, the same decision might be less so in a study of syntax. The analyst must make a choice as to how her own study will proceed. Whatever the decision, it should be transparent enough for comparison with earlier research as well as future replications. Procedures for how the type-token question is resolved differ across studies and, unfortunately, in many the decisions have not been made explicit in published works. To date, the relevance of type-token decisions has not, to my knowledge, been fully explored in the published literature.

ILLUSTRATING LINGUISTIC VARIABLES

A requisite component of a variation analysis is to illustrate the linguistic variable. At the beginning, it is important to substantiate the crucial characteristics of equivalence and distribution as well as intra-speaker and inter-speaker variation. In the ideal situation you will find a 'super token': alternation of variants by the same speaker in the same stretch of discourse. Examples of variable verbal *-s* from Samaná English (Poplack and Tagliamonte 1989a: 49) show that both *-s* and zero occur in the same speaker. Examples (42a–b) are uttered by speaker 'E'.

Third person singular ▮▮▮▮▮▮▮▮▮▮▮▮▮▮▮▮▮▮▮▮▮▮▮▮▮▮▮▮▮▮▮▮▮▮▮▮

(42)
a. And sometimes she **go** in the evening and **_come_** up in the morning. (SAM/E)
b. She **goes** to town every morning and **_comes_** up in the evening. (SAM/E)

Tip

Whenever I construct a handout I always look for the most interesting, funny, informative examples I can find in my data. The reasons are: 1) to convey a sense of what the variety under investigation is like; and 2) if the audience is bored, they can at least enjoy the data!

Examples of variable adverbial *-ly* from York English, as in (43) (Tagliamonte and Ito 2002), show that both *-ly* and zero occur in the same speaker as well as in the same stretch of discourse.

(43)
I mean, you go to Leeds and Castleford, they take it so much more **_seriously_** ...
They really are, they take it so **_serious_**. (YRK/T)

Providing examples of intra-speaker variation is important because it demonstrates that the linguistic variable under investigation is endemic to individual sample members, not simply the result of amalgamating data from speakers who are categorical one way or another.

Cross-variety comparisons illustrate that variation exists within individuals *and* across the communities under investigation. In (44a) you see intra-speaker variation for African Nova Scotian English in rural Nova Scotia, Canada, and in (44b), for Buckie English in rural Scotland (Tagliamonte and Smith 2000).

(44)
a. And we *was* the only colour family. We *were* just surrounded. (GYE/l)
b. We *were* all thegither ... I think we *was* all thegither. (BCK/h)

Similarly, example (45) illustrates variable verbal -*s* in third person plural in Samaná English and Devon English (Godfrey and Tagliamonte 1999).

(45)
a. They *speak* the same English. But you see, the English people *talks* with grammar. (SAM/G)
b. Yeah they *drives* 'em ... They *help* out. (DVN/d)

SUMMARY

Where does all this leave you with regard to defining the linguistic variable? The main thing is simply 'know them by their colours'. In other words, the onus is on the analyst to determine and defend the linguistic variable under investigation. If the variable is bona fide, this should become evident during the investigation. This means establishing at the outset that the linguistic variable is authentic, meeting the criteria of 1) functional equivalence; 2) distribution and 3) structural embedding. These criteria are often outlined in research papers as part of the methodology section. As part of the process of *doing* variation analysis, data anomalies may arise, further observations may become apparent and correlations may reveal themselves. Such discoveries can then be incorporated into the analysis, sometimes becoming part of the story. Indeed, as the field has evolved, circumscribing the variable context has become an important starting point and, as Labov says (to appear), it is an important end point too.

In sum, the systematic study of competing forms of variation analysis requires not only the identification of these forms, but also the individual contexts in which differences between them are neutralised. This, in turn, leads to the interpretative component of variation analysis, i.e. deciding how to circumscribe the context and identifying the places in which variation between forms for the same function may occur. I turn to this phase of research in Chapter 6.

Exercise 5: Locating and circumscribing a linguistic variable

One of the key measures of success in the study of language variation and change is to locate an appropriate linguistic variable to analyse. In this exercise you will pay particularly close attention to the data you have targeted and, based on your own observations of variation in your data (as you experienced with Exercise 2), choose the linguistic variable that you would like to study.

The variable should be relatively frequent in the data and have linguistic and/or sociolinguistic implications.

You must establish that the linguistic feature you choose is a *bona fide* linguistic variable, i.e. a linguistic feature which can be *shown* to co-vary systematically with some features of the linguistic or extralinguistic environment.

Your report should include the following:

Identification of your variable

What is it? How many variants are there? What are they? Which are standard? Which are non-standard/dialectal? Describe them and provide examples. If you can find a 'super-token', that is ideal.

Definition of the variable context

Include a precise definition of all contexts which will be included in your analysis.

Exclusions and exceptional distributions

Exclude any forms which are not part of the variable context:

* invariant forms (e.g. a context that is always one variant or the other)
* exceptional distributions (e.g. metalinguistic commentary, quoted speech, etc.)
* ambiguous contexts (e.g. false starts, neutralisation, etc.)
* forms that do not have the relevant function

Illustrate each of these and justify why they should be excluded. Read sections entitled 'Circumscribing the variable context' in the following:

Godfrey, E. and Tagliamonte, S. (1999). **98–100**.
Poplack, S. and Tagliamonte, S. (1989). **47–84**.
Sankoff, G. and Thibault, P. (1980). **315–30**.
Tagliamonte, S. (1998). **159–61**.
Tagliamonte, S. and Hudson, R. (1999). **154–7**.

6 Formulating hypotheses/ operationalising claims

> What do you do with a *linguistic variable* once you've found one?
> This chapter will provide a step-by-step procedure for setting up an analysis of a linguistic variable. It will detail the procedures for coding, how to illustrate the linguistic variable and how to test claims about one variant over another.

Once you have decided on a linguistic variable to study and have a good idea how you will circumscribe it, the next step is to begin the extraction phase.

DATA EXTRACTION

Data extraction refers to the process and procedures involved in sifting through your data in order to find and select the relevant tokens, i.e. each and every instance of each variant within the context of variation (Chapter 5), and place each token into a data file. A number of procedures have evolved over the years which greatly facilitate the extraction process. To be very practical about exactly how this is done, I will make use of the data shown earlier in Chapter 5, example (12). Suppose we were to extract the tokens of variable (ing) from this material; the data could be listed as in (1) with the word containing the variable along with some of the context in which it occurred displayed in each line. I have found that putting the word containing the variable in capital letters makes it easier to see what is going on in the data. It also helps to distinguish which item is the relevant one, when two (or more) are present, as in (1r–s).

Extraction of variable (ing) from example (12) in Chapter 5:

(1)
a. sort-of-like just sat in Fibbers, HAVIN' a pint
b. she said, 'If- w - - what are you DOING?'
c. So, I said, 'Well, I'm HAVIN' a beer'

d. So, I said, 'Well, why are you HASSLIN' now?'
e. So, she said, 'Well, I want SOMETHING on my desk by five o'clock.'
f. So I said, 'Don't worry, there'll be SOMETHIN' on your desk . . .
g. That night w – was- a few of us from work . . . GOIN' out for a drink
h. all these horror stories start COMIN' about . . .
i. and the TRAINING bit
j. and everybody's BITCHIN' about this woman
k. I said, 'That's it, I'm 'ANDING my notice in tomorrow.'
l. they're all GOIN' like, 'Nah, . . .'
m. FOLLOWIN' mornin', I got up
n. following MORNIN', I got up
o. I've said there'd be SOMETHIN'
p. by nine-o-clock tomorrow MORNIN'
q. You-know everybody's GOIN', 'Oh, you won't . . .
r. FOLLOWIN' mornin', I got up
s. Followin' MORNIN' I got up
t. I said, 'Joanne, you wanted SOMETHIN' on your desk . . .

Similarly, if were to extract the tokens of variable (t,d) from this material; the data would look like as in (2):

Extraction of variable (t,d) from example (12) in Chapter 5:

(2)
a. So . . . sort-of-like JUS' sat in Fibbers
b. havin' a PINT and the phone rang
c. TOL' everybody I'd gone t'pub
d. how Joanne's treated DIFFERENT
e. There's a RECRUITMENT bit
f. I was sort of like TUCKED
g. I didn't get to see much of what WENT on downstairs
h. You-know, and I JUS' said so
i. I'd TOLD 'em about w - - this phone call
j. I got up, shirt and tie on, suit as normal, TOOTLED around the corner
k. tootled around the corner, WALKED into the office
l. and I said, 'Joanne, you wanted somethin' on your desk by nine-o-clock, there's my time sheet, I quit.' . . . And I WALKED out
m. And you could JUS' see everybody's face like drop

EXTRACTION STRATEGY

One of your earlier decisions will have been a sample design consistent with your research questions (Chapter 2). At the outset, put into place a strategy for extraction in order to manage the sequence through which you will find and select the tokens from your speakers. You can ensure that your data file always represents a relatively balanced sub-sample of the total sample planned for your study. For example, if you are studying a variable with implications for linguistic change, you will undoubtedly have planned a sample from a cross-section of the population in your corpus by age and sex. However, it would be foolhardy to start extracting from your data haphazardly or even to extract the data from all the old people first, or all the younger people first. Instead, extract first from one older male, then one younger male, then one older female, then one younger female. In this way you build your sample evenly. The advantage to an extraction strategy is that you can conduct a distributional analysis of your data (see Chapter 9) at any point during the extraction process. This will provide you with a preparatory view of how your linguistic variable is distributing across the speakers in your data, as well as the relevant external factors, long before your analysis is completed. Every extraction phase must start with someone. Had you begun with the data from the speaker, as in (1) and (2) above, you would then turn to a female speaker in a different age bracket, and so on.

HOW MUCH TO EXTRACT?

The next question is precisely how much to extract. Obviously, you need to extract the individual tokens of the linguistic variants. Make sure you select all relevant contexts that you will ever need for the particular variable under investigation. This is imperative. To go back and relisten to the data, or even to go back and search for individual tokens a second or third time, is extremely time-consuming. Another question is whether or not to extract some of the surrounding context and, if so, how much of the context to import into the data file? The best rule of thumb is to take from the data source as much context as you need for interpreting the meaning of the utterance and for coding it later for all the relevant contextual characteristics. To go back – because you do not have enough context – to code for a particular factor later on is also very time-intensive. Instead, ensure that you only need *one* pass of the material at this phase.

For example, in (1) and (2) above I have made sure to extract not only the word in which variable (ing) and (t,d) are contained, but also the preceding and following word. Moreover, I have included enough of the context to make sense of what is being said. This information is critical for coding these data for the grammatical category of the word containing (ing). For variable (t,d), even more context has been extracted for some contexts. This is because I knew in advance that I would code for iconic order in past tense verbs, i.e. the order in which the events actually occurred. This means I had to have access to the preceding verb, hence more context. In other words, how much of the discourse around your variable you need to extract depends on the types of factors that you will eventually code.

Phonological variables

If your linguistic variable is a phonological variable, your coding system will necessarily involve natural classes of sounds, cluster composition and other phonologically reasonable categorisation schemas. In this case, it is wise to record relevant phonetic details during the extraction phase such as the phonetic composition of the item itself and the surrounding phonological contexts. Broad phonetic transcription for a phonological variable is usually sufficient. As you extract the data, attend to lexical exceptions and type–token ratios (see Chapter 5). For example, in extracting variable (ing) and variable (t,d), we put a limit on the number of tokens that were extracted for certain frequent lexical forms for each speaker. In the case of (ing), words such as *something*, *doing*, etc. were extremely frequent, so we only included three of each type per speaker. In the case of (t,d), words such as *went, just* and *told* were extremely frequent. Again, in order not to skew the data with too many of one type of word and not enough of infrequent others, we limited the number of tokens of each lexical item for each speaker.

Morphosyntactic variables

When it comes to morphosyntactic variables, even more context may be required in order to facilitate the future coding of syntactic and semantic factors. For example, the extraction of contexts for variable (have/got) are as in (3). We needed to record what the object was in order to determine whether it was concrete or abstract. This requires sufficient context to determine this. When this information was not in the immediate discourse, as in (3b), we devised a strategy of including the referent in the context, within square brackets, e.g. [a lovely family bible]. Similarly, the data file for variable (ly) is as in (4). Here, it was necessary to code whether the manner adverb encoded 'concrete', (4a–b), or 'abstract' meaning, (4c). Therefore, enough of the discourse was extracted in order to make this decision.

(3) Excerpt of extraction for variable (have/got), (CLB/a)
a. (CaTG8--C*2A And they GOT *a lovely family bible* you-know that's gien to Thomas,
b. (CaBHpN-C*2A Thomas HAS it [a lovely family bible]
c. (CaNH^-GA-/N Young yins ... They HAVE no *interest*.
d. (CaBH3--C//A And he plays- tries to play the- what you call *the thing* he HAS now?

(4) Excerpt of extraction for variable (ly), (YRK)
```
a.(Y%YQ/VFMC//  I know all little bits of hedges and things so I
   can do it [clipping the hedge] really QUICKLY.
b.(Y1YQ/VFMC//  I-mean obviously must have read fairly QUICKLY
c.(YEYQ/VAMA//  the young people say they've- the time flies
   QUICKLY
```

Discourse/pragmatic variables ▪▪▪▪▪▪▪▪▪▪▪▪▪▪▪▪▪▪▪▪▪

The study of discourse/pragmatic variables are notoriously difficult for traditional quantitative methodology. This is because the non-applications (the places where the discourse-pragmatic feature could have occurred, but *did not*) are very difficult to circumscribe (see further explanation in Chapter 5). Nevertheless, these variables can be studied by alternative methods. For example, they can be studied within the context of narrative structure, a discourse type with a highly circumscribed structure in which discourse-pragmatic features can be studied accountably. In such cases, the narrative is coded into the data file finite clause by finite clause, as in (5). Then, the data can be coded for narrative section (e.g. complicating action, evaluation, orientation, etc. (Labov and Waletzky 1967)), or other structural components (e.g. background vs foreground). In this way, whatever discourse-level feature is under investigation can be studied accountably with a base-line of: 1) clauses in the narrative discourse, or 2) clauses within each of the narrative sections.

```
(5)
a.(1yAPF2-  This WAS
b.(1yAPF2-  when I WAS still in high school.
c.(1yOGF2-  I WAS WALKING to class one day,
d.(1yCPF2-  the bell RANG
e.(1yOPF2-  So the hallways WERE empty
f.(1yOGF2-  and I WAS COMING from the upstairs
g.(1yOGF2-  I WAS WALKING down the stair case
h.(1yOmF2-  and I CAN HEAR people TALKING.
i.(1yOPF2-  And at the bottom of the staircase WAS the vice
            principal
j.(1yCGF2-  and he WAS YELLING at two students
k.(1yOPF2-  and I kind of KNEW the students
l.(1yEPF2-  they WERE losers
m.(1yEPF2-  and I really DIDN'T LIKE them
n.(1yrGF2-  So I WAS WALKING down the stairs
o.(1yCPF2-  and for some reason I SAW a reflection
p.(1yCPF2-  so I LOOKED up
q.(1yCPF2-  and I SAW this girl walking down the stairs
```

```
  r.(1yCPF2-  and after that I jus-  I FELL
  s.(1yCPF2-  I TRIPPED on one of the stairs
  t.(1yCPF2-  and I SLID down all the way on my knees
  u.(1yCPF2-  and FELL right in front of the vice principal
  v.(1yCPF2-  and then he STOPPED yelling at those people
  w.(1yCPF2-  and he TURNED over
  x.(1yCPF2-  and he HELPED me up
  y.(1yOGF2-  and those two students WERE LAUGHING at me.
  z.(1yQPF2-  And he TOLD me
 aa.(1y$/F2-  'It's those damn heels!'
 bb.(1yEPF2-  Then I WAS embarrassed
 cc.(1yCPF2-  and I WENT to class [ST3]
```

When the entire narrative structure is coded into the data file, many discourse-level patterns become visible. Most especially, notice how features of the discourse beyond the level of the sentence can now be coded into the material. In (5n), *so* appears in a clause that is a near identical repeat of an earlier one in (5f). Interestingly, this occurs immediately after a digression from the main story line (5h–m). Also note the extensive use of *and*, occurring in seventeen out of twenty-nine finite clauses, the strategic placement of adverbial *then*, and the use of quotative *told* by the principal compared with the use of quotative *be like* used by most young people (see Chapter 5, examples (16) and (17). Any of these observations might lead to an analysis of the feature in question and to a series of hypotheses about relevant correlations that might be tested.

In sum, your strategy for how much of the actual language material to input into the data file will depend on the level of grammar of the variable you have targeted for investigation.

Once this initial phase of extraction and coding is complete, you will need to move on to coding the contextual factors which may condition the choice of one variant over another.

FACTOR GROUPS AND FACTORS

A factor group is some aspect of the context (either internal linguistic or external social) which affects whether or not a variant occurs. Each factor group can also be thought of as a hypothesis about what influences the choice process. In this way, a factor group is also a constraint on the dependent variable. For example, a factor group in the analysis of consonant cluster simplification is following phonological segment. Here, the hypothesis about the choice process is that consonant clusters will be influenced by the surrounding phonological constituents. Given the universal tendency toward CVCV order, following consonant may be hypothesised to promote consonant cluster simplification. Given this hypothesis, a test for this hypothesis can be devised or 'operationalised'. The factor group is set up by categorising the data into a set of reasonable linguistic divisions defining the nature of the phonological context. Each of these categories, or factors, delimit well-defined attributes of the factor group. For the factor group 'following phonological segment', a number of different categorisation schemas might be used. Factors might include general grouping of consonant, vowel, pause, as in the first column in (6), or this schema could be elaborated to distinguish between voiced and voiceless consonants as in the second column in (6), or even between stops, fricatives, liquids and laterals, as in the third column. Alternatively, the phonological context might be more finely categorised by individual type of consonant, vowel, etc.

The coding system adopted for a particular factor group will depend on what the analyst deems relevant to the choice between one variant or another. In the case of following phonological context the relevant dimensions might be simply the contrast between consonants and vowels. It might also be voicing, point of articulation or some other phonological contrast. It is up to the analyst to find out what is explanatory for the variable process under investigation.

(6)

Factor group	Possible coding systems			
	Factor(s) i	Factor(s) ii	Factor(s) iii	Factor(s) iv
Following phonological context	Consonant	Voiced consonants	Stops	[p]
	Vowel	Voiceless consonants	Fricatives	[t]
	Pause	Vowels	Liquids	[k]
		Pause	Laterals	[b]
			Vowels	[d]
			Pause	[g]
				etc. ...

A factor group may encode any type of conditioning factor, from characteristics of the phonological environment, for example, following phonological context as in (6), to features of the morphology, as in (7), to configuration, as in (8), to external aspects such as the speaker's social, cultural or other characteristics.

(7)

Factor group	Factor(s)	Example
Type of adjective	Attributive	**blue** sky
	Predicative	The sky is **blue**

(8)

Factor group	Factor(s)	Example
Negation	Synthetic	I know **nothing**
	Analytic	I **don't** know **anything**

In sum, factor groups are the explanatory or independent variables, while the choice variable (i.e. the linguistic variable involved in the choice process) is the variable which is dependent on these factors. In other words, the factors constrain the choice. The word 'choice' is not meant to imply a conscious choice on the part of the speaker, but is a more abstract notion of selection in the grammatical system (see Chapter 7).

PROCEDURES/STRATEGIES FOR EXTRACTION

Over the years, I have developed a number of protocols that enable me to extract and code data efficiently.

WHERE TO EXTRACT TO?

In my experience, you save time and energy if you extract your data directly into the variable rule program (i.e. Goldvarb token file). There are numerous advantages to this method. One of them is that you are able to process the data any time you want to. This keeps you on top of the material at all times. Other researchers use their own methods for the extraction phase. Some extract data into an Excel document, coding the data by column. When extraction is complete, they concatenate the columns and then import into the variable rule program (Young and Bayley 1996: 260-1). Other researchers use search programs (e.g. Goldsearch (Boas et al. 2002)) to specify speaker characteristics. Detailed information about the format of a data file is found in Chapter 7.

ORDER OF EXTRACTION AND CODING

The first rule of thumb is to code for at least three factor groups as you extract: 1) the community or data set; 2) individual speaker; and 3) the dependent variable. This will produce a data file as in (9). Notice the super-token in lines (9f–g).

```
(9)
a.(3BS   it's just SO SPONTANEOUS
b.(3B-   There's something 0 WRONG with this picture
c.(3BS   I got SO SCARED of that thing
d.(3B-   Whoa these are 0 HILARIOUS
e.(3B-   they make a 0 NEW one every so often
f.(3BR   this REALLY RECENT one is just so hilarious
g.(3BS   this really recent one is just SO HILARIOUS
```

All the adjectives have been extracted (along with their context), and coded for the corpus from which they have been taken, in this case the corpus which is designated with the code '3', and the speaker, 'B', followed by the dependent variable, which is presence or absence of intensification in pre-adjectival position. In factor group three, the dependent variable is coded as '-' for no intensification and a series of codes for the particular lexical intensifier employed, e.g. *so* = 'S', *really* = 'R'. In the next phase of this research I would code for additional independent factor groups in successive columns (see Chapter 8).

You may ask: Why not code for *all* the factor groups at this stage? There is a very good reason. Extracting data is a challenge in itself, involving not only paying strict attention to the data so that you notice each and every possible context, but also attending to detailed char-acteristics of the data such as lexical idiosyncrasies, exceptional dis-tributions and other anomalies that typically arise. If you also had to code for a series of contextual factor groups at the same time, it would increase the margin of error of your phase exponentially. A more efficient way to handle this phase of research is to devote yourself entirely to extracting the data and circumscribing the variable context first.

Once this phase is complete, you can move on to coding for all the other bits of information relevant to your linguistic feature. Do this one factor group at a time. This ensures consistency in the coding for each individual factor group through the entire data set because it means making the same single decision over and over again as you go through the data file. This method has far less margin for error than coding each token for a long series of different factor groups, which requires making a lot of different decisions one after another.

Tip

The optimal way to set up a coding system is to use mnemonic codes. For example, 'M' = main clause, '1' = first person singular, 'N' = negation, etc. Further, I typically use capital letters for categories, e.g. 'S' = subordinate clause; but lower case letters for types within categories, e.g. 'w' = subordinate clause with *when*. If you use the same codes for the same factor groups across studies, these codes will become second nature to you. Of course, your codes cannot always be mnemonic, but making sure the main ones are will make your job a lot easier.

CODING THE DEPENDENT VARIABLE

The dependent variable is the linguistic variable under investigation. It alternates (i.e. varies) when some independent variable changes. Independent variables can be external (e.g. sex, socioeconomic class, age, etc.) or internal (e.g. lexical item, clause type, semantic or syntactic features). For example, alternates of the variable (ing) will vary according to the grammatical category of the word containing (ing): [ŋ] will occur more often with nouns, [n] more with verbs. This is the primary task of variation analysis – to correlate the dependent variable with independent variables (see Chapter 1).

All variants are assigned a separate code: for example, variant [n] is given the code 'N'; variant [ŋ] is given the code 'G', as in (10). If other variants occur, assign another code, e.g. 'K' for [Ink], 'E' for [in], etc.

```
(10)
  a.(N  sort-of-like just sat in Fibbers, HAVIN' a pint
  b.(G  she said, 'If- w- - what are you DOING?'
  c.(N  So, I said, 'Well, I'm HAVIN' a beer'
```

It is not necessary that the dependent variable be the first factor group, as in (10), where the code occurs in the first column after the open parenthesis. In (11)–(13) the dependent variable is coded into factor groups 2 or 3.

Coding the variant forms of some linguistic variables can be relatively straightforward, i.e. presence vs absence of a form, as with verbal -s, (11), complementiser *that*, (12), and variable (t,d), (13):

(11)

Verbal *-s*

FG3	Presence of *-s* marking	
S	*-s* marking is present	*youngsters **gets** far too much*
0	No *-s* marking	*they **get** things sorted out*

(12)

Complementiser *that*

FG3	Variation between *that* and zero in complement clauses	
T	'that'	I honestly believe ***that*** he has a good heart
0	zero	I think *Ø* he's nice

(13)

Variable (t,d)

FG2	Realisation of (t,d)	
t	[t]	... beans on ***toast*** or toasted teacake
d	[d]	the house the Terry's ***lived*** in
0	zero	I ***slepØ*** through lot
?	glottal stop	it was totally ***differen[?]*** experience

However, coding the variant forms of the dependent variable can get much more complicated depending on the linguistic variable itself and what level of detail the analyst deems necessary. For example, variable realisations of the definite article (Tagliamonte 1997) require a much more elaborated coding system, as in (14).

(14)

The definite article

FG1	Realisation of the definite article	
T	standard 'the'	I found out, ***the*** *fella* that I worked for
t	[t]	when he comes in to ***t'*** *house* ...
0	omitted 'the'	... as long as *Ø wagon* and you's alright
?	glottal stop	We'll claim *[?] window* on *[?] insurance*

Analysis of future temporal reference (Tagliamonte 2002) involves coding for several different lexical items, e.g. *shall, will, going to*. Further, because phonological variants of *going to* are implicated in ongoing grammaticalisation, e.g. *gointa, goina, gonna, onna, gon*, etc., variant forms were coded separately. In addition full (e.g. *will*) and contracted (e.g. *'ll*) variants of *will* were distinguished, as in (15).

(15)

Future temporal reference

FG1	Future temporal reference	
W	will + simple infinitive	Pam **_will_** answer it upstairs
L	'll + simple infinitive	I'**_ll_** be flying out there next week
O	won't	I **_won't_** do it this week
D	'd + simple infinitive	**_It'd_** take me a week to do that
d	would + verb	he thought I **_would_** take him up on it
S	shall	'Where **_shall_** I take her tonight?'
G	be going to + simple infinitive	What are we **_going to_** do
§	goin/a (glottal stop for 't')	We're **_goin/a_** move up
g	gointa	It's **_gointa_** rain today
N	gonna	I'm **_gonna_** protest it
o	gonta	things are **_gonta_** change
u	gonnu	It's **_gonnu_** upset me
i	goin	We were **_goin_** have a rest
n	gon	I'm not **_gon_** tell you ...

Once all the tokens of the dependent variable have been extracted and coded for the data set, speaker and variant, you are ready to code the data in such a way as will most felicitously test your hypotheses.

CODING THE INDEPENDENT VARIABLES

After extracting the dependent variable and coding the speaker and data set, it is time to code the independent factors.

Note

Coding is widely agreed to be 'the most tedious and time-consuming' (Young and Bayley 1996: 260, see also Milroy and Gordon 2003: 137) task of variation analysis. Imagine coding over 15,000 tokens of verb phrases with past temporal reference for 30 different factor groups, as I did for my dissertation, as in (i):

```
(i)
(----A-811MP-FNPP-TQ--RAH-S-QFN   190  [when] my
daughter WENT
(----C-91UXPOP1PP0CTPMPW-ES-QFN   190  [well then]
I COME out here
(----k-311MP-P1PP-2CPXP---S-QFN   191  I BOUGHT
this property
```

This coding system must be 'linguistically principled' (Wolfram 1993: 216). In other words it must be consistent with the organisation of linguistic structure and informed by solid linguistic understanding. Further, the pattern of variability in your data should be treated as a type of evidence which can be applied to broader questions of linguistic patterns and contribute to basic linguistic insight. In fact, the coding schema is where your analysis resides. It is a set of reasoned hypotheses (encoded in factor groups) about which variant of your variable occurs where. These hypotheses come from the relevant theoretical, descriptive, synchronic and historical literature (Poplack and Tagliamonte 2001: 91).

Tip

Make sure you know what each factor group is testing and why! If you do not have a reason for testing something, why do it? The results will mean very little if there was no hypothesis motivating the test in the first place.

How do you arrive at a coding schema for your linguistic variable? This is where the goals of the analysis come into play. The linguistic variable must be coded in a way that is consonant with the goals of the study (Wolfram 1993: 208). If your goal is to determine patterns of social and linguistic correlation, stylistic shifting or linguistic change, then the variants need to be coded in a way that has the highest potential for revealing these patterns. Relevant factor groups will vary tremendously across different linguistic variables. On the other hand, some factor groups will be relevant for many variables. But how do you decide what the likely factors are?

THE REVIEW OF THE LITERATURE

The most important source of information for determining the coding system is the extant literature on the subject. Nothing is more important than knowing everything that has ever been written about the linguistic variable you have targeted for investigation. Only rarely will you have found a variable that no one else has noticed before. Typically, you will be able to find support for your investigation somewhere in the public domain, either historical or contemporary.

Begin with an extensive literature search. A good way to start is by finding the feature you are investigating in a grammar book and familiarising yourself with its standard prescriptive description. Compare this with its formulation in theoretical models. Find out whether or not it has been uncovered in dialect surveys, old grammars or odd dialects. Determine how old the feature is by consulting the *Oxford English Dictionary*. What is the earliest attestation? Scour old grammars to determine if early grammarians made note of the feature (Poplack et al. 2000b). Contemporary academic journals in the field are also rich resources. Make yourself aware of any recent work on the topic. Research that has been conducted in the tradition of variation analysis will provide you with optimal data for comparison. This is not always possible. Every linguistic variable will have its own idiosyncratic history and character depending on whether it is standard or non-standard, what level of grammar it involves, whether it is stable or changing, obsolescent or incipient, etc. Browsing the internet can be useful. There are tremendous resources available there. It can also be worthwhile to spend some time in the stacks at the library browsing and checking tables of contents and indexes. This is particularly useful when your variable has historic implications.

Tip

The archives of the American Dialect Society, which originated in 1889, and its journal, *American Speech*, provide great ideas. The journal has been published since 1925.

OPERATIONALISING HYPOTHESES

As you comb the literature, pay particular attention to authors' observations of trends, patterns and collocations, etc. relating to your variable. Such nuggets should be highlighted and recorded with relevant page numbers. These observations form the foundations of your coding system.

Tip

Always record the source and page number of relevant quotes when you first find them! I don't know how much time I have spent, frustratingly, searching for the source and page number of important quotes. Save yourself time and energy. Do it from the beginning.

Perhaps the most well-known observation in the variation literature is that enunciated by Murray (1873: 211), who says: 'When the subject is a noun, adjective, interrogative or relative pronoun, or when the verb and subject are separated by a clause, the verb takes the termination -s in all persons.' This is illustrated in (16):

(16) The burds *cums* an' paecks them but They *cum* an' teake them (Jespersen 1909/1949: 15)

How is such an observation translated into variable terms? First, you would have to code the data for the grammatical person, as in (17), distinguishing full noun phrases, adjectives, interrogatives and relative pronouns from personal pronouns. Second, you would need a coding system for intervening elements, as in (18). Murray's observation predicts that verbal -s would be favoured after non-adjacent nominal or pronominal subjects and disfavoured after adjacent pronominal subjects.

```
(17)
;FG5: Grammatical person
;    P=personal pronoun
;    N=full noun phrase
;    R=relative pronouns
;    J=adjective
;    I=interrogative
```

```
(18)
;FG6: Adjacency
;    A=adjacent subject verb
;    X=intervening material
```

Another example comes from the relative marker system in Early Modern and Modern English. Contemporary grammar books prescribe that *who* occurs with human (or personal) antecedents and *which* with non-human (or non-personal) antecedents (e.g. Quirk 1957: 97–8). Typical statements read as follows:

> *That* for persons and things, ... *who* for persons; *which* for things. (Curme 1947: 166)

Studies of relative markers repeat this prescription:

> *Who* refers to people and *which* to things; *that* can refer to both people and things. (Swan 1995: 473)

> Restrictive relatives with human antecedents show a strong predilection for *who* in subject function. (Denison 1998: 278)

These statements can be 'translated' into a coding schema for a factor group you could call 'animacy of the antecendent', which tests the hypothesis that *who* encodes human antecedents, *which* encodes non-animate antecedents and *that* encodes both, as in (19).

```
(19)
;FG7 the nature of the antecedent
;    H = human
;    A = non-human animate, e.g. dog
;    T = non-animate, i.e. thing
```

THE CODING SCHEMA

Once you have familiarised yourself with the literature on your linguistic variable, you will be able to synthesise the main trends that have been observed, tested or hypothesised about it and create a coding schema, or coding system, for your data. This is the set of instructions for how to code the data. The relevant questions you should ask yourself are: 1) What are the factors that are known to condition the variable; and 2) How, precisely, does each factor condition the variation?

EXAMPLE: VARIABLE (t, d)

Consider the example of variable (t,d). A review of the extensive literature on this feature reveals three main linguistic factors conditioning the variable: 1) the preceding phonological context; 2) the following phonological context; and 3) the morphological structure of the word. The next question is: Exactly how do these factors condition the variation? For variable (t,d), the literature is quite straightforward.

Preceding phonological context

For preceding phonological context, variable (t,d) varies roughly in proportion to the sonority of the preceding segment: less sonorous segments (stops and fricatives) tend to favour deletion, while more sonorous segments disfavour deletion. You may then hypothesise that there will be more deletion in contexts such as in (20) than those in (21).

(20)
They ***stopØ*** making bricks. (YRK/#)

(21)
It had all ***spille[d]*** over. (YRK/Ω)

Following phonological context

As for following phonological segment, this has consistently proven to be the strongest linguistic constraint operating on variable (t,d). Obstruents (and nasals) trigger the most deletion, followed by liquids, then glides, and finally following vowel or pause, the latter two contexts varying in order between dialects. Therefore, you may hypothesise that there will be more deletion in contexts such as (22) than in (23).

(22)
We ***handcuffØ*** somebody to somebody in a pub in York once and ***dropØ*** the key down t' drain. (YRK/™)

(23)
I've been ***bombed***, I've been ***shelled***, I've been torpedoed. (YRK/>)

Morphological status

Finally, the morphological status of the word is also important. Previous studies have found systematic variability according to the morphological identity of the word. Uninflected or monomorphemic words, such as in (24), undergo deletion at the highest rate, and regular weak past tense forms, as in (25), undergo deletion at lesser rates. Irregular so-called 'semi-weak' verbs, which have stem vowel alternation in addition to a coronal stop past tense suffix, as in (26), pattern in between, with more deletion than weak past tense forms but less deletion than monomorphemes. Past participles, as in (27), tend to pattern with regular weak verbs. For most speakers the highest deletion rate is found for monomorphemes, then an intermediate effect for semi-weak verbs, and the lowest rates of (t,d) deletion are found for regular weak verbs. Once again, you are able to formulate a ready hypothesis: realised (t,d) will occur most often with past tense forms (either simple past or past participles), less often with semi-weak verbs and most often with monomorphemes.

(24)
He came for a **weekenØ** 'cos he'd had a fall. (YRK/g)

(25)
They **knocked** it down. (YRK/g)

(26)
But we still **kepØ** corresponding all the time. (YRK/≠)

(27)
I've **workØ** for Laing's. (YRK/S)

Notice how the observations and trends reported in the literature each make predictions about how variable (t,d) will be conditioned. Further, for each conditioning effect, there is a specific trend or ranking of factors within the factor group that is crucial. For preceding and following segment, vowels are more likely than consonants to appear with realised (t,d). For grammatical category, monomorphemes are more likely than semi-weak verbs to appear with unrealised (t,d), which are in turn more likely than past tense. This is referred to as the 'constraint ranking' or 'hierarchy of constraints'. The coding schema for each factor group should allow for this relative ranking of categories to be tested.

For each factor group, assign a unique code for all the relevant categories. I will typically allow for even more distinctions into the coding system than the literature suggests (see also Guy 1988). This gives you the opportunity to extend the findings that already exist. In the coding schema for variable (t,d) in (28), notice that each individual phonological segment preceding and following the /t,d/ has a separate code. This permitted us maximal flexibility in re-coding these factor groups for different criteria (voice, point of articulation, etc.). Having each segment coded separately means that we can merge categories or keep them separated. As we shall see (Chapter 8), this is ideal for assessing the contribution of individual segments.

(28)
Coding schema for variable (t,d)
```
;FG4: FOLLOWING PHONOLOGICAL
;    n = /n/
;    l = /l/
;    t = /t/
;    g = judge
;    k = /k/
;    Ø = thought
;    † = church
;    © = sing
;    # = rather
;    b = /b/
;    ß = wish
;    v = /v/
;    z = /z/
;    s = /s/
;    d = /d/
;    m = /m/
;    f = /f/
;    p = /p/
;    ? = glottal stop
;    V = vowel
;    R = vowel but r in orthog.
;    Q = pause
;    r = /r/
;    Σ = /w/
;    G = /g/
;    j = /j/
;    h = house
;
;FG5: MORPHOLOGICAL STATUS
;    P = bimorphemic
;    A = word final + vowel
;    a = word final + vowel, participle
;    À = word final + vowel, other
;    M = monomorpheme
;    R = participles
;    J = adjectives
;    Z = passive participles, got or 'be'
```

EXAMPLE: VARIABLE (ly)

Another example comes from variable (ly) (Tagliamonte and Ito 2002). A review of the literature revealed a diachronic angle due to the development of this suffix in earlier stages of English. Moreover, earlier research had been done on the variable in historical corpora. At least two internal factors were implicated in variable use of (ly): 1) adverb function; and

2) the semantics of the adverb. Once again, the relevant question is: What is the nature of these contextual influences on variant choice?

Adverb function

At earlier stages of English, the intensifier use of adverbs (i.e. adverbs which modify adjectives) tended to be zero marked, as in (29), whereas adverbs which modified verbs (i.e. manner adverbs) tended to be marked with *-ly*, as in (30) (Nevalainen 1997: 148).

(29)
Intensifier adverbs
And then he had an ***awful*** big sheep. (YRK/5)

(30)
Manner adverbs
He fell ***awkwardly*** on the floor. (YRK/S)

Semantics of the adverb

The zero variant was used more with a concrete or objective sense, as in (31). In contrast, the *-ly* form was used with abstract or subjective sense, as in (32). This distinction, of course, is only relevant for manner adverbs.

(31)
Concrete
I've walked upstairs dead ***quick***. (YRK/s)

(32)
Abstract
Thursday was meat and potato pie, if I remember ***rightly***. (YRK/R)

Each of these constraints is then coded for the relevant categories (extrapolated from the literature), as in (33). A number of other divisions have been made in order to account for additional types of adverbs as well as frequent and/or anomalous trends visible in the data.

WHERE TO KEEP YOUR CODING SCHEMA?

When I first starting setting up coding schemas, I set them up in a separate computer file that looked like (33) and I called them 'coding instructions'. Subsequently, I began putting this schema directly into the Goldvarb data file, as in (34). Both (33) and (34) contain the same information; however, when the coding schema is contained in your data file it never gets lost – it is right there along with all the tokens.

---

(33)

Coding schema for variable (-ly) – type 1

FG8	Adverb type	
I	intensifier	So he didn't go for an ***awful*** long time (YRK/O)
r	*really* + adjective	***Really*** long time
M	manner	but there again I-mean er you look at life er ***different*** (YRK/2)
S	sentence adverb	Yeah, ***honest*** they did. (YRK/9)
e	adv + 'enough'	e.g. ***funny*** enough we had a telephone call- (YRK/2)
		e.g. ***funnily*** enough we go out more now (YRK/O)

FG9	Semantics of adverb	
C	concrete	e.g. they were just gently moved up and down, very ***slowly***
A	abstract	e.g. I worked very ***closely*** with the organisers of the papal-visit.

---

(34)

Coding schema for variable (-ly) – type 2

```
FG8  ADVERB TYPE
;
;    I = Intensifier
;    r = 'really''
;    S = Sentence adverbial
;    e = followed by 'enough'
;    M = manner adverb
;
; FG9 SEMANTICS OF ADVERB
; MANNER ADVERBS ONLY
;
;    C = Concrete/Physical meaning, e.g. Pigs root foul
;    A = Abstract/mental/feelings, etc. e.g. Men sin foully
```

Whatever system you devise, make sure you do not lose your coding schema. As time goes by you will not remember what all those codes mean. I will never forget the first time I conducted an updated analysis from a study I had conducted many years earlier. Imagine my dismay – faced with a token file looking like (35), and no coding schema to be found!

```
(35)
(01BZCVDPONNOBBOOODZOOOOOB 953 boil
(11BZCCCPONNOCOOOODZOOOOOB 956 boils
(01DZCCCPONDOOOOOOHZOOOOAB 807 call
(11DZCVDPONDOOOOOOHZAOOOQB 1140 calls
(11BECVDPONNOOOOFOHZOOBBOB 1052 catches
(01BZVVVPONNOBBOOODZOOOOOB 1137 do
```

This is the data file for my original analysis of verbal -s (Poplack and Tagliamonte 1989), long before I had figured out all these tips I am giving you. Returning to the data file some ten years later and finding it like this made me realise just how far I had come. This is why I advocate keeping the coding schema right in your data file. For ease of coding, print it and have it in front of you while you code. Revise it as you go.

Tip

Somewhere alongside the coding schema for each factor group, record why you are testing this factor and where you got the idea from. Sometimes I will even include a relevant quote from the literature.

Keep your coding schema up to date. Include relevant examples. Insert important information such as what the linguistic variable is, what the data is, a list of good examples, etc., as in (36), at the beginning of a data file focusing on variable intensifiers. This practice will ensure that your data file is usable for posterity.

```
(36)
;INTENSIFIERS
;
;TORONTO: COMBINED ROP AND IN-TO-VATION DATA
;
;
;FG1: CORPUS
;
;    2 = ROP 2002
;    3 = ROP 2003
;    I = IN-TO-VATION 2003
;    N = IN-TO-VATION 2004 [selected speakers]
;
;FG2: SPEAKER - see TO speaker codes protocol
;
;FG3: LEXICAL INTENSIFIER - see coding protocol_INT
;
;FG4: MULTIPLE INTENSIFICATION
;
```

```
;    - = single intensifier
;
;    V = very × 2
;    v = very × 3
;    R = really × 2
;    r = really × 3
;    Q = quite × 2
;    P = pretty × 2
;    T = too × 2
;
;
; FG5 : LEXICAL ADJECTIVE - see coding protocol
;
; GOOD EXAMPLES
;
; SUPER-TOKENS : 2yP-  That's 0 GOOD, that's PRETTY GOOD.
;                2yV-  I had a 0 TERRIBLE chemistry OAC teacher,
;                      VERY TERRIBLE.
;                2a--  Like, I would feel 0 OFFENDED. I would feel
;                      REALLY OFFENDED.
;                2wR-  it was SO BAD 'cause I was REALLY NERVOUS.
;
; *** DATA START HERE ***
;
;    ** ROP 02 **
;
;Vivian Bustamante, F, [02], (b), 16
;Antonio Silvaggio, M, [03], ©, 16
;
(2b--j  Oh, I heard that's GOOD.
(2c--y  That was HILARIOUS.
(2cP-C  It was PRETTY CRAZY.
(2bR-O  I heard it was REALLY FUNNY.
(2c--O  I know it was FUNNY.
(2cJ-y  it was JUST hilarious.
[data file continues for 8,763 more lines ...]
```

Of course, none of these coding schemas enables you to *explain* the variation. That is something that must come from interpreting the analysis in the context of external and internal factors, and putting these all together (see Chapters 11 and 12).

CODING FOR LEXICAL ITEM

It is rare to find a linguistic variable that does not have some kind of lexical conditioning. Lexical effects are particularly germane to a number of broader issues, including lexical diffusion and for testing the effects of frequency. Most linguistic variables involve linguistic categories such as nouns, verbs, adjectives, adverbs, etc., which can be coded separately by type. Indeed, without strict accountability to lexical differences, you may miss dramatic contrasts between forms. This is so important that, as a matter of course, I always code for lexical item.

Coding schemas for lexical item are unavoidably cumbersome; however, they are not complicated. It is simply a matter of coming up with a systematic way of representing each form. For example, the coding system in (37) shows a subset of lexical codes used for coding matrix verbs involved with variable complementiser *that*.

(37)

FG10: Main clause verb			
a	admit	A	appreciate
b	believe	B	bet
c	convince [somebody]	C	accept
d	decide	D	discover

In Appendix D on the companion website I have included the full coding schema I use for verbs and, more recently, for adjectives (Tagliamonte and Roberts 2005). Once you have created a system for a particular part of speech, you can then use it as a template for other studies. My own template for lexical verb codes has been used dozens of times.

Tip

One of the great things about Goldvarb token files is that they are simply ASCII files. You can import the data into other programs easily. For example, if you want to know which lexical items occur frequently, you can import the data file into a concordance program and sort the data by alphabetical word. However, now that Goldvarb X is operational you can search the token file for words or phrases directly within the program.

Coding for lexical item has proven indispensable. For example, in the study of variable (that) as a complementiser, the collocation of certain verbs and the zero complementiser was critical for explaining the variation (Tagliamonte and Smith 2005). Similarly, coding for lexical adverb in the study of variable (ly) revealed an important contrast between the adverb *really* and all other adverb types

(Tagliamonte and Ito 2002). Coding for lexical adjective in a study of intensifiers enabled us to chart the grammaticalisation of incoming intensifier *so* (Ito and Tagliamonte 2003). Knowing the distribution of your variable by lexical item enriches your research. Moreover, it gives you the ultimate flexibility when you analyse your data. Finally, it often contributes key information for understanding what is going on with linguistic variables and for telling their story.

CODING FOR EXTERNAL FACTORS

Most linguistic variables will have external conditioning, either by sex, education, style, socioeconomic class or other social factor. However, none of these need to be part of the coding schema. This information comes (almost) for free within another factor group. Each individual in your sample should be coded separately as a matter of course (i.e. speaker code). Once this is accomplished, all external characteristics of the speakers can be coded via re-coding in the condition file in the variable rule program. For further detail on this procedure, see Chapter 8.

SOME TYPICAL CODING SCHEMAS

Some internal (contextual) factors are implicated in the conditioning of many different linguistic variables. Grammatical person is such a factor. Whether the relevant hypothesis contrasts first person vs third person, noun phrase vs pronoun, singular vs plural, all these divisions can be accomplished with a coding system for grammatical person that is categorised something like (38a). I have used this coding schema for years with minimal modifications. Other people may find this too complicated and split the relevant categories into two factor groups: one for grammatical person, (38b), and the other for subject type, as in (38c). Whatever suits you. There is more than one way to cut a pie!

(38)
a.

FG4: Grammatical person

1	first person singular
N	third person singular – FULL NP

3	third person singular – PERSONAL PRONOUN
E	third person singular – OTHER PRONOUN
X	third person singular – EXISTENTIAL
T	third person singular – EXISTENTIAL 'it' in place of 'there'
I	third person singular – EXISTENTIAL 'it'
2	second person singular
4	first person plural
f	second person – indefinite
5	second person plural
n	third person plural – FULL NP
6	third person plural – PERSONAL PRONOUN
7	third person plural – OTHER PRONOUN
t	third person plural – EXISTENTIAL 'it' in place of 'there'
x	third person plural – EXISTENTIAL
Ø	No overt subject

b.

FG4: Grammatical person

1	first person singular
2	second person singular
3	third person singular – PRONOUN
4	first person plural
5	second person plural
6	third person plural – PRONOUN

c.

FG5: Subject type

N	FULL NP
X	EXISTENTIAL there
I	EXISTENTIAL it
P	PRONOUN
Ø	No overt subject

Similarly, a coding schema for humanness and/or animacy might be set up, as in (39):

(39)

FG7:	Animacy of noun phrase head	
H	+ human, + animate	it was *my sister* THAT was looking after us
A	−human, + animate	one day there were *a raven* Ø landed
T	−human, −animate	is this *the train* THAT's going to Ostend
C	collection of humans	*The company* THAT'll get it
		e.g. family, band, group, committee
p	'people'	most *people* WHO never heard of it ...

A coding schema for type of clause might be categorised as in (40):

(40)

FG4:	Type of sentence	
N	negative	I *haven't* any contact with her
−	affirmative	I *got* one old cow there
n	interrogative, negative	*ain't* you *got* no one yet?
A	interrogative, affirmative	*Have* you *got* any tabs?

Tip

A time-saving strategy when coding a factor group in which the vast majority of tokens are of one type is to code only the rarer categories, not the common one. Leave the default blank. As you will see in Chapter 7, the variable rule program permits you to change all these blanks automatically to a specific code later on.

The relevant hypothesis for each factor group must be lucid. For example, the animacy of the antecedent is claimed to determine the choice of relativiser in English. *Who* is used for animate/human subjects in English; *which*, with non-humans; and *that* can be used with both animate/human and non-animate/things. The coding schema in (39) tests for all these possibilities. But what happens if the results are not as expected? You must be prepared to interpret any result vis-à-vis the observations and claims in the literature.

Note

Be sure to distinguish between 'claim' and 'observation'. In many cases, the observations in the literature are simply that – observations. A claim is a much stronger statement.

USING A 'FLAGGING' FACTOR GROUP

Not all factor groups need to be constructed as tests about the linguistic variable under investigation. I will typically devote one factor group for simply encoding 'flags' for the researcher. It may also serve to keep track of good examples, particularly 'super-tokens', anomalous items, exclusions and the like.

SUMMARY

The outline in (41) summarises the steps for researching the linguistic variable and for devising a coding schema for your data.

(41)
Find and read all previous analyses of the linguistic variable.
Can these studies be categorised into different types, different traditions, different analytic methods, different results? Are the results conflicting or corroborating? Why? Why not? Does the linguistic variable have historical implications? Are there implications for linguistic change? Origins and development?
Pay particular attention to the data and methods in earlier research What data was used and how? How was the linguistic variable circumscribed? Does this differ across studies? Why?
How was the data coded? Why?
What type of analysis was performed? What was the justification?
Gain a synthetic view of the findings from all the studies you have found.
    How do they compare with each other?
    What are the predominant results?
    What are the trends that emerge?
Write a critical commentary of your findings.
    How can the results be explained? What have the studies demonstrated?
Highlight the theoretical significance of the findings.
Make a proposal for how the extant research might be extended. What are its deficiencies? Can they be addressed in your own research?
Highlight the extent to which further study might make a novel contribution and at what level – i.e. To language variation and change studies only? To other domains of linguistics? To the field of linguistics more generally?

Exercise 6: Devising a coding schema

The purpose of this exercise is to design a coding schema for your data. The coding schema details the categories for each of the linguistic and/or extralinguistic constraints (i.e. factor groups, *aka* independent variables) which may operate on your linguistic variable (i.e. the dependent variable).

With these constraints in mind, start setting up a coding schema. Begin by asking yourself: What are the factors which constrain the choice of one variant or the other? The factors may be external (e.g. sex, education) or internal (e.g. phonological environment, syntactic structure). Each feature will constitute a factor group for analysis.

Each factor group must be configured to test a specific claim made about the linguistic feature in the literature, or even a hypothesis arising from your own observation. Internal linguistic factors can be quite complex and will depend on the variable. For example, a variant may be influenced by clause type, whether main or subordinate, or by subject type, whether full NP or pronoun. For every factor group, justify and explain your decisions linguistically and link each one to the literature.

Come up with a preliminary list of factors which typify each factor group. The factors should comprise linguistically principled categories.

Note

While you need not code characteristics such as age, sex, socioeconomic class in the token file (see Exercise 8), the schema for re-coding the individual speaker codes into relevant external categories should be detailed in your coding schema.

Start thinking about what the correlation of factor groups to the dependent variable may mean for understanding and explaining the linguistic variable.

7 The variable rule program: theory and practice

Why variable rule analysis?
This chapter will introduce the statistical analysis of variable rules.
It will cover the terms 'input',' log likelihood' and 'significance', and
describe what they mean.

> The fact that grammatical structures incorporate choice as a basic
> building block means that they accept probabilization in a very
> natural way, mathematically speaking. (Sankoff 1978: 235)

This chapter is written in two parts. The first part is theoretical,
designed to tell you about the variable rule program, variable rules
and their history. Importantly, I address the issues of why to use the
variable rule program at all. The second part is practical, providing
you with an overview of how the fundamental characteristics of the
variable rule program function in the Goldvarb series of programs.

First, here is where you can download the variable rule program
(Rand and Sankoff 1990, Robinson et al. 2001, Sankoff et al. 2005):
http://www.crm.umontreal.ca/~sankoff/GoldVarb_Eng.html; http://
www.york.ac.uk/depts/lang/webstuff/goldvarb/; http://individual.
utoronto.ca/tagliamonte/Goldvarb/GV_index.htm (Goldvarb 2.1,
Goldvarb 2001, Goldvarb X).

THEORY

Much of what is mysterious about variationist sociolinguistics comes
from the often arcane technical descriptions of its primary analytic tool,
the variable rule program. Like many things that involve numbers, reading about the variable rule program often incites a negative response.
However, the variable rule program is an incredible tool, not only for
conducting sophisticated statistical analyses, but also for helping you to
make sense of linguistic data, and even for simply organising it.

The variable rule program

The variable rule program was developed by the combined efforts of a number of different mathematicians through several rounds of technical improvements. It is one of the most appropriate methods available for conducting statistical analysis on natural speech (Sankoff 1988c: 987). Once you get the hang of how the program works, you will find that nothing is better than having every minute detail of your data at your fingertips and organised in a way that makes it maximally accessible and analysable. After months of extracting and coding, the joy of 'running your marginals' and finding out what is going on in your data (Chapters 9 and 10) cannot be underestimated.

I will begin with a historical overview of how the variable rule program works and why it should be your (analytic) tool of choice. I also hope to give you an insider's perspective on how the program came into existence. Should you wish to pursue further explanation or wish more detail on any of what is discussed in this chapter, go directly to the early descriptions of the program (Cedergren and Sankoff 1974, Sankoff and Labov 1979, Sankoff and Rousseau 1979, Sankoff 1988c).

The most in-depth discussion of variable rules is found in Sankoff (1988c). An adapted version was included with the documentation for Goldvarb 2.0. Subsequent digests of variable rule methodology can be found in Guy (1988, 1993), whose aim was explicitly to demystify what had been passed on by 'word of mouth'. The same can be said of Young and Bayley (1996), who document the procedures of variable rule analysis very lucidly. Their 1996 chapter is perhaps the most straightforward, 'user-friendly' writing on doing variation analysis in the literature (see also Bayley 2002). Paolillo's (2002) is perhaps the most detailed, with a focus on statistical terms and explanations.

Let us now turn the clock backwards and try to understand the intellectual climate in sociolinguistics in the 1960s.

A history of variable rules

What we now refer to as 'variable rules' are founded in the notion of 'orderly heterogeneity' (Weinreich et al. 1968: 100), the idea that variation in language is not random or free, but systematic and rule-governed.

> The analysis of speech behaviour has repeatedly revealed that the possibilities represented by abstract optional rules are distributed in a reproducible and well patterned way in a given speaker and in a given speech community. (Cedergren and Sankoff 1974: 333)

Variable rules were first introduced by Labov (1969a), arising from his fundamental observation that speakers make choices when they use language and, further, that this choice is systematic. Due to the systematicity of the process, the relative frequency of selection can be predicted. The variable rule was designed as an accountable, empirical model for this phenomenon, thus introducing a probabilistic component into the model of language.

To some researchers, the introduction of statistical concepts was a natural and logical addition to study of inter-individual, dialectal and historical variation in language. However, the idea of 'probability' in language was met with intense criticism: 'though "probability of a sentence (type)" is clear and well-defined, it is an utterly useless notion' (Chomsky 1957: 195).

There are fundamental epistemological questions involved here. Does choice exist in linguistic competence? Some people argue yes; some argue no. This book is not the place for such questions (for further discussion, see Sankoff 1988b). Instead, I will focus on the development of probabilistic theory in sociolinguistics and the mathematical issues that led to refinements of the original formulation of variable rules.

In his study of contraction and deletion of the copula, Labov made an interesting discovery – the choice process operates regularly across a wide range of contexts, both external and internal: 'we are dealing with a set of quantitative relations which are the form of the grammar itself' (Labov 1969a: 759). Cedergren and Sankoff (1974: 336) elaborated on the mathematical significance of this discovery, showing that 'the presence of a given feature or subcategory tends to affect rule frequency in a probabilistically uniform way in all the environments containing it'. Thus, a broader (statistical) generalisation can be made. If a given feature tends to have a fixed effect independent of the other aspects of the environment, then this can be formulated mathematically.

However, statistical procedures such as analysis of variance, or ANOVA, were unsuitable for language data. It was necessary to construct 'probabilistic extensions of the extant algebraic linguistic models' (Sankoff 1978: 219). In order to model a grammar that has heterogeneity with contextually conditioned 'order' to it as well as innumerable blank regions, a mathematical construct had to be devised that would suitably mirror it.

Variable rule analysis

Variable rule analysis was first developed as a quantitative extension of generative phonological analysis and notation (Labov 1969a, 1972b: 93,

Cedergren and Sankoff 1974). In the early descriptions, you will find variable rules presented as formal expressions compatible with the apparatus of formal language theory of the time (Chomsky 1957), i.e. 'rules'. However, the reference to variation as 'rule' has more to do with variation being systematic (i.e. rule-governed) than with any specific formalism. Indeed, variable 'rules' do not necessarily involve rules at all (Sankoff 1988c: 984). This terminology is an inheritance of its early contextualisation within formal theories of language, which at the time involved 'rules'. Instead, variable rules are actually 'the probabilistic modelling and the statistical treatment of discrete choices and their conditioning' (Sankoff 1988c: 984).

The prerequisites for variable rule analysis are: 1) choice, 2) unpredictability and 3) recurrence (Sankoff 1988c: 984). First, the analyst must perceive that there is 'a choice between two or more specified sounds, words or structures during performance'. Second, the choice must be seemingly haphazard based on known parameters. Third, the choice must occur repeatedly in discourse. Given these conditions statistical inference can be invoked.

The apparent randomness of the choice process makes it appear that the variation has no structure and has many more exceptions that it really does. Statistical inference by its very nature extracts regularities and tendencies from data presumed to have a random component. In order to accomplish this, the inference procedures must be applied to some sample containing the outcomes of the choice repeated many times (your token file/data) usually in a variety of contexts, each context being defined as a specific configuration of conditioning factors (your coding schema). In variation analysis terminology, the choice of one variant over the other is the 'dependent variable'. The independent variables, features of the linguistic or extralinguistic context which impinge on the choice of one variant over the other, are the 'factors' or 'factor groups'.

The null hypothesis

How can we distinguish those factors which have a genuine effect from those whose apparent contribution is an artefact of the particular data sample?

The starting point is the null hypothesis, the idea that no genuine effects exist in the data. Statistical methods are used to distinguish bona fide contrasts and trends from accidental data patterns due to statistical fluctuation, often referred to as random error, or 'noise'. In order to establish that a real effect exists, the null hypothesis must be falsified. In the variationist approach to language, the type of data which interests us are 'choice frequencies in contexts made up of cross-cutting factors' (Sankoff 1988c: 987). The null hypothesis is that none of the factors has any systematic effect on the choice process and that any differences in the choice outcome among the various contexts is to be attributed to statistical fluctuation. As Sankoff (1988c: 987) says, 'if we can prove that random processes alone are unlikely to have resulted in the pattern of proportions observed, we may be able to attribute this pattern to the effect of one or more of the factors'. How can we identify systemic deviations from randomness? This is where the mathematics underlying the variable rule program become complicated.

Sankoff (1988c: 987–92) elaborates on the steps taken towards arriving at the special case of logistic regression embodied in the variable rules program. I simplify greatly in my overview of this process here and draw heavily on Sankoff's description. For readers who feel no need to understand the logic behind the mathematical process, skip to the section on practice.

Models and link functions

Separating the effects of different contextual factors requires knowing how they jointly influence the choice process in a given context (Sankoff 1988c: 987). The simplest way of combining effects is additive and this is the model that Labov had originally used. However, the additive model is not useful for situations in which 'the application frequencies are very different in different environments, or when there are a large number of different environments' (Cedergren and Sankoff 1974: 337) – exactly how language always is! Therefore, the simple additive model that is often used for statistical procedures, e.g. the analysis of variance, is not appropriate for sociolinguistic data analysis.

In typical natural language performance there are many cross-cutting factors. An additive model applied to such data – say, the combined effect of preceding phonological segment, grammatical category and following phonological segment – may well produce percentages in excess of 100 per cent and below 0 per cent. As Sankoff (1988c: 988) points out, 'such "impossible" predictions' are a major problem. 'The solution is to use a model where the sum of the factor effects is not the predicted percentage of a given choice, but some quantity related to this percentage' (Sankoff 1988c: 988) – the link function. This function is such that it can take on any value without the risk that the corresponding percentage will be less than 0 or more than 100. In variable rule analysis the link function is the logit of the percentage (Sankoff 1988c: 988). The logit has two properties which make it superior to other link functions: 1) the predicted percentage always lies between 0 and 100 – this condition does not automatically hold for other link functions; 2) it is symmetrical with respect to binary choices. It doesn't matter which value is the application value; the model has the same form. This logit link function (i.e. logit-additive model) underlies the variable rule program and distinguishes it from other statistical models. For more information, read the section on 'Models and link functions' in Sankoff (1988c: 987–9).

The likelihood criterion

How do we find a set of values which best accounts for the observed data? In statistics, how well a model with given factor effects fits a data set can be measured by several criteria.

Variable rule analysis uses the likelihood criterion because it can account for the extreme distributional imbalances, including contrasting full vs near-empty cells, in corpus-based data. In the second half of this chapter, you will see some practical examples of what such 'lumpy' data look like.

The likelihood measure indicates how likely it is that a particular set of data has been generated by the model which has the given values for the factor effects. Different sets of factor effects will have different likelihood measures for the same set of data. The principle of maximum likelihood provides a means to choose the set of values which is most likely to have generated the data (Sankoff 1988c: 990). As we shall see in the second half of the chapter, the likelihood criterion is critical for establishing which combination of factors is the best 'fit' of the model to the data.

The estimation of maximum likelihood is carried out by logistic regression. This type of analysis is not unique to linguistics. In fact, it is widely used and many statistical packages can do it. However, variationist sociolinguistics, which relies on the badly distributed cells of language in use, requires a modified version of it. The variable rule program was written specifically for this, calculating the results 'in a form most useful in these studies' (Sankoff 1988c: 990).

The variable rule program is an incredible tool; however, it is important to keep in mind that it is only a tool. Statistical analysis does not, in itself, explain the variability in the data nor its origins: 'Varbrul only performs mathematical manipulations on a set of data. It does not tell us what the numbers mean, let alone do linguistics for us' (Guy 1988: 133).

In fact, the choice mechanism that the variable rule program models could originate in the grammatical generation of sentences, in the processes of production and performance, in the physiology of articulation, in the conscious stylistic decision of speakers, or even in an analytical construct on the part of the linguist. On the other hand, the *linguistic* significance of the analysis does, of course, depend on the nature of the choice process. This is where the important interpretative component of variation analysis comes in. The question of the linguistic (structural) consequences of the choice process must be addressed prior to the formal, algorithmic, statistical procedures. This is done in the collection (Chapter 2) and coding of the data (Chapter 6), the decision about what choice is to be studied (Chapter 5) and what is to be considered the context (defining the variable context). In the end, it is the relevance of the choice process to linguistic and social structures that must inform the discussion, interpretation and explanation of the results (see Chapters 11 and 12).

PRACTICE

Today, variable rule analysis is more readily available than ever before. All of the Goldvarb programs are available for free download, along with documentation, from the web. All you have to do is double-click, and get going.

In the next section, I review some of the foundational aspects of the variable rule program and show how these operate in practice.

The choice process in linguistic data

In order to understand the need for variables rules it is necessary to return to the nature of linguistic data. Language gives us options (see Chapter 1). This is the fundamental starting point for variable rules.

> Whenever a choice among two (or more) discrete alternatives can be perceived as having been made in the course of linguistic performance, and where this choice may have been influenced by factors such as: features in the phonological environment, the syntactic context, discursive function of the utterance, topic, style, interactional situation, personal or socio-demographic characteristics of the speaker, other participants, then it is appropriate to invoke the statistical notions and methods known to students of linguistic variation as 'variable rules'. (Sankoff 1988c: 984)

Labov's thesis was that this variation is part of an individual's linguistic competence. But until we can view these choices statistically, natural speech data often look like a big mess (i.e. 'apparent random-ness', one of the key criteria for a probabilistic model).

Modelling the choice process ▬▬▬▬▬▬▬▬▬▬▬▬▬▬▬▬▬

What does this choice process look like in practical terms? Let us look at the 'marginal results' for variable (t,d) as produced by the variable rule program. Marginal results, *aka* 'comparison of marginals analysis' (Rand and Sankoff 1990: 4), refer to the relative frequencies and per-centages of the variant forms in the data of the dependent variable, either alone, as in (1), or with the independent variable(s) that have been coded into the token file, as we shall see. The marginals reveal the factor-by-factor correlations in the data.

Note

The term 'run' is used for any computation performed by the variable rule program, e.g. 'run your marginals' refers to producing distributional results from a condition file. 'Run the variable rule program' refers to the statistical procedure of the binomial or binomial step-up/step-down regression.

First, consider the 'overall distribution' of variable (t,d) in (1). Overall distribution refers to the relative frequency of each variant of the variable without consideration of anything else.

```
(1)
   Dependent variable [t/d] deletion in British English
Group                  T        0       ?      Total
- - - - - - - - - - - - - - - - - - - - - - - - - - - -
TOTAL       N        795      291      59      1145
            %         69       25       5
```

The choice process revealed in (1) involves a full cluster, the pro-nunciation of the final [t] or [d], 't', absence of a closure, '0', or glottal stop [?], '?'. At the top of the table you will see 't', '0' and '?'. These are the symbols I selected for the variant forms. The column underneath each of these symbols shows you the frequency of each of these variants and their proportions (percentages). There are 1,145 tokens of the variable overall, 795 are realised [t] or [d], 291 are unrealised, here represented by the symbol '0', and 59 are glottalised, here repre-sented by the symbol '?'. The overall distribution of unrealised (t,d) (*aka* 'deletion') in British English is 25 per cent.

Now consider the dependent variable according to one of the independent variables, following phonological context, as in (2). Notice how this independent variable influences the choice process.

```
(2)
   Dependent variable [t/d] deletion in British English with
   independent variable following phonological context [V = vowel;
   C = Consonant; Q = pause]
```

Group		t	0	?	Total	%
1 (new)						
V	N	456	44	20	520	45
	%	88	**8**	4		
C	N	227	240	31	498	43
	%	46	**48**	6		
Q	N	112	7	8	127	11
	%	88	**6**	6		
Total	N	795	291	59	1145	
	%	69	25	5		
TOTAL	N	795	291	59	1145	
	%	69	25	5		

Note

The variable rule program shows the 'Total' distributions for each factor group as well as for the overall total, 'TOTAL N'. In example (2), these are identical. As we shall see, they need not be.

The table in (2) now shows the distribution of variants of the dependent variable, (t,d), unrealised forms and glottal stop, '?', according to following phonological context. Here the following phonological context is categorised into three main divisions: vowels, 'V', consonants, 'C', and pause, 'Q'. Note the number and proportion of each of the dependent variants in each of these contexts separately. There are two rows for each context. The first is labelled 'N' and records the actual number of tokens. The second, labelled '%', shows you the percentage that these tokens represent of the total number for each cell. For example, consider the context of following vowels, the first row of results inside the table. The second column from the end, titled 'Total', shows you that there are 520 tokens that have a following vowel in the data. The last column, titled simply '%', shows you that this represents 45 per cent of the total data, 520/1145. Now turning back to the column titled 't', the dependent variable is realised as [t,d] 456 times. The next column titled '0', shows 44 unrealised tokens, and finally the next column, titled '?', shows 20 glottal stops. These represent 88 per cent, 8 per cent and 4 per cent of the context respectively.

However, the important thing to observe is the contrast between 'V', 'C' and 'Q' contexts. It is clear how following phonological context influences variable (t,d). When the following context is a consonant, the proportion of unrealised consonants is relatively high, 48 per cent (240/498). In contrast, when the following context is a vowel or a pause, unrealised consonants are relatively low, 8 per cent (44/520) and 6 per cent (7/127).

The marginal results in (2) also highlight the aspect of language data that makes it difficult for statistical modelling – it is badly distributed. Notice that the distribution of contexts is not equally represented. While following consonants and following vowels represent a good proportion of the data (45 per cent and 43 per cent respectively), the following pause context represents only 11 per cent. In real language data, this uneven distribution of categories is typical. The number of occurrences of each context depends on its relative frequency in discourse. Hence, the number of cases per context is highly variable and many combinations of factors may not occur at all. This is why standard statistical procedures such as ANOVA, which assume even distribution, are not ideal for language in use. This type of data contrasts with that found in psycholinguistic studies, which are usually based on experimental data, rather than on corpus work. In this tradition the same number of examples is collected for all contexts, ensuring balanced cells and permitting analysis by standard statistical procedures. This highlights one of the fundamental differences between sociolinguistics and psycholinguistics – the nature of the data. 'It is a tenet of corpus-based sociolinguistics that data analysis should make use of the naturally occurring frequencies of the contexts, even if these are not statistically examined in the same way or at the same time as the choice variable' (Sankoff 1988c: 986).

Further, it is a natural aspect of speech to have dependence among factor groups. Lexical, functional and phonological factors, for example, may have a particular relationship. Certain forms may appear more often than others, and in particular constructions more often than others.

Following pauses are not nearly as frequent as following consonants or vowels. Full noun phrases occur more often in subject position than in object position. Predicate adjectives are more frequent than attributive adjectives. This type of natural interaction is why examination of marginal results alone may be misleading. Consider again the

(3)

Horizontally - function of word containing [t,d] is:
monomorpheme [M], past tense form [P], ambiguous verb [A]

Vertically - preceding phonological context:
nasal [N], liquid [L], fricative [F], sibilant [S], stop [P]

```
          M    %     P    %     A    %     Σ    %

     + - - - - + - - - - + - - - - + - - - -
N 0:     63  21:    12  25:     0   0|    75   21
  -:    233  79:    36  75:     6 100|   275   79
  Σ:    296   :     48   :      6   |    350

     + - - - - + - - - - + - - - - + - - - -
L 0:     11  23:     8  20:     8  19|    27   21
  -:     36  77:    33  80:    34  81|   103   79
  Σ:     47   :     41   :     42   |    130

     + - - - - + - - - - + - - - - + - - - -
F 0:      0   0:     6   8:     9  23|    15   12
  -:     11 100:    71  92:    30  77|   112   88
  Σ:     11   :     77   :     39   |    127

     + - - - - + - - - - + - - - - + - - - -
S 0:    109  44:    33  32:     4  29|   146   40
  -:    141  56:    70  68:    10  71|   221   60
  Σ:    250   :    103   :     14   |    367

     + - - - - + - - - - + - - - - + - - - -
P 0:      5  22:    16  13:     6  22|    27   16
  -:     18  78:   103  87:    21  78|   142   84
  Σ:     23   :    119   :     27   |    169

     +---------+---------+---------+---------
Σ 0:    188  30:    75  19:    27  21|   290   25
  -:    439  70:   313  81:   101  79|   853   75
  Σ:    627   :    388   :    128   |   1143
```

marginal results from variable (t,d) in (3), which now shows preceding phonological context with the categories 'N', nasals, 'L', liquids, 'F', fricatives, 'S', sibilants, and 'P', stops, along the vertical axis. These contexts are cross-tabulated with the functional categories of past tense (e.g. *walked, stopped*), 'P'; monomorpheme (e.g. *found, mist*), 'M'; and verbs such as *kept* and *left*, 'A' – displayed across the horizontal axis. When two factor groups are cross-tabulated in this way the analyst can view how they intersect with each other. Within each context on the vertical axis, the data are divided into two categories: the symbol '0' represents unrealised [t,d]; whereas '–' now represents presence of consonant [t,d] *or* glottal stop. In this run, these latter two categories have been combined, i.e. collapsed, into one category. The symbol 'Σ' is the sum or total of each category.

Overwhelmingly, monomorphemes have word-final clusters whose first consonant is a nasal, 'N', or a sibilant, 'S'. Nasals represent 296 tokens; while sibilants represent 250 tokens. Other clusters are rare. Liquids (L) represent 47 tokens, fricatives (F) 11 tokens, and stops (P) 23 tokens. Past tense forms, on the other hand, ending in sibilant and stop clusters, occur 103 and 119 times respectively. Ambiguous verbs hardly ever end with a nasal, *lend*, N = 6. Moreover, two cells are categorical: monomorphemes with a preceding consonant, 'F', and ambiguous verbs with a preceding consonant that is a nasal, 'N'. Even though the factor groups are themselves independent in principle, i.e. preceding phonological environment and morphological status, the individual factors they are comprised of reveal 'lumps' and 'clumps', 'hollows' and 'dips', in the data. Such interactions are often not readily apparent until cross-tabulations of this type are performed. Then, the uneven patterning of language is revealed.

The question is: How do we deal with these very real aspects of naturally occurring language? Sometimes the interactions are a normal by-product of the language that the variable rule program is designed to handle. But sometimes the interactions are so severe that they obscure underlying effects on the variable that are explanatory. In these cases, a different model must be configured. I will talk more about interaction in Chapter 10.

Types of variable rule analysis

The Goldvarb series of applications offer two ways of conducting analyses of variable data: 1) binomial one-step and 2) binomial step-up/step-down. The binomial one-level analyses all groups and all cells at the same time. This permits you to examine each of the cells and see how much each combination differs from the expected. This type of information can help you to understand what is going on with your analysis, particularly by allowing you to determine which cells fit the model least well. Such cells may represent tokens that can be excluded from the model as exceptions. The binomial step-up/step-down performs a levelled analysis in which computations are done one step at a time. The majority of studies employing variation analysis use the latter. This method supplies you with 'three lines of evidence' (see Chapter 11), statistical significance, relative strength and constraint ranking of factors, all of which are instrumental for interpreting the model of the data. Here, I focus on the step-up/step-down analysis in order to demonstrate how multiple regression works. Further discussion of the one-step analysis can be found in Chapter 10.

Step-up/step-down analysis

The step-wise procedure of the multiple regression embodied in the variable rule program is easily visible when you run it. First, you will see the regression step up. Then you will see it step down.

The first step in fitting the model to the data is to find the group which makes the most significant change to the model when it is added or subtracted from the rest. All factor groups are tested, in order to determine which one increases the likelihood most significantly.

The program retains the most significant group and tries to add a second group, which increases the likelihood as significantly as possible. It continues in this way until no further additions result in a statistically significant improvement. The collection of groups incorporated in the model this way is referred to as the step-up solution.

A series of diagrams on the companion website schematises the operation of the variable rule program. These diagrams were constructed by me under the direction of David Sankoff for a workshop on variable rule analysis at the 32nd New Ways of Analysing Variation Conference (NWAVE 32) in Ottawa in 1993. They give you a means to conceptualise the variable rule program. In the next sections, I will show you how it all works in practice.

Step-up

Consider the following step-up analysis of variable (t,d) in British English (Tagliamonte and Temple 2005), testing the following three factor groups: 1) preceding phonological context, 2) following phonological context and 3) functional category of the word containing (t,d), as in (4). I have added some extra commentary to this output (annotation), so that you can understand what the symbols for each category mean.

First, a few notes on what you will see. The 'Input', also known as 'corrected mean', is a global measure of rate of rule application (Guy 1988: 126) and can be thought of as an 'overall indication of the strength of the rule' (Young and Bayley 1996: 270) or 'an average frequency of occurrence of the application value of the dependent variable' (Paolillo 2002: 79). This value varies a little from level to level, but hovers near .236 throughout. This means that the overall probability of [t,d] deletion in British English is about .24, a value which is in this case identical to the overall distribution we saw earlier. The 'iterations' show you 'an account of the program's progress in finding the "maximum likelihood" estimation of the factor weights to a certain degree of accuracy, at which point "convergence" is indicated' (Rand and Sankoff 1990). The iterations for each run are different. Depending on the factor groups being considered in a particular iteration, the computations required to achieve this accuracy level may take longer.

The step-up analysis begins at Level '0' and continues to build from one level to the next, as shown in (4).

(4)
Variable (t,d) with three factor groups, step-up
```
Stepping Up ...

--------- Level #0 ---------
Run #1, 1 cells:
Iterations: 1 2
Convergence at Iteration 2
Input 0.236
Log likelihood = -673.480

--------- Level #1 ---------
Run #2, 2 cells:
Iterations: 1 2 3 4 5
Convergence at Iteration 5
Input 0.223
Group #1, Other consonant [O]; Preceding Sibilant [S]
- - O: 0.413, S: 0.697
Log likelihood = -637.748   Significance = 0.000

Run #3, 3 cells:
Iterations: 1 2 3 4 5
Convergence at Iteration 5
Input 0.177
Group #2, Following phonological context:
Vowel [V], Consonant [C], Pause, [Q]
- - V: 0.285, C: 0.795, Q: 0.202
Log likelihood = -547.430   Significance = 0.000

Run #4, 3 cells:
Iterations: 1 2 3 4
Convergence at Iteration 4
```

```
Input 0.235
Group #3, Functional Category of word containing [t,d]
Monomorpheme [M], Past tense form [P], Ambiguous past tense form [A]
--M: 0.539, P: 0.439, A: 0.466
Log likelihood = -669.676  Significance = 0.024
Add Group #2 with factors VCQ

-------- Level #2 --------
Run #5, 6 cells:
Iterations: 1 2 3 4 5
Convergence at Iteration 5
Input 0.170
Group #1 - - O: 0.426, S: 0.670
Group #2 - - V: 0.294, C: 0.787, Q: 0.202
Log likelihood = -526.649  Significance = 0.000

Run #6, 9 cells:
Iterations: 1 2 3 4 5 6
Convergence at Iteration 6
Input 0.175
Group #2 - V: 0.287, C: 0.796, Q: 0.192
Group #3 - M: 0.544, P: 0.447, A: 0.417
Log likelihood = -543.529  Significance = 0.020
Add Group #1 with factors OS

-------- Level #3 --------
Run #7, 17 cells:
Iterations: 1 2 3 4 5
Convergence at Iteration 5
Input 0.170
Group #1 - - O: 0.428, S: 0.664
Group #2 - - V: 0.295, C: 0.786, Q: 0.200
Group #3 - - M: 0.527, P: 0.458, A: 0.478
Log likelihood = -525.291  Significance = 0.262

No remaining groups significant

Groups selected while stepping up: 2 1
Best stepping-up run: #5
```

The regression begins with the overall probability of 0.236 at
Level #0. This is the model with no factor groups included. At Level #1,
each factor group is tested independently by adding it in turn to the
model and comparing the resulting model to the model at Level #0.
In Run #2, preceding phonological context is added; in Run #3, following phonological context; in Run #4, functional category. The addition
of each of the three groups results in a significant change to the model,
as the significance levels show. At the end of Level #1, Group #2
(following phonological context) is selected since it results in the
log likelihood closest to zero (−547.430, as compared to −637.748

and −669.676 for the other two factor groups) and is added to the model. At Level #2 the basic model includes Group #2 (following phonological context). As in Level #1, each of the two remaining factor groups is added to the model in turn and the resulting model is compared to the basic model with only Group #2. Again, the addition of each group results in a significant change to the model (check the significance levels), but Group #1 (preceding phonological context) results in a higher log likelihood and so is selected. At the end of Level #2 the basic model now contains Groups #2 and #1. Finally, in the last stage the remaining factor group, #3 (functional category), is tested. In this case, adding the group to the model does not result in a significant improvement (the significance level is .262) and so this group is not added. At the completion of this step-up process, the best fit is assessed as Run #5. Two factor groups are statistically significant at the .05 level, preceding phonological segment and following phonological segment.

Step-down

The step-down analysis is based on the same principle as the step-up, but in reverse, as in (5). The program starts by calculating the likelihood of the model when all the factor groups are included in the regression simultaneously. Thereafter, it discards the group whose loss least significantly reduces the likelihood (using the chi-square test).

```
(5)
Variable (t,d) with three factor groups, step-down
Stepping Down ...
-------- Level #3 --------
Run #8, 17 cells:
Iterations: 1 2 3 4 5
Convergence at Iteration 5
Input 0.170
Group #1 - - O: 0.428, S: 0.664
Group #2 - - V: 0.295, C: 0.786, Q: 0.200
Group #3 - - M: 0.527, P: 0.458, A: 0.478
Log likelihood = −1525.291

-------- Level #2 --------
Run #9, 9 cells:
Iterations: 1 2 3 4 5 6
Convergence at Iteration 6
Input 0.175
Group #2 - - V: 0.287, C: 0.796, Q: 0.192
Group #3 - - M: 0.544, P: 0.447, A: 0.417
Log likelihood = −543.529   Significance = 0.000

Run #10, 6 cells:
Iterations: 1 2 3 4 5
```

```
Convergence at Iteration 5
Input 0.222
Group #1 - - O: 0.413, S: 0.696
Group #3 - - M: 0.524, P: 0.446, A: 0.530
Log likelihood = -635.556  Significance = 0.000
```

```
Run #11, 6 cells:
Iterations: 1 2 3 4 5
Convergence at Iteration 5
Input 0.170
Group #1 - - O: 0.426, S: 0.670
Group #2 - - V: 0.294, C: 0.787, Q: 0.202
Log likelihood = -526.649  Significance = 0.262
```

```
Cut Group #3 with factors MPA
```

```
---------- Level #1 ----------
Run #12, 3 cells:
Iterations: 1 2 3 4 5
Convergence at Iteration 5
Input 0.177
Group #2 - - V: 0.285, C: 0.795, Q: 0.202
Log likelihood = -547.430  Significance = 0.000
```

```
Run #13, 2 cells:
Iterations: 1 2 3 4 5
Convergence at Iteration 5
Input 0.223
Group #1 - - O: 0.413, S: 0.697
Log likelihood = -637.748  Significance = 0.000
```

```
All remaining groups significant
Groups eliminated while stepping down: 3
Best stepping-up run: #5
Best stepping-down run: #11
```

This step-down analysis begins at Level #3. All the factor groups are tested together. The overall probability is 0.170. At Level #2, the program begins removing factor groups, testing for whether this improves or worsens the log likelihood. In Run #9, the preceding phonological category has been discarded. The log likelihood worsens. In Run #10, following phonological context is discarded and the log likelihood worsens dramatically at −635.556. In Run #11 the functional category is removed and the log likelihood improves again. Clearly, this is the factor group to throw out entirely, and notice that this is where the program cuts the group. We now come back to Level #1, where each factor is tested independently one at a time. At the completion of this step-down process, the best fit is assessed as Run #11. One factor group has been eliminated, the functional category. Only two factor groups are significant: preceding and following phonological context.

In the normal case, the best step-up and step-down stops discarding groups when it is left with just the set of groups that were added in the step-up analysis. In other words, the run which is the best fit of the model to the data in the step-up analysis should be precisely the same as the one for the step-down analysis. Check this by comparing Run #5 in (4) with Run #11 in (5). They are identical.

Favours/disfavours

Factor weights obtained from a multivariate analysis can be values anywhere from 0 to 1. When a factor weight is closer to 1, it is interpreted as 'favouring' the application value, whereas if it is closer to zero it is interpreted as 'disfavouring' the application value. In some places in the literature you will find analysts saying that anything over .50 favours the application of the rule and anything under .50 disfavours. While this is generally true, it is not the most accurate way to conceive of factor weights. Instead, it is the *relative* position of factor weights, vis-à-vis each other, that is the relevant criterion for interpreting the results.

Significance within factor groups

In the Goldvarb series of programs there is no automatic procedure for testing for significance *within* a factor group. However, this can be accomplished by separate runs with your data arranged in different ways and comparing the log likelihood values for the best step-up/ step-down run (see Sankoff and Labov 1979: 199, Guy 1988: 132–3).

For example, you may have wondered why in the step-up/step-down analysis of variable (t,d) in (4) and (5), I ran the data for preceding phonological context as sibilants vs other, or the following phonological context as consonants, vowels, pause. The configuration of the analysis was arrived at through many runs of different arrangements of the same data with the aim of achieving the best model of the data. In order to carry out this testing I began with a much more elaborated set of factors across three factor groups, as in (6). Preceding phonological context was originally coded for the actual form of the consonant, e.g. 'n' for [n], 'm' for [m]. Each of the original coding symbols can be seen in the single-digit codes appearing after 'COL 3'.

```
(6)
(0
; PRECEDING SEGMENT
; nasal
(0 (COL 3 n))
(0 (COL 3 ©)))
```

```
(O (COL 3 m))
;liquid
(O (COL 3 l))
;sibilant
(S (COL 3 Z))
(S (COL 3 S))
(S (COL 3 J))
(S (COL 3 †))
(S (COL 3 z))
(S (COL 3 s))
;stop
(P (COL 3 t))
(P (COL 3 g))
(P (COL 3 k))
(P (COL 3 b))
(P (COL 3 d))
(P (COL 3 p))
(P (COL 3 ?))
;non-sibilant fricative
(F (COL 3 Ø))
(F (COL 3 #))
(F (COL 3 v))
(F (COL 3 f))
)
```

The same schema was applied for following phonological context, as in (7). Here the original coding symbols appear after 'COL 4'. However, for the variable rule analysis in (4) and (5), these detailed (what I refer to as 'elaborated') divisions are collapsed into the major relevant divisions for each factor group. Preceding phonological context is re-coded as follows. Nasals and liquids were re-coded as 'O'. Sibilants are all treated together as 'S'. Stops are coded as 'P' and non-sibilant fricatives as 'F'. Following phonological context is coded as in (7). All consonants are coded as 'C', vowels as 'V' and pause as 'Q'.

```
(7)
(0
;FOLLOWING PHONOLOGICAL CONTEXT
;obstruents
(C (COL 4 n))
(C (COL 4 S))
(C (COL 4 t))
(C (COL 4 g))
(C (COL 4 k))
(C (COL 4 Ø))
(C (COL 4 b))
(C (COL 4 v))
(C (COL 4 z))
```

```
(C (COL 4 s))
(C (COL 4 d))
(C (COL 4 m))
(C (COL 4 f))
(C (COL 4 p))
(C (COL 4 ?))
(C (COL 4 h))
;lateral
(C (COL 4 l))
;rhotics
(C (COL 4 r))
;following glides
(C (COL 4 j))
(C (COL 4 w))
;VOWELS
(V (COL 4 V))
;PAUSE
(Q (COL 4 Q))
)
```

Finally, the functional category of the word containing the [t,d] cluster is re-coded into the usual three-part division treated in the literature on this subject, as in (8). Here, too, the first coding schema was much more elaborated, differentiating many different types of preterite contexts.

```
(8)
(5
;REGULAR BI-MORPHEMIC PRETERITE
(P (COL 5 P))
(P (COL 5 p))
(P (COL 5 Z))
;SEMI-WEAK PRETERITES
(A (COL 5 A))
(A (COL 5 a))
(A (COL 5 n))
;STRONG PRETERITES
(M (COL 5 S))
;REPLACIVE PRETERITES
(M (COL 5 B))
;TRUE MONOMORPHEMES
(M (COL 5 M))
)
```

The results from different runs of the same data set using five unique configurations of the three factor groups are shown in (9).

Each analysis is shown in the columns from left to right in the table. A variable rule analysis of the data re-coded as in (6) to (8) produced the factor weights in Analysis #1. Successive analyses in which the preceding phonological segment factor group was collapsed are shown in Analyses #2 to #5.

(9)

	ANALYSES				
	#1	#2	#3	#4	#5
Factors considered	Factor weight	Factor weight	Factor weight	Factor weight	Factor weight
Preceding phonological segment					
Sibilant	.67	.67	.67	.67	.67
Obstruent	.45	.45	.43	.43	.43
Stop	.45				
Non-sibilant fricative	.31	.31			
Following phonological segment					
Consonant	.79	.79	.79	.79	.79
Vowel	.29	.29	.29	.29	.28
Pause	.20	.20	.20	.20	
Morphological status					
Monomorpheme	[ ]	[ ]	[ ]	[ ]	[ ]
Past tense form	[ ]	[ ]	[ ]	[ ]	[ ]
Ambiguous past tense	[ ]	[ ]	[ ]		
LOG LIKELIHOOD	−524.68	−524.67	−526.65	−526.65	−527.42

Notice that when you compare the log likelihood values for these analyses at the bottom of the table, Analysis #2 looks like it has the best overall log likelihood, i.e. the value closest to 0. Different configurations of the factor groups in Analyses #3 through to #5 do not greatly change the fit of the model to the data.

However comparing log likelihoods in this gross manner does not take into account that the more factor groups you put into an analysis, the more complicated it becomes. It is also necessary to take into account the 'degrees of freedom' of the model. These are the number of adjustable parameters of the model, i.e. 'the number of independent pieces of information available or used in an analysis of the observed data' (Paolillo 2002: 109). In other words, the more factors that are involved in a variable rule analysis, the greater the degrees of freedom. At the same time, the fewer factors used to predict the data, the less well it will fit the model. For both these reasons, comparing log likelihoods is only rudimentary. In (9), for example, direct comparison of log likelihood is obscured by the fact that Analysis #1 and Analysis #2 differ with respect to the number of parts to the analysis, i.e. the degrees of freedom. Degrees of freedom is 'calculated by subtracting the number of factor groups from the total number of factors' (Young and Bayley 1996: 273). In the case of Analysis #1, there are 10 factors minus 3 factor groups, which equals 7 degrees of freedom. In the case of Analysis #2, there are 9 factors minus 3 factor groups, which equals 6 degrees of freedom. Despite this difference, Analysis #1 has a log likelihood value that is virtually identical to Analysis #2. The comparison could be taken further by assessing whether or not the different log likelihood values are *significantly* different from each other.

Here is the procedure, somewhat simplified, based on Young and Bayley (1996: 272–3) and Guy (1988: 133):

i. Given the degrees of freedom of the revised analysis, how many factors have been eliminated? This will be the 'degrees of freedom' for this test.
ii. Calculate the difference between the log likelihoods of the two analyses.
iii. Multiply by 2.
iv. Use this value and the degrees of freedom of the model and look it up in a chi-square table (readily available in any introductory statistics textbook, from the internet, or see Paolillo (2002: 231–2).
v. Is the value more or less than .05? If less, then the difference between the factors combined was significant. If more, then the difference was not significant.
vi. If the new, combined factor group is linguistically and/or extra-linguistically justified and the fit of the model is better, then the revised analysis is likely a better analysis.

Following these procedures, you can compare one analysis to another. For example, let us compare Analysis #1 and #2.

i. Analysis #1 degrees of freedom = 7; Analysis #2 degrees of freedom = 6.
ii. Difference between log likelihoods = .01.
iii. .02.
iv. When this value is viewed in a chi-square table, under 1 degree of freedom (df), the p-value is found to be more than .05.

    v. This means the difference between the two factors combined was not significant.

    vi. Conclusion: Analysis #2 is a better analysis.

Compare Analysis #2 and #3.

    i. Analysis #2 degrees of freedom = 6; Analysis #3 degrees of freedom = 5.

    ii. Difference between log likelihoods = 1.98.

    iii. 3.96.

    iv. P-value is greater than .05.

    v. The difference between the two factors combined was not significant.

    vi. Analysis #3 is a better analysis.

These comparisons reveal that the difference between obstruents, stops and non-sibilant fricatives is not significant. Technically, they should be collapsed for the most parsimonious model. Yet in the published version of variable (t,d), Analysis #1 was selected for presentation. Why? It enabled us to show the detail of how each of the major categories performed in the regression, particularly in demonstrating that stops patterned with obstruents. We opted to present the full spectrum of categories in the analysis so that the contribution of each one could be viewed in relation to all the others (and for comparison with other studies), even though some of the factors were not significantly different from each other (Tagliamonte and Temple 2005: fn. 14).

Subjecting the data to successive analyses in this way leads you to discover the relevant distinctions in the data. In this case, we found that the distinction between vowels and pause is relevant in this data, as is the difference between past tense forms and ambiguous verbs. We also demonstrated that the relevant categories for the preceding phonological context are sibilants vs obstruents (including stops), and non-sibilant fricatives. More broadly, we were able to establish that, no matter which way we run the data, morphological class is not significant. Such findings lend support to one of the more important findings of this analysis – that this variable in British English is phonological. This makes it similar in some respects to the same variable phenomenon found in North America. At the same time, this variable operates quite differently than it does in North America. There, the functional category is also statistically significant, making this variable a morphophonological feature. See Tagliamonte and Temple (2005) for further discussion.

In sum, there are two goals for finding the 'best' analysis for your data. On the one hand, you must be driven to find the best fit of the model to the data. This means, in part, combining factors that do not differ significantly from each other. On the other hand, you also want to explain (and demonstrate) how the variation is embedded in the subsystem of grammar as well as in the community. Sometimes this is more effectively accomplished with a more 'fleshed-out' model. It may be fitting to show that certain internal or external categories pattern similarly.

Interaction

Unlike other statistical programs, the variable rule program does not check overtly for interaction between factors. However, there are a number of ways to spot interaction. The simplest way is to compare the probabilities (i.e. factor weights) assigned by the variable rule program to the proportions calculated in the marginal results. Is the same order from more to less apparent? Such an observation should be supplemented by a detailed examination of the regression and cross-tabulation. As the step-up/step-down regression proceeds, interaction between factors, if it exists, will often be visible. You will see it as notable shifts in the factor weights from one level to another. In the step-up analysis, as each significant factor group is added, the estimated factor effects of the previously incorporated factor groups will change to some extent. When these changes are small, e.g. if they do not affect the way in which factor effects are ordered by size, then we may generally attribute them to sampling fluctuation. In another case a particular factor group may be marginal. If so it may flip from .48 to .51 back and forth as the regression proceeds, but never reach statistical significance. This, too, does not seriously compromise the model. Go back and look at the weights for each factor in each factor group in the step-up and step-down runs in (4) and (5). Notice that they hover near the same values throughout.

However, if one or more of the changes is large, then you may suspect that the new factor group and the one(s) subject to this change are not independent, i.e. they interact. This can be verified by examining the distribution of contexts through cross-tabulations of factor groups. This should not be perceived as a defect in variable rule analysis. Cross-tabulation is a key element of a variation analysis (Tagliamonte 1998: fn. 22).

When you search for interaction in your model, you may uncover some of the most important findings. In Chapters 8 and 10, you will find additional practical demonstrations of how to spot interaction.

Some other things you may see

There are a number of other things that you will inevitably come across while conducting variable rule analysis. I detail these in the next sections.

Tip

Students sometimes end up with variable rule outputs that I have never seen before. Fortunately, the really weird stuff is usually due to some inadvertent mistake. If something strange happens, just quit out of the program and start again. Usually this works.

KnockOuts

When you see the term 'KnockOut' surrounded by stars, this may look severe, as in (10). However, these should not bother you. A KnockOut simply means that there is a 0 per cent value or a 100 per cent value in one of the cells in your analysis. You cannot run a variable rule analysis when either of these cases exist because it means that the data, so configured, is not variable. In most cases, knockouts can be handled by removing them or re-coding them in a sound linguistically justified way.

```
(10)
Group         L    A    O    B    S    0    Total    %
- - - - - - - - - - - - - - - - - - - - - - - - - - - - - - - - - -
2 (2)
   1      N    1    2   65    0    0    9     77      18
          %    1    3   84    0    0   12             *KnockOut*
   3      N   30   14   65    7    4  115    235      56
          %   13    6   28    3    2   49
   2      N    0    0   14    0    0   10     24      6
          %    0    0   58    0    0   42             *KnockOut*
   0      N   10   10   30    1    1   32     84      20
          %   12   12   36    1    1   38
Total     N   41   26  174    8    5  166    420
          %   10    6   41    2    1   40
- - - - - - - - - - - - - - - - - - - - - - - - - - - - - - - - - -
```

In (10) you are viewing the distribution of *whatever* types (the columns) in four age groups of adolescents in Toronto (the rows). Here, *whatever* has been coded for words that it collocates with, e.g. *like*, *and*, *but*, *so* and *or*, as in *like whatever*, *and whatever*, *so whatever* and *or whatever*, as in (11a). If *whatever* occurs alone, as in (11b), it is coded as '0'.

(11)
a. They came to visit me and like, they're all cute ***and whatever***. (ROP4/a)
b. Fine ***whatever*** this is useless (ROP4/f)

The four age groups are 9- to 11-year-olds, '0', 12- and 13-year-olds, '1', 14- to 16-year-olds, '2', and 17- to 19-year-olds, '3'. Now, you can understand why the KnockOuts occur and what they mean. Neither the 12–13s nor the 14–16s have any tokens of *but whatever*. This is a very low-frequency item in the data overall. Part of the research process involves finding out how to deal with KnockOuts.

Singletons

This is another item that will appear surrounded by stars, as in (12). You are looking at the same data as in (10); however, in this run of the data factor group 3 is included, which, as you can clearly see, contains only one factor, 'W', *whatever*. A singleton simply means that there is only one factor in a factor group. Singletons should not bother you, either, but you will have to take care of them somehow (i.e. removing them or collapsing them with other like categories) before running the variable rule program. See Chapter 8.

```
(12)
    Number of cells: 21
    Application value(s): LAOBS0
    Total no. of factors: 11
Group        L    A    O    B   S    0   Total  %
- - - - - - - - - - - - - - - - - - - - - - - - - - - -
3 (3)
   W     N   41   26  174   8   5  166    420  100
         %   10    6   41   2   1   40          *Singleton Group*
Total   N   41   26  174   8   5  166    420
        %   10    6   41   2   1   40
- - - - - - - - - - - - - - - - - - - - - - - - - - - -
```

Non-convergence

Convergence at each iteration (run) of the step-up/step-down analysis is the ideal; however, sometimes this level of accuracy has not been met, even by the twentieth iteration. If it goes this far, the program will stop, make an estimate and move on to the next level, as in (13). In this case, I was running 7 different internal factors groups on a large data set of nearly 3,000 tokens. At Level #3 of the step-up analysis when Group #6 is added to #1, #4 and #5, the program tries twenty times, then issues a 'no convergence' signal and moves on to the next iteration.

```
(13)
--------- Level #3 ---------
Run #18, 19 cells:
Iterations: 1 2 3 4 5 6 7 8 9 10 11 12 13 14 15 16 17 18 19 20
No Convergence at Iteration 20
Input 0.021
Group #1 - - R: 0.905, S: 0.335
Group #4 - - P: 0.583, N: 0.545, O: 0.373
Group #6 - - P: 0.530, S: 0.333, C: 0.266
Log likelihood = -459.946  Significance = 0.608
```

When non-convergence occurs, the estimations in the run may not be as accurate as desired. What does this mean? It is likely that some factors within factor groups overlap with each other in the model defined by the condition file or there is some 'unnoticed chance maldistribution' of the data (Guy 1988: 128). In other words, the factors may be overlapping. In the example above, such a problem is exacerbated by the very low application value. Notice how low the input values are. In cases like this, where variation is so infrequent, an accurate statistical model is difficult. In most cases, however, non-convergence, in itself, does not invalidate your analysis.

Negative change in log likelihood

When many different factor groups are being investigated, a situation may arise in which there is a 'negative change in the log likelihood', as in (14). Here, I was running 7 different factors groups of both internal and external factors on a small data set of just over 600 tokens. Not a good idea at the best of times. At Level #0 of the step-up analysis in Run #6 a warning is issued. The three dots simply indicate material omitted for illustration purposes.

```
(14)
Stepping Up ...
--------- Level #0 ---------
...
Run #6, 2 cells:
Iterations: 1 2
Convergence at Iteration 2
Input 0.876
Group #5 - - A: 0.497, -: 0.501
*** Warning, negative change in likelihood (-0.02020264) replaced
    by 0.0.
Log likelihood = -238.647  Significance = 1.000
```

This looks very ominous when you see it in your regression. It is the result of the program attempting to achieve a particular mathematical status. However, the model has many factors and some of them are overlapping. As you saw earlier in the schemas of the program, it will 'do its best' to find the best fit of model to data, but if the data are badly distributed like this, the task for the program becomes exponentially more difficult. In either case, copious cross-tabulation of factor groups will reveal interactions. It is up to the analyst to determine how to deal with these problems. In this case, the run never made it past the 'cutting-room floor', so to speak. More practical tips on dealing with interaction problems are covered in Chapters 8 and 10.

SUMMARY

It has been nearly forty years since Labov first proposed variable rules. Since then, there has been an astounding outpouring of studies, all of which have demonstrated the value of the quantitative model for data ranging from historical texts of written English, to large-scale corpora of naturally occurring language to television commercials and programmes. At the same time, many new theoretical issues have arisen: Are all variable rules the same? Do they originate in the same area of grammar? For example, certain variables, such as agreement, word order and certain reduction phenomena can implicate structure. How far does this go? Where is the choice process in the grammar? Are the variants of a variable simple lexical choices, optimal structures, parametric differences? If variation is predictable and constrained, then what is the underlying principle (or principles) that account for it?

From their conception, the regularities and tendencies modelled by variable rules have been conceived as multiplex and diverse. Phonological variability is undoubtedly 'a direct consequence of natural articulatory processes' (Sankoff 1978: 235). Here, variable rules may be conceived as quantitative outcomes of natural physiological tendencies. On the semantic level, on the other hand, probabilities are 'clearly dependent on features such as the topic of discourse, style of conversation, the relationship among speakers and other psychological and sociolinguistic factors' (Sankoff 1978: 235). Thus, while the literature on variable rules states quite unequivocally that they are 'analytical abstractions rather than components of language' (Sankoff 1978: 235–6), in some areas of grammar, particularly semantics, the lines may be more blurred. Indeed, as Sankoff concluded, 'Variation theory is in large part the study of to what extent these probabilities are intrinsic to language as a system, and how extrinsic considerations impinge' (Sankoff 1978: 236).

FREQUENTLY ASKED QUESTIONS

What is a 'factor weight'?

A factor weight (*aka* probability) measures the influence that each factor has on the presence of the variant in question. In other words it answers the question: How probable is it that the application value will occur in this context?

What's the 'input'?

The overall tendency of rule application, regardless of proportion (*aka* 'corrected mean').

What does 'input and weight' refer to?

This calculation is found only in the one-step analysis. It represents the combined effect of the percentage and the factor weight. In cases where you want to compare two variable systems – one with higher frequency, one with much lower frequency – this value may make a more accurate measure of the variation.

What does 'expected' in the one-step analysis refer to?

This is a calculation of the number of occurrences of the variant in question (the application value) based on the factor weights calculated by the program.

What does 'error' refer to?

This measures how well the predicted data match the observed data.

What does the 'log likelihood' measure?

It measures the goodness of fit of the analysis. Figures closer to 0 represent better models than those further removed from 0.

How do you find the best run?

Goldvarb finds it for you. The best stepping-up run is recorded at the end of the stepping-up analysis and again when the regression finishes, along with the best stepping-down run.

Is it true that points over .5 favour and those under disfavour?

In the literature, you will often find absolute reference to factor weights over .5 being favouring and those under .5 as disfavouring. In actuality, this is not the whole truth. The contrast is not black and white, but relative. While a factor that has a weight of .59 may be said to favour the application value, its relative position in the constraint ranking is more important. For example, if it is only one factor in a group of three categories, where another factor has a weight of .85, and the other a weight of .31, then the factor with the weight of .59 is intermediary between the two.

How does Goldvarb select factor groups?

It picks weights which make the expected values in the cells as close as possible to the observed value, where 'close' means the most likely value, given the data. Technically, the program maximises a measure of likelihood.

Is it better to have one big factor group containing many contrastive factors, or is it better to have a large number of factor groups, each having a binary contrast?

A binary factor group makes a stronger linguistic hypothesis. However, if it is only partially right, the fit of the model to the data will not be as good.

If you throw everything into one factor group, it can be termed the 'kitchen sink effect'. While such a model might fit the data better, it will not tell you as much if it misses linguistically valid generalisations elsewhere.

Exercise 7: Running the variable rule program

In this exercise you will run the variable rule program.
Do a binomial analysis.
Do a step-up/step-down analysis.
What problems and/or questions arise? Are there errors? How many? Where? Can you explain them?
Begin to ask the question: What do my findings mean? Interpret them in terms of how they illuminate linguistic and extralinguistic processes. Situate your research in the context of the issues you have identified from the literature.
Your ultimate goal is an explanatory account of the patterning of the variability in the data. Attempt to ground your interpretation within the literature, prescriptive and descriptive, both contemporary and historical, on the subject.
Consider in detail the decision-making process that has gone into creating viable condition files. These analyses will be used as testable models of your data that will be subjected to multiple regression.
Finally, document your procedures for annotating and managing the innumerable files you will generate as you run various configurations of the data.

8   The how-to's of a variationist analysis

How do you code the data? How do you write a condition file?
This chapter will detail the day-to-day steps of a variationist research project.
It will also show you how to troubleshoot your results.

Now that I have explained the history, development and nature of variable rules and the variable rule program, let us now work directly with the program. The prototype program, Varbrul 2 S, was written in Fortran by David Sankoff (1975). It was revised by researchers at the University of Pennsylvania, including Don Hindle and Susan Pintzuk. Refinements to the program were also conducted by Pascale Rousseau at the University of Quebec in Montreal. When Goldvarb 2.0 was released in 1988, it was based on these versions of the program, but was partially reprogrammed in Pascal by David Rand (1990). Other versions of the program also exist, including MacVarb (Guy 1993) and R-Varb (Paolillo 2002). Goldvarb 2001 provides users with a Windows version of the original Macintosh application. Goldvarb X has been available since October 2005. It is an update of Goldvarb 2.1 for Macintosh or Windows in which the entire program has been translated into C++ (Sankoff et al. 2005).

In this chapter, I will abstract away from the various individual attributes of these different packages. Details of their workings can be found in the users manuals, documentation and online help menus which come with various applications. Here I outline basic operations and frame these in terms of the later, most widely used packages, Goldvarb 2.1 and Goldvarb X.

THE VARIABLE RULE PROGRAM IN PRACTICE

To begin with, I will review the files which comprise the variable rule program – the token (or data) file, the condition file, the cell file and the results file. When you are inside the variable rule program with all these files open, your screen will look something like as in (1).

(1)

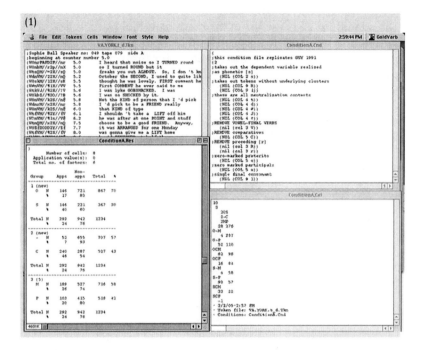

THE TOKEN FILE (Tkn)

The main file, which is in the top left corner, is the data file, *aka* token file. The dependent variable, the coding strings for each of the independent factors, reference markers and contexts are contained here. In the example, the token file from variable (t,d) in York, you see two comment lines beginning with semicolons, followed by a series of lines which begin with an open parenthesis and contain a long list of letters and symbols. These letters and symbols are the coding strings. When there is at least one space after the coding string, this signals to the program that the relevant part of the token has ended. I will typically insert additional spacing. This makes it easier to spot where the coding string ends and the data starts. In this data file, you see the tape counter number, followed by the context in which the dependent variable occurs.

THE CONDITION FILE (Cnd)

The second file, which is in the top right-hand corner, is the condition file, 'ConditionA.Cnd'. This is the place where the analyst tells the program precisely how the data in the token file are to be configured. The condition file is the list of instructions to Goldvarb. It is written in the form of a LISP list, a high-level computer programming language, in which statements and data are in the form of lists enclosed in parentheses. For further discussion, see the Goldvarb 2.0 user's manual (Rand and Sankoff 1990: 41–3). The condition file runs on the data file to produce the cell file. In the example, a number of comment lines are interspersed in the file. These comments are for the humans who want to understand what the condition file is doing. In this case, the comments relate to a series of contexts which the program is instructed to remove from the analysis, e.g. tokens without underlying clusters, neutralised contexts, vowel-final verbs, comparatives, etc. All these are outside the context of variation (see Chapter 5).

Application values

When you run the conditions, the program will check the data file for errors, prompt you to save the soon-to-be-produced cell file, and then request that you choose an application value. The program is capable of producing marginal results for up to nine different application values. These are the variants in the dependent variable factor group. You may choose which variant (or combination of variants) to view. Whichever variant's symbol you enter first will be the 'application' value. In this example, I entered the value '0' into the 'choose Application value' window. This is faithfully reproduced in the 'results' file as 'Application value(s): 0'.

The Goldvarb versions of the variable rule program are capable of binomial analysis only. Thus, only one application value is possible when you run the variable rule program. At the beginning phase of your analysis, however, it is worthwhile to examine all your variants. For example, in a study of relativisers, we coded for six different relativisers, *that*, 'T', *who*, 'O', zero, 'Z', *whose*, 'S', *which*, 'C', and *what*, 'A' (Tagliamonte et al. 2005). Since this is how the data were coded in the token file, these very symbols will come up in the 'choose application' window. I simply order the program to go ahead. The results in (2) are produced.

```
(2)
Group      T        O        Z        S    C    A    Total %
- - - - - - - - - - - - - - - - - - - - - - - - - - - - - - - - -
1 (1)
Total N    611      234      268      3    2    1    1119
      %    55       21       24       0    0    0
```

In another run, I type 'TOZ' into the 'choose Application value' box. This produces the results in (3).

```
(3)
Group         T           O           Z        Total       %
- - - - - - - - - - - - - - - - - - - - - - - - - - - - - - - -
1 (1)
Total N       611         234         268      1113
       %      55          21          24
```

The infrequent *which, whose* and *what* tokens have simply disappeared from the total N. The total N of 1119 in (2), changes to a total N of 1113 in (3). In the next analysis, I opt to run *that* as the application value against the two others. To do this, I type in the code 'T' only into the choose Application box. This produces results in (4). Now, the non-applications include both zero 'Z' and *who* 'O'.

```
(4)
    Number of cells: 368
       Application value(s): T
       Total no. of factors: 56
Group        Apps       Non-apps      Total       %
- - - - - - - - - - - - - - - - - - - - - - - - - - - -
1 (1)
Total N      611        502           1113
       %     55         45
```

Alternatively, you may want to type in two different codes, e.g. 'TO'. In this case, the first one will be considered the application value, the second will be treated as the non-application, and every other code will be ignored, as in (5). Notice that the total N now reflects the total of *that* and *who* tokens only. This time only the zero tokens have not been taken into account.

```
(5)
    Number of cells: 288
       Application value(s): TO
       Total no. of factors: 56
```

Group	T	O	Total	%
1 (1)				
Total N	611	234	845	
%	72	28		

Note the effect these different configurations of the variants in the data file have on the overall distribution of forms. In (2), the proportion of *that* was 55 per cent; in (3), 55 per cent; in (4) 55 per cent; and in (5), 72 per cent. These proportions are a reflection of how you have asked the program to process the data. In sum, choose the most suitable application value for your dependent variable. Your decision determines how the results will be displayed.

THE CELL FILE (Cel)

Now, take a look at the cell file, which is named after the condition file that produced it, 'ConditionA.Cel'. The cell file is the input to the variable rule program. The variable rule program can interpret and run on these results. In the example, you see numbers and letters representing the factor groups and factors in each group and how many of each cell occurred in the data. When this cell file is 'loaded to memory', the marginal results are produced in the results file. A set of file names arising from this process might look as in (6) or (7), or, as in the case under scrutiny, 'ConditionA.Cnd; ConditionA.Cel; ConditionA.Res'.

```
(6)
York.td.Tkn
York.td.001.Cnd
York.td.001.Cel
York.td.001.Res
```

```
(7)
York.ing.Tkn
York.ing.001. Cnd
York.ing.001.Cel
York.ing.001.Res
```

Whatever name you choose for your condition file, this will be reproduced automatically for the cell file (Cel) and the results file (Res). This helps you to keep your files organised.

THE RESULTS FILE (Res)

The type of analysis produced in the results file is called the 'comparison of marginals' (Rand and Sankoff 1990: 4). It displays the overall number and percentage of each variant of the dependent variable for each of the independent factor groups and factors in the analysis. See the Goldvarb 2 manual for further discussion (Rand and Sankoff 1990: 23).

Each of the factor groups in a results file will be listed in the order it was in, in the condition file, followed by a record of its original position in the token file, in parenthesis, as in (8). Here, (8a) means that the factor group was the first one in the condition file, but the fifth one in the token file. (8b) means that the factor group was the sixth one in the condition file, but the third one in the token file.

```
(8)
a. 1 (5)
b. 6 (3)
```

When the designation 'new' appears, as in (9), which is what you saw in the diagram in (1), this simply means that you have created a new factor group out of an old one.

```
(9)
a. 1 (new)
b. 6 (new)
```

For each factor in each factor group is the number and proportion of its use, the total number of tokens and finally the proportion this particular factor represents out of all the data. In the diagram, you see three factor groups: 1) preceding phonological context re-coded as 'O' and 'S'; 2) following phonological context re-coded as 'C' and '-'; and 3) function category, re-coded as 'M' and 'P'. The actual output is replicated in (10).

```
(10)
Group              Apps      Non-apps    Total      %
- - - - - - - - - - - - - - - - - - - - - - - - - - - - -
1 (new)
O          N        146        721         867        70
           %         17         83
S          N        146        221         367        30
           %         40         60
Total      N        292        942        1234
           %         24         76
- - - - - - - - - - - - - - - - - - - - - - - - - - - - -
```

```
2 (new)
-         N      52      655       707      57
          %       7       93
C         N     240      287       527      43
          %      46       54
Total     N     292      942      1234
          %      24       76
- - - - - - - - - - - - - - - - - - - - - - - - - - - - - -
3 (5)
M         N     189      527       716      58
          %      26       74
P         N     103      415       518      42
          %      20       80
Total     N     292      942      1234
          %      24       76
- - - - - - - - - - - - - - - - - - - - - - - - - - - - - -
TOTAL     N     292      942      1234
          %      24       76
Name of new cell: ConditionA.Cel
```

The application values may also appear as the codes of the variants in the token file, e.g. *was* vs *were*, 'S' and 'R', as in (11), *-ly* vs zero, for adverbs, 'Y' and '0', as in (12).

```
(11)
    Number of cells: 18
       Application value(s): SR
       Total no. of factors: 8
 Group   S       R      Total     %
- - - - - - - - - - - - - - - - - - - -
```

```
(12)
    Number of cells: 57
       Application value(s): Y0
       Total no. of factors: 18
 Group   Y       0      Total     %
- - - - - - - - - - - - - - - - - - - -
```

I will return to further discussion of the results file later on in this chapter.

TOKEN FILES AS DATA FILES

The data for variation analysis is comprised of individual instances of a linguistic variable. This is the listing of each context in which the speaker had a choice (the variable), and a record of which choice was actually made (the variant). These individual instances are known as tokens and this is why researchers typically refer to the data file as the 'token' file. Each line of a token file must begin with an open parenthesis, followed by the single-digit codes which record the categories of the dependent and independent variables. For further discussion of the format of the data file, see Chapter 6. For many researchers, a token file will look something like (13).

```
(13)
(adnVS
(a0lkM
(adnVS
(adnVS
(advVP
(adlwP
```

A token file may also include comment lines. These must be preceded by a semicolon(;), as in (14):

```
(14)
;this is my token file for variable [x]
(adnVS
(a0lkM
(adnVS
(adnVS
(advVP
(adlwP
```

What's a 'coding string'?

In traditional formulations of token files in the literature you see only the 'coding strings', as in (13) and (14). These are the strings of individual codes running horizontally in each line of the data file beside the open parentheses, representing all the contextual environments (factor groups) that have been coded for each of the tokens. For example, the coding string 'adnVS' represents five different factor groups.

Each of the symbols after the parenthesis is a 'factor group', as in (15). For example, factor group 1 records the individual speaker, in this case speaker 'a'. Factor group 2 records the dependent variable, in this case a [t] or [d] or zero, here encoded as 't', 'd' and '0'. Factor groups other than the one encoding the dependent variable represent a hypothesis about some feature that conditions the dependent variable (see Chapter 6).

(15)

	FG1	FG2	FG3	FG4	FG5
(	a	d	n	V	S
(	a	0	l	k	M
(	a	d	n	V	S
(	a	d	n	V	S
(	a	d	v	V	P
(	a	d	l	w	P

Goldvarb permits up to thirty factor groups, including the dependent variable. The dependent variable may be anywhere in the string of codes.

Token file tips

A number of enhancements to the token file will facilitate your research process. Note the excerpt from my (t,d) data file in (16). A reference to the precise coordinates of the datum is recorded just after the coding string. This may be in indication of line numbers, dates or whatever referencing system works for your data. This ensures you can always get back to the original context. There is also a record of the actual linguistic variant (token) as well as its surrounding context. This enables coding of independent factor groups in the initial phase of your research, and at later phases facilitates understanding what the coding string represents while at the same time keeping you close to your data. (Compare the listing in (16) with that in (13) for comprehensibility.) Finally, the relevant item is highlighted in capitals. It is remarkable how much easier this makes it to see the variants (see Chapter 6). All these additions have made a tremendous difference to me for understanding and interpreting the results of an analysis. Further, note the use of the comment lines to elucidate various aspects of the analytic process – for example, the speaker name, Maureen Londry, and speaker number, 001. A token which has been excluded is also noted (here neutralisation contexts of [t,d] are those followed by / θ, ð, t, d, n, tʃ, dʒ /). The ready availability of this information in the data file means that it can be easily retrieved when the research is written up. In a methods section describing the variable context, you can easily illustrate the types of contexts that have been excluded. Without recording some of these in the data file, as in (16), you would have to go back to the data to find them, and that would take a very long time!

```
(16)
;Maureen Londry 001
(adnVSOFF2P//nV    5.4     And the reason they FOUND out
   about the Viking thing was
;the following token was excluded due to neutralisation
;a0k#PAFD2         5.4     they KNOCKED the Candy-Land
   down.
(a01kM//o2X//1K    5.6     while they were knocking down
   the OLD Craven's
(adnVSAFF20//nV    5.7     they FOUND all this stuff
(advVPODD20//vV    6.1     And um- LOVED it
```

Another example of a data file is shown in (17). In addition to the enhancements noted above, notice that a little more context was required to fully interpret the variants. Notice, again, the notes about the data in comment lines in (17). During the extraction and coding phase relevant notes have been inserted as guideposts to support and inform data processing at a later stage.

```
(17)
Example of data file, possessive have/have got
;iferguson[m, speaker u[021]] with eferguson[f/m,
   speaker v[022]]
;
;NOTE:these two excerpts are from the same
   conversation,
;so I knew what speaker u was referring to
(AuGVnA-C//A[1] And you forget what the real coal fire looks like
;cos you're so used to-[021] Oh you do.
;You ken some of the gas yins HAVE GOT the-
(AvTG8--C//A Oh that' right- they GOT the wee flame and that aye.
;Deontic modality
;Av///////∞/ You've got to have a vice of some kind.
(AvOV3--C//A But I says, ''you forget she'S GOT a husband
(AvHH%-GC//A we HAVE nice shops in- in Scotland.
(AudH1--C+/N I know when I DON'T HAVE any sweeties in the
   house-
;NOTE: VERY COOL example of variation!!!!
(AuHH@-GA*/A But then the time comes again when you're granny
   and Grandad
;cos then-[021] And then you HAVE the time.
;[022] And you'VE GOT all the time.
```

While these enhancements, including the possibility of including the coding schema within the token file (see Chapter 6), increase the size of the data file, they are well worth it. Neither contemporary computers nor the program itself has any problem with token files of 1000 K or more.

> ## Note
>
> Another useful technique is to incorporate 'super-tokens' directly into the top of the token file so that they are readily found when needed; for example, writing an abstract or reporting preliminary results.
>
> ```
> ;GOOD EXAMPLES
> ;
> ;VARIABILITY: 2yP- That's 0 GOOD, that's PRETTY GOOD.
> ;          2wR- it was SO BAD 'cause I was REALLY NERVOUS.
> ;          2gR- Yeah, VERY BORING, REALLY BORING.
> ;          2fR- REALLY HIGH heights. EXTREMELY HIGH heights.
> ;          2aR- if he's REALLY DULL, but he's like, SO HOT
> ;          2ha- so it wasn't THAT BAD but, it was PRETTY BAD.
> ```

CODING FOR INDIVIDUAL SPEAKER

Individuals should always be coded separately so that the results from each individual can be checked, compared and contrasted.

However, because an analysis of variation might include data from hundreds of speakers, you should keep a separate record of the codes associated with each individual in your sample. In my own research, speaker codes are stored in a relational database (see Chapter 4), whose contents can be searched or tables printed for easy access. A listing for the first three speakers ordered alphabetically by pseudonym from the York English Corpus is shown in (18). The listing includes their speaker codes, speaker numbers, as well as a number of social characteristics. These speaker codes are used in every analysis that includes these speakers.

(18)

Speaker code	Speaker pseudonym	Speaker number	Sex	Age	Education
X	Aileen Stone	024	F	75	Up to age 16
¢	Albert Jackson	081	M	66	Up to age 14
N	Carl Beckett	040	M	29	Up to age 18

HOW TO WRITE CONDITION FILES

The condition file gives instructions to the program about how to configure the analysis of the factor groups and factors in the data file.

These instructions will include which factor groups to include in the analysis, which factor group is the dependent variable, what independent variables to include and how each factor group is to be re-coded. This is also the place where you will exclude factors or factor groups, combine factors and factor groups and even create new factors and factor groups (Rand and Sankoff 1990: 16). In Goldvarb 2.1, Goldvarb 2001 and Goldvarb X these tasks are facilitated by re-code set-ups whose operations are discussed in the respective manuals. Condition files can also be typed by hand by the analyst. In my own experience, a combination of strategies is most effective. Generate the initial condition file using the re-code set-up embodied in the program, then make changes manually thereafter (see also Rand and Sankoff 1990: 20).

No-re-code

The most basic condition file is simply a listing of the factor groups in your data file. The condition file in (19) is a no-re-code of the York (t,d) token file for the first six factor groups.

```
(19)
(
; Identity re-code: All groups included as is.
(1)
(2)
(3)
(4)
(5)
(6)
)
```

Recall that, whatever column the dependent variable occurs in, the number of this factor group must always appear first in the condition file. In the re-code in (20), factor group 1, '(3)', is placed first. Further, only those factor groups specified in the condition file will be used to build the cells for analysis. If you do not want to include a factor group, you simply do not list it in the condition file. If you wanted to include only factor groups 1, 4 and 6 in the analysis, the condition file would look like (20).

```
(20)
(
; Identity re-code: All groups included as is.
(3)
(1)
(4)
(6)
)
```

Re-coded conditions

I would usually never run the variable rule program on my data under a 'no-re-code' condition for all factor groups. This is because I will typically have coded an overabundance of information into my token files, including some things that were never intended for variable rule analysis.

For example, for variable (t,d), the dependent variable was initially coded for a number of different renditions of the word-final consonants, including [t], [d], glottalised variants and a number of low-frequency others, as in (21).

```
(21)
   Number of cells: 8
      Application value(s): d0t#N?M
      Total no. of factors: 6
Group        d      0      t      #      N      ?      M    Total    %
- - - - - - - - - - - - - - - - - - - - - - - - - - - - - - - - - - - -

TOTAL    N   319    291    497    30     11     83     1    1232
         %   26     24     40     2      1      7      0
```

Notice that the vast majority of forms are [d], [0] or [t]. For this reason, the condition file was modified, as in (22). Each element in the LISP list consists of two parts: a group number, which is the column number in the token file; and an optional set of re-code conditions. Here I am re-coding factor group 2 (which was originally categorised into 'd, t, #, N, ?, †, M, 0') into two main categories: realised (t,d) forms, 'T'; and unrealised forms, '0'. Read the condition file something like this – Re-code factor group 2 into 'T' and '0'; Each of the 'd, t, #, N, ?, †, M' are to be treated as 'T', and '0' stays as '0'.

```
(22)
(
(2
   (T (COL 2 d))
   (T (COL 2 t))
   (T (COL 2 #))
   (T (COL 2 N))
   (T (COL 2 ?))
   (T (COL 2 †))
   (T (COL 2 M))
   (0 (COL 2 0))
)
```

Of course, there must be linguistic justification for these modifications. In this case, the major forms were 'd' and 't', both realisations of the consonant cluster. Other realisations were rare, e.g. '#, N, ?, †, M'. The glottal variant, '?', occurred fairly frequently, but implicated a whole other set of facts. In the end we opted to abstract away from these details and contrast realised forms with unrealised forms, as in (22). This produced the results in (23).

```
(23)
    Number of cells: 3
    Application value(s): 0
    Total no. of factors: 3
Group        Apps    Non-apps    Total    %
- - - - - - - - - - - - - - - - - - - - - - -
TOTAL   N    291     941         1232
        %    24      76
```

In sum, from the beginning the condition file must be modified from the 'no-re-code', which simply reproduces the factor groups in the order they occur in the data file.

FLAGGING FACTOR GROUPS

Certain factor groups may simply be 'flagging' factor groups for sorting the data (see also Rand and Sankoff 1990: 16). I typically set aside one factor group for recording good examples. Questionable tokens, unusual configurations, etc. can also be flagged for additional scrutiny, as in (24), which shows a fairly elaborate system to identify contexts that are likely to be excluded from the variable context of relative markers.

```
(24)
;FG7 ''flags''
;        * = GOOD EXAMPLE
;        p = ''place'' -relatives: ''the place/area that''
;        l = all that/Ø
;        @ = need coding decision
;        ? = possible non-restrictive, need coding decision
;        u = unfinished
;        a = ambiguous
;        n = non-restrictive, mostly proper noun antecedents
```

EXTERNAL FACTORS FOR FREE

As mentioned earlier, in every analysis I code individual speakers uniquely. While this is necessary for its own sake, there are also a number of add-on advantages. Once each speaker has a unique code, this factor group can be used to re-code the speakers into any number of extralinguistic categories. These can be coded in the same condition file for whatever factor groups are relevant to your analysis. For example, a re-code for sex is shown in (25), for age in (26), and for occupation in (27). For illustration purposes I have listed only the first ten speakers.

Pay particular attention to the format of the re-codes. In (25) to (27) I am re-coding factor group 1, which contains a large number of individual speaker codes. Each re-code condition is a LISP list. The first part is the re-code value. This is the value that the original symbols in factor group 1 will be re-coded to. So, for example, '(F (COL 1 a)' in (25) means re-code everything that is 'a' in factor group 1 as 'F' (i.e. female), and so on. In other words, this tells the program that speakers 'a' and 'c' are female and speakers 'r' and 'K' are male, etc. I follow the same basic procedure to re-code each individual for age. Note the annotation in (26). The lines beginning with a semicolon record the groupings for age: speakers between 14 and 34 are re-coded as '1'; between 35 and 54 as '3'; between 55 and 74 as '5' and anyone over 75 is re-coded as '7'. Similarly, in (27), I have re-coded the speakers by occupation. Speakers in professional level jobs are re-coded as 'P', in white-collar jobs are re-coded as 'M', skilled manual jobs as 'W', semi- or un-skilled jobs are re-coded as 'L', and college students as 'S'. Three speakers whose education is unknown are removed, '/'.

The number of each of the factor groups, i.e. the number immediately after the first open parenthesis, is '0'. This simply means it is a new factor group that has been re-coded out of another in the data file.

```
(25)
; SEX
(0 (F (COL 1 a)))
  (F (COL 1 c)))
  (M (COL 1 r)))
  (M (COL 1 K)))
  (F (COL 1 o)))
  (M (COL 1 Σ)))
  (M (COL 1 N)))
  (M (COL 1 y)))
  (F (COL 1 ;)))
  (F (COL 1 i))) ...)
```

```
(26)
; AGE
; 14-34  1
; 35-54  3
```

```
;55-74  5
;75+    7
(0
     (7 (COL 1 >))
;91
     (1 (COL 1 %))
;17
     (1 (COL 1 i))
;33
     (7 (COL 1 b))
;82
     (3 (COL 1 ¶))
;50
     (1 (COL 1 ™))
;24
     (3 (COL 1 V))
;53
     (1 (COL 1 Z))
;22
     (3 (COL 1 z))
;51
     (1 (COL 1 ;)) ... )
;28
```

```
(27)
;OCCUPATION, based on Macaulay 1976
;P = professional and managerial
;M = white collar
;W = skilled manual
;L = semi- or un-skilled manual
;S = college students
(0
   (S (COL 1 Π))
   (L (COL 1 a))
   (M (COL 1 b))
   (L (COL 1 c))
   (L (COL 1 e))
   (P (COL 1 f))
   (M (COL 1 g))
;occupation unknown
   (/ (COL 1 d))
   (/ (COL 1 h))
   (/ (COL 1 &))
```

In each case the individuals in the data file are being grouped and regrouped by different social criteria. This is why there is no need to code this information separately. You get it for free. Moreover, you have the flexibility of coding and re-coding speakers however you like.

Tip

Inevitably you will miss out one of the individuals in these elaborate re-codes. This is easy to spot and fix. Run the individual speaker factor group as a no-re-code along with the others. Cross-tabulate with the re-coded factor groups. The missing speaker's code will stand out on its own. Go back to the condition file and enter the missing speaker into the LISP list re-codes.

ANNOTATING CONDITION FILES

For each re-code, I have added explanations for precisely how the re-code was done, along with justification. This way you have a permanent record of what you have done. In (26) I have inserted the actual age of each of the informants. This will facilitate further modifications to the conditions in the event that I should decide to re-code the data into alternate age groupings – old vs young, for example, or a more finely graded categorisation schema. Further, note that my re-code schema for occupation in (27) is based on Macaulay (1976). Such justification is necessary, particularly for external factors where judgements about socioeconomic class and education are notoriously subjective.

In sum, re-codes of any type are very important. The condition files in which they are formulated should always be saved and named so that you can retrieve them easily when you need them. Indeed, some condition files are invaluable templates for continual use as you move from one analysis to another in the same corpus. For example, the condition file which records all the re-codes for the York English Corpus by age, sex, education and occupation is a condition file with over 300 LISP list re-codes. However, it is stored safely and can be used over and over again in any study of variation on the York data. The condition file which contains all the re-codes for age and sex in our growing Toronto English Corpus is even more complicated, because there are so many speakers that we have had to duplicate speaker codes. An excerpt from this massive condition file is shown in (28), where factor group 1 codes the year of data collection (2, S, $), and factor group 2 codes the individual speaker.

```
(28)
;RE-CODE BY SEX
(2
   (F (AND (COL 1 2) (COL 2 a) ))
   (F (AND (COL 1 S) (COL 2 a) ))
```

```
(F (AND (COL 1 $) (COL 2 a) ) )
(F (AND (COL 1 2) (COL 2 b) ) )
(F (AND (COL 1 S) (COL 2 b) ) )
(F (AND (COL 1 $) (COL 2 b) ) )
(M (AND (COL 1 2) (COL 2 c) ) )
(F (AND (COL 1 S) (COL 2 c) ) )
```

Note

Goldvarb 2.1 and Goldvarb 2001 do not copy the careful annotations of the condition file into the results file. To see this, you must go back to the condition file that produced it. However, Goldvarb X copies all this information into the results file for easy viewing.

WHAT DOES A CELL FILE LOOK LIKE?

The token file along with the condition file are used to create the cell file. Unlike the other files, the contents of this file are not transparent. This is because it is configured for readability by the computer, not humans. The first line of (29) indicates that there are 10 cells and the second that there are 3 factor groups. Then each of the factor groups is listed by number followed by its codes, e.g. 2FM, 45137 and 2– +. Then the cells are listed on two lines each. The first line records the number of applications and the total number of contexts in the cell, e.g. 16 43. The second line records the values of the cell, e.g. F1+, and so on. If you want to know more about what it all means, read the relevant sections of the Goldvarb 2.0 manual (Rand and Sankoff 1990: 23). It is likely sufficient to know that the program reads from the cell file in order to produce the marginal data and, subsequently, the variable rule analysis. Let us take the condition file of the variable (t,d) data and run the conditions for sex, age and education that were partially illustrated in (25)–(27). The cell file is shown in (29).

```
(29)
10
 3
 2FM
 45137
 2-+
 16  43
F1+
 18  93
F1-
```

```
   3   20
F3+
  22   54
F3-
   2   21
F3/
   3   19
F5+
  27   83
F5-
  26   75
F7-
  38   81
M1+
  10   12
M1-
  15   40
M3+
   3   19
M3-
   4   19
M3/
  40   67
M5-
  30   62
M7-
  -1
● 6/19/04 ● 3:32 PM
● Token file: YORK.td.Tkn
● Conditions: eg9.Cnd
```

In order to produce the marginal results and later run the variable rule program, the cell file must be 'loaded to memory'. This produces a results file.

READING A RESULTS FILE

The results file is shown in (30).

```
(30)
● CELL CREATION ● 6/19/04 ● 3:50 PM
  ●●●●●●●●●●●●●●●●●●●●●●●●●●●●●●●●●●●●●●●●●●●●●●●●●
  Name of token file    : YORK.td.Tkn
  Name of condition file: eg12.Cnd
(
CONDITION FILE REMOVED FOR ILLUSTRATION PURPOSES
)
        Number of cells : 26
```

```
      Application value(s)    : 0
      Total no. of factors    : 13
Group                Apps      Non-apps    Total      %
- - - - - - - - - - - - - - - - - - - - - - - - - - - - - - - -
1 (new)
F            N       138       503         641        56
             %        22        78
M            N       152       350         502        44
             %        30        70
Total        N       290       853        1143
             %        25        75
- - - - - - - - - - - - - - - - - - - - - - - - - - - - - - - -
2 (new)
5            N        75       197         272        24
             %        28        72
1            N        93       292         385        34
             %        24        76
3            N        65       207         272        24
             %        24        76
7            N        57       157         214        19
             %        27        73
Total        N       290       853        1143
             %        25        75
- - - - - - - - - - - - - - - - - - - - - - - - - - - - - - - -
3 (new)
-            N       196       548         744        69
             %        26        74
+            N        87       254         341        31
             %        26        74
Total        N       283       802        1085
             %        26        74
- - - - - - - - - - - - - - - - - - - - - - - - - - - - - - - -
4 (new)
L            N        87       198         285        28
             %        31        69
M            N       114       398         512        50
             %        22        78
S            N        14        53          67         7
             %        21        79
P            N        24        87         111        11
             %        22        78
W            N        23        30          53         5
             %        43        57
Total        N       262       766        1028
             %        25        75
- - - - - - - - - - - - - - - - - - - - - - - - - - - - - - - -
TOTAL        N       290       853        1143
             %        25        75
Name of new cell file: eg12.Cel
```

The program copies various bits of information into the file for your convenience, including the date and time, the name of the token file and the name of the condition file used for the analysis. You will find this very handy. Below these identification strings is a listing of the condition file used to produce the results. Because the particular condition file used for this run was huge, I have removed it for illustration purposes. The marginal results follow this listing of conditions. First, you will find the total number of cells, the application value(s), here '0', and the total number of factors, '13'. Beneath this, the marginal results begin. 'Group' refers to the factor groups that have been included in this run. 'Apps' refers to the application value; 'Non-apps' groups the remainder of the variants. 'Total' refers to the total number of tokens per cell and '%' refers to the proportion that each cell represents of the total number of tokens.

The factor groups will appear in the same order as they appear in the condition file that produced them. The column number of the factor group in the token file is recorded in parentheses. Here, since I have re-coded several different external factors on the same factor group, these new factor groups are listed as '(new)'.

Read through these marginal results, trying to understand what they mean. Can you spot any patterns? A great way to do this is to get a highlighter and colour the percentage of applications for each factor group. Then compare the proportions for the factors within each factor group. For example, for the first factor group, sex, notice that females, 'F', have 22 per cent unrealised consonants whereas males, 'M', have 30 per cent. This means that, overall, the men in the data delete (t,d) more than the women. On the other hand, when you perform the same comparison for factor group 2, age, notice that the proportion of unrealised consonants hovers at about 25 per cent across all age groups. Are these results expected? Why? Why not? What do they tell you about variable (t,d) in York? I will return to these questions in Chapters 9 and 10.

Why mismatched totals?

The total number of tokens at the very bottom of the results file equals 1143. Why then do the 'Total Ns' for each individual factor group sometimes differ from this overall total? For example, Total N for sex is 1143, for education 1085, for socioeconomic class 1028. The reason for this is that some data have been removed from consideration in each of these factor groups. In the re-code for education, speakers whose education was unknown were omitted.

Exclusions of this type are easily accomplished by using the 'slash' function in the LISP list format of the condition file, as in (31). See also (27) above.

```
(31)
(/ (COL 1 u))
(/ (COL 1 V))
(/ (COL 1 R))
(/ (COL 1 T))
(/ (COL 1 "))
(/ (COL 1 @))
```

In (31), the tokens from these speakers do not show up in the factor group, in this case 1, in which they are 'slashed'. However, since we knew the age and sex of these speakers they can be included in the re-codes for sex, as in (32), and age, as in (33). In the case of factor group 4, several of the speakers who were unemployed have similarly been removed, leaving the total here somewhat less than the others, i.e. 1028. These exclusions account for the different totals you see in the marginal results in (30).

```
(32)
(M (COL 1 u))
(F (COL 1 v))
(F (COL 1 R))
(F (COL 1 T))
(M (COL 1 "))
(F (COL 1 @))
```

```
(33)
(7 (COL 1 u))
(7 (COL 1 v))
(3 (COL 1 R))
(3 (COL 1 T))
(5 (COL 1 "))
(5 (COL 1 @))
```

Mismatches between Total Ns for factor groups may also arise if certain tokens in the data file have features which make one of the factor groups non-applicable. In this case, a slash will be inserted for that category in the factor group. Earlier in (30) this was due to external information that was not known about certain speakers. Such non-applicability may also be due to internal factors. Factor groups 6 and 7 in (34) recorded information about the narrative structure of verbs. In the case of tokens that were not verbs, these factor groups were simply not applicable. Such tokens are coded as '/', underlined in (34), so as not to be included in the analysis of either of these factor groups in the results.

```
(34)
a. (a0sgM//j2J//sG    9.9    I used to JUST go and give
                                 the envelope
b. (a0lmM//o2X//lm   10.0    there used to be all OLD men
c. (atsVM//j2J//sV   10.4    It was JUST offices
```

Tip

'Ns' refers to 'number'. Number of what? Either 1) the total 'number of tokens' in the data set; or 2) 'N' could also mean the total 'number of tokens in a cell'. I once received a paper from a student who, following explicit instructions, faithfully reported to me the 'ends' in her analysis.

EXCLUDING AND INCLUDING TOKENS

When it comes to including and excluding tokens from an analysis, there are at least two choices. You may wish to exclude an token entirely. To do this, use the NIL function. The NIL function is always placed at the beginning of the condition file to ensure that the tokens specified are removed from the whole analysis. Take, for example, the variable (t,d) token file discussed previously, where the dependent variable was coded in factor group 2. If you wished to remove all the tokens which were realised as the glottal stop, coded '?' in factor group 2, the re-code would be written as in (35).

```
(35)
(
  (2 (NIL (COL 2?)))...
```

However, the trickier case is when you want to exclude the token only with respect to one factor group. In this case, you use the slash, '/', as described above. Suppose you wished to remove all the tokens realised as glottal stop, '?'. However, you only wanted to remove them from the consideration in preceding phonological context, factor group 3. In this case, the re-code would be written as in (36).

```
(36)
(
(2)
(3 (/ (COL 2 ?))) ...
```

This has the effect of removing all tokens coded as '?' in factor group 2 from consideration in factor group 3. However, it does not remove them from any other of the factor groups.

Note

If a category is excluded using 'NIL' or '/', e.g. (NIL (col 1 X)), at the beginning of the condition file *and* it occurs later on in the condition file in another LISP list, e.g. (Y (col 1 X)), then from that point onwards it will reappear in the analysis. Be careful!

ORTHOGONALITY OF FACTOR GROUPS

In order to achieve reliable results using the variable rule program, factor groups must be 'orthogonal' (Guy 1988: 126–7). This means that factor groups should be independent of each other. They should not be subgroups of each other or supercategories of each other. This is easy enough to say, but in most research this ideal may not be achieved for one reason or another. It might be the case that a given cell was simply not filled in the data collection phase. For example, no males between 30 and 40 agreed to be interviewed, or no women of a certain age had achieved a certain level of education, or no highly educated speakers are under 30. These types of sampling issues can sometimes never be resolved. They are an intrinsic part of a given situation, of a particular generation when these were the sociocultural facts. In other cases, a combination of factors may simply not exist in a language or dialect. Again, such structural impossibilities are just the way it is. The best example of this I can think of is the use of verbal *-s* in contemporary standard English dialects. It only occurs in third person singular. Why? Nobody knows for sure. That's just the way it is. Another example is that the contrast between personal pronouns and full noun phrases only exists in the third person in English. These are some of the natural asymmetries of language. Natural data and corpus-based research have incalculable potential for data overlap, interaction and difficult distribution issues. Be on the look out for these.

As far as I know, Guy (1988: 126) is unique in having addressed the question of how far an analysis can deviate from the standard of strict orthogonality and still obtain valid results. As Guy points out, 'a few empty cells in a table do not always create a problem of ortho-gonality' (1988: 127). The important question then becomes: How do you find non-orthogonality in your data and what to do about it if you find it?

Cross-tabulation

In order to spot overlap, interaction and non-orthogonality, you must examine the intersection of factor groups by using cross-tabulation, as schematised in (37). This schema displays the intersection between speakers divided into two categories – age (young and old) and sex (male and female).

(37)

	Male	Female
Young	A	B
Old	C	D

My standard method is to cross-tabulate every factor group with every other factor group. Why? Not only does this practice ensure that you know your data inside out; it also permits you to see exactly how the data are distributed for each intersection of factors. In the process you may observe interactions, badly distributed cells, empty cells, and even coding errors (which can then be corrected in the token file).

The worst-case scenario of non-orthogonality is when every token of one thing is the same as another. For example, all males that are 'old' are also less educated, '–'. All speakers that are 'young' are also 'students'. Guy's example is the factor group of individual speaker and sex (Guy 1988: 128). This perhaps goes without saying. If you code for the individual and you also code for the sex of the speaker, you should not, ever, run these two factor groups together. Of course, if individuals are coded separately, then any combination of the factor group encoding individual speaker will be non-orthogonal with any social factor. This dictates removing one of the factor groups from the analysis – typically, individual speaker.

Note

Recall that individual speakers are coded uniquely for at least two reasons. First, this enables you to check for intra-speaker variability as well as inter-speaker variability. Second, this enables you to re-code for whatever external factors you choose, in any way you choose.

The more likely situation is that data will be badly distributed in one way or another. How much is too much? In (38), I have cross-tabulated factor group 2, age, and 3, education, based on the results file in (30). The age groups are divided into four groupings, from youngest to oldest groups – 1, 3, 5, 7 – as discussed earlier. The education level has been collapsed into two groupings, '+' and '−'. Recall also that you are looking at variable (t,d), in which the application value '0' means that the consonant cluster has been reduced. These are the unrealised (t,d) forms, e.g. *walk, jus', tol'*. The realised forms have been re-coded as dash, '-'. The per cent sign, '%' heads the columns showing the proportions. The total N for each category is represented by the symbol 'Σ'. Other numbers are Ns.

```
(38)
Variable (t,d)

Group #2 -- AGE

Group #3 -- EDUCATION


        5    %      1    %      3    %      7    %      Σ    %

    +  -  -  -  -  +  -  -  -  -  +  -  -  -  -  +  -  -  -  -  +  -  -  -  -  -

-  0:   67   31:   28   21:   25   26:   56   29|   176   27

   -:  150   69:  105   79:   73   74:  137   71|   465   73

   Σ:  217    :   133    :    98    :   193    |   641

    +  -  -  -  -  +  -  -  -  -  +  -  -  -  -  +  -  -  -  -  +  -  -  -  -  -

+  0:    3   14:   54   30:   18   23:    0   --|    75   27

   -:   19   86:  124   70:   60   77:    0   --|   203   73

   Σ:   22    :   178    :    78    :    0    |   278

    +  -  -  -  -  +  -  -  -  -  +  -  -  -  -  +  -  -  -  -  +  -  -  -  -  -

Σ  0:   70   29:   82   26:   43   24:   56   29|   251   27

   -:  169   71:  229   74:  133   76:  137   71|   668   73

   Σ:  239    :   311    :   176    :   193    |   919
```

There is one entirely empty cell, represented by three zeros and two sets of dashes. The cell should comprise speakers in the highest age group, the over-75s, who have been educated beyond the age of 16. However, there simply are no speakers with these two attributes in the sample. Note too that in the second highest age group, 5, the 55–74s, there are very few tokens from anyone educated beyond the

(39)

- CROSS-TABULATION • 6/19/04 • 3:57 PM

••

- Cell file: eg12.Cel
- 6/19/04•3:51 PM
- Token file: YORK.td.Tkn
- Conditions: eg12.Cnd

Group #2 -- AGE

Group #4 -- OCCUPATION

	5	%	1	%	3	%	7	%	Σ	%
L 0:	47	**29**:	13	**33**:	27	**32**:	0	--|	87	31
-:	114	71:	27	68:	57	68:	0	--|	198	69
Σ:	161	:	40	:	84	:	0	|	285	
M 0:	18	30:	23	23:	29	18:	44	24|	114	22
-:	43	70:	79	77:	135	82:	141	76|	398	78
Σ:	61	:	102	:	164	:	185	|	512	
S 0:	0	--:	14	21:	0	--:	0	--|	14	21
-:	0	--:	53	79:	0	--:	0	--|	53	79
Σ:	0	:	67	:	0	:	0	|	67	
P 0:	10	20:	5	14:	9	38:	0	--|	24	22
-:	40	80:	32	86:	15	63:	0	--|	87	78
Σ:	**50**	:	**37**	:	**24**	:	0	|	111	
W 0:	0	--:	10	**42**:	0	--:	13	**45**|	23	43
-:	0	--:	14	58:	0	--:	16	55|	30	57
Σ:	0	:	24	:	0	:	29	|	53	
Σ 0:	75	28:	65	24:	65	24:	57	27|	262	25
-:	197	72:	205	76:	207	76:	157	73|	766	75
Σ:	272	:	270	:	272	:	214	|	1028	

age of 16 (N = 22). This is because elderly speakers in York in 1996 tended not to be educated to this level.

What happens if you cross-tabulate occupation and speaker age? This is shown in (39). There are five occupation groups –, 'L', 'M', 'S', 'P' and 'W' – as discussed earlier. The education level has been collapsed into two groupings, '+' and '–'. The cross-tabulation reveals, not just one, but a number of 'holes' in the data. Elderly people in York are either white-collar workers, 'M', or skilled manual workers, 'W'. None are students, 'S', or professionals, 'P', or semi- or un-skilled manual workers, 'L'. Students are represented only amongst the under-35s. Few individuals in the sample are professional, as is obvious from the sparse tokens in these cells (N = 50, 37 and 24).

This gives you a sense of the types of interactions that may typify a data set that has been coded for a number of external factor groups.

Resolving interaction

How should interaction problems be resolved? In the case of (38), we simply did not test education in our analysis. First, education is not well represented across age groups. Second, even if it is represented, education does not seem to influence the variable. The only context in which education is explanatory, and there is sufficient data to make a comparison, is amongst the youngest speakers. You could focus on these speakers only and re-run the analysis with education as a factor group. However, in this particular study, we did not pursue this. In the case of (39), there is a much more serious problem. One option is to collapse the socioeconomic classifications into broader groups. First, you could collapse the category 'W', which represents skilled manual labourers with 'L', which represents semi- or un-skilled manual labourers. The justification for this is that 'W' has small Ns, and these categories are comparable occupationally. Further, the proportion of (t,d) is somewhat comparable across the available cells, and is generally higher than for 'M', white-collar workers. Further, you may collapse the rare professional individuals with 'M'. The students are a difficult choice. You could simply remove them due to their ambiguous status with respect to occupation or include them as a separate group in order to observe their behaviour vis-à-vis the others. Here, for illustration purposes, I have simply removed them. Doing all these re-codes, you end up with a configuration of the data with no 'holes', as in (40).

```
(40)
 • CROSS-TABULATION • 6/19/04 • 4:13 PM
 •••••••••••••••••••••••••••••••••••••••
 • Cell file:  eg13.Cel
 • 6/19/04•4:13 PM
 • Token file: YORK.td.Tkn
 • Conditions: eg13.Cnd

Group #2 -- AGE
Group #4 -- OCCUPATION


        5    %    1    %    3    %    7    %    Σ    %
   + - - - - + - - - - + - - - - + - - - - + - - - - -
L 0:   47  29:   23  36:   27  32:   13  45|  110  33
  -:  114  71:   41  64:   57  68:   16  55|  228  67
  Σ:  161   :    64   :    84   :    29   |  338

   + - - - - + - - - - + - - - - + - - - - + - - - - -
M 0:   28  25:   28  20:   38  20:   44  24|  138  22
  -:   83  75:  111  80:  150  80:  141  76|  485  78
  Σ:  111   :   139   :   188   :   185   |  623

   + - - - - + - - - - + - - - - + - - - - + - - - - -
Σ 0:   75  28:   51  25:   65  24:   57  27|  248  26
  -:  197  72:  152  75:  207  76:  157  73|  713  74
  Σ:  272   :   203   :   272   :   214   |  961
```

The regular pattern across the board – more (t,d) deletion amongst
blue collar workers, 'L', than white collar workers, 'M' – is consistent
with other research on this variable, providing support and
justification for this particular configuration of the data. However,
notice the distributional asymmetry for age groups 1, 3 and 7. If you
calculate what proportion of the data occurs in each age group,
you find that in age group 7, 86 per cent of the data is white collar (185/214). In age group 3, 69 per cent (188/272). In age group 1,
68 per cent (139/203). This is the very type of badly distributed
data that lead to the variable rule program. But is it too badly
distributed to analyse? Guy's (1988: 131) rule of thumb is the
following:

A 90 per cent overlap is tolerable, although one should realise that some distortion of results is probably occurring, and the analysis is already taking a lot longer. 95 per cent is probably the absolute limit of reasonable analysability.

Despite the badly distributed cells in our York (t,d) data, it is still feasible to run a variable rule analysis.

The variationist lab book

The steps involved in conducting a variation analysis are complex and involve many different decisions, revisions to decisions and even more revisions to decisions. I often tell my students that if they do not make any mistakes they must be doing it wrong. This is all part of the process. Beginning with the judgements that go into circumscribing the variable context right through to checking for interaction, as I just discussed, you will be engaged in a long process of observation and problem-solving. But how do you keep track of it all? You need to have some central place to record procedures, note exceptions and document your decision-marking process. You need to be able to refer back to what you did, so that you can remember how you did it. This is where the 'lab book' comes in.

Record your research process in minute detail – in part so that you maintain consistency, in part so you can replicate the process or improve upon it. Just as a chemist or an inventor records the minute steps of each experiment in ink so that the actual process undertaken cannot be amended or erased from the record, so too in variation analysis. Get yourself a lab book or make yourself an observations file, or create a mini-database. Whatever suits your inclinations. The important thing is to have a place to keep track of everything. Date and record your decisions. When you make a mistake, refine your process and record the revision. When you notice an exception, record the example, with reference, so that you know what types of things you should exclude as you move forward. When you come to the same problem again, go back to the lab book to find out what you decided to do about it. Apply the update consistently every time. I still go back to my earlier lab books in order to understand precisely what I did.

The lab book can also be used to maintain a list of Goldvarb files (token, condition, cell and results) and their names. It is a good idea to name your files so that you will be able to glance at them and know what they are and what they were configured to do. I use a 'naming protocol', which I apply in the same way for each analysis. For example, each corpus in my archive has a three-place code, as in (41). Each variable has a two- or three-place code, as in (42). This makes it easy to name token files consistently, as in (43). To this, you can always add dates, in order to keep track of the most updated version of files, as in (44). Whatever naming protocol you use will go a long way to helping you remember what each token file contains. It also makes global searches for files much easier.

(41)
a. York English Corpus   YRK
b. Devon English Corpus   DVN
c. Roots Corpora   ROO

(42)
a. Variable (ing)   ing
b. Variable (t,d)   td
c. Variable (have/have got)   got

(43)
a. YRK_ing.Tkn
b. DVN_-s.Tkn
c. ROO_got.Tkn

(44)
a. YRK_ing_24_8_04.Tkn
b. DVN_-s_2_6_97.Tkn
c. ROO_got_12_10_01.Tkn

The lab book serves many purposes, not the least of which is simply to remember where you left off. If even a day or two goes by, you will forget what you did the last time you worked on your data. The lab book also ensures consistency in circumscribing the variable context, in coding the factors and in producing the condition files. It should also hold the coding schema for your variable in hard copy, a list of speaker codes, and as you produce results files these can be included as well. I recommend this practice to you; it will save you time and frustration. It may even help you figure out what is going on in the data. Sometimes the observations you note down, scribbled over the marginal data months previously, actually hold the key to understanding and explaining the data later on.

Note

You will accumulate an incredible number of small files when you use the variable rule program. Of course, you will keep your token files and your coding schema. However, never delete your condition files; this is where your analysis is. You can always recreate cell files or results files, but token files and condition files are priceless!

SUMMARY

It takes a lot of work before you reach the point of running the variable rule program. The long process from data extraction and coding, to running the marginal data one way and another, until finally arriving at a condition file (analysis) that is suitable for deploying the variable rule program, involves many small steps. I think of this part of the research process as 'honing' the analysis. Indeed, it is not unusual to create hundreds of files before you finally arrive at the set of condition files that will be the final series of 'runs' for your analysis. And, even then, this is only the beginning!

Exercise 8: Honing a variationist analysis

1 The base-line ...

Create a no-re-code condition file. Load the cells (i.e. Cel file). Save the results file. Does your coding schema require you to modify this basic re-code? How? Create your own base-line condition file. Name it mnemonically. This is the beginning.

On a hard copy, annotate each factor group with the factors it contains (I usually write the full forms of each factor contained in each factor group listed).

Make observations and interpretations for each. Where is the bulk of the data? Where are the singletons? Do you see any problems, errors, etc.? What are the trends? Make as many observations as you can. The no-re-code analysis of your data will reveal where and how you should re-code it.

2 Honing the analysis ... re-coding

Re-coding involves honing your coding schema so that it embodies the best, most explanatory, analysis for your linguistic variable.

This will involve some or all of the following:

* collapsing factors within a factor group
* removing factors altogether
* combining factor groups
* re-coding individual speakers by age, sex, education, social class, etc.

Conduct a number of re-code condition files that are relevant to your data. Notice the ramifications of each re-code on the data. Which is the best analysis?

3 Record-keeping – the lab book

Begin putting together a binder (or other type of volume) where you will organise the data analysis phase of your research.
This should contain the following:

1. A copy of all your Tkn, Cnd, Cel, and Res files. Remember to back up!
2. A copy of the fully annotated coding schema corresponding to your token file.

Annotate with updates, changes, revisions, hypotheses being tested, etc. You must always have an updated copy in order to manage ongoing developments to your research.

Record the progress of your research in dated entries. The lab book may also include a list of re-coded condition files that you have created and why, observations, ideas, good examples, etc.

9 Distributional analysis

How do you do a distributional analysis? Cross-tabs?
This chapter will cover how to conduct a factor by factor analysis.
It will also demonstrate how preliminary distributional analyses can pinpoint difficulties in research design and/or data anomalies.
It will focus on techniques for resolving data, computational and linguistic problems.

Now that you have some basic understanding of how the variable rule program works, let us now turn to the step-by-step procedures involved in performing an analysis. I will begin with distributional analysis.

FUNDAMENTALS

All too often when students first set out to do a distributional analysis, they do it the wrong way round. In order to do it right, distinguish between the roles of the dependent variable and the independent (explanatory) factors. Recall that in every variation analysis the focus is the tendency for the dependent variable to occur in a series of cross-cutting independent factors: 'The essence of the analysis is an assessment of how the choice process is influenced by the different factors whose specific combinations define these contexts' (Sankoff 1988c: 985).

THE WRONG WAY TO DO DISTRIBUTIONAL ANALYSIS

Many students make the mistake of reporting how the variants are distributed across the explanatory factors. Consider the results file for variable (t,d) in (1).

(1)
```
● CELL CREATION ● 6/24/04 ● 11:35 AM
●●●●●●●●●●●●●●●●●●●●●●●●●●●●●●●●●●●●●●●●●●●●●●●●●●●●●●
    Name of token file: YORK.t_d.Tkn
  Name of condition file: ch9.eg1.2.Cnd
  Number of cells: 9
      Application value(s): CVQ
      Total no. of factors: 6
```

Group		C	V	Q	Total	%
1 (2)						
t	N	162	537	117	816	66
	%	20	**66**	14		
0	N	232	52	7	291	24
	%	80	**18**	2		
?	N	66	47	12	125	10
	%	53	**38**	10		
Total	N	460	636	136	1232	
	%	37	52	11		

In this view of the data, I have purposefully run one of the independent variables as the dependent variable. As you will see, it is not the right way to view the distributions, at least not for variation analysis! The application values across the top of the table are categories (i.e. factors) of the following phonological context factor group: consonants, 'C', vowels, 'V', and pause, 'Q'. The three dependent variants 't', '0' and '?' have been re-coded in the condition file, 'ch9.eg1.2.Cnd'. They are listed along the leftmost side of the table. The numbers and proportions of these cross-cutting categories are shown in the lines below (for further discussion of how to read the data in a results file, i.e. the marginal data, see Chapter 8).

The total number of contexts in the data file is 1232. Of these, consonants, vowels and pause represent 37 per cent, 52 per cent and 11 per cent of the data respectively. These total N figures are shown on the bottom line. Now, read the vertical columns across. Take for example, the [Ø] variant. Under 'Total', you see that it occurs 291 times. The percentage at the end of the row tells you that the [Ø] variant represents 24 per cent of the data. Of these, 80 per cent, occur with consonants while 18 per cent occur in following vowel contexts and 2 per cent with following pause. However, this is *not* the relevant observation. For the analysis of variation you are not interested in how the variants are distributed across following phonological contexts. You are interested in the tendency of following phonological environments to constrain the appearance of [t, d], [Ø] or [ʔ]. In other words, what phonological context leads to more [Ø]? This cannot be determined based on the marginal data shown in (1).

Consider, in particular, the bolded percentages in (1). These do not tell you how the variants are constrained by the following phonological context. Instead, they simply tell you how many instances of the variant in question are found in each of the contexts. For example, 66 per cent in the 't' row does not mean that [t] occurs 66 per cent of the time in the context of a following vowel. It only means that of all the [t] tokens, the majority occur before a following vowel. There is no way to tell whether or not following vowels influences the use of variable (t,d). In order to find how the following phonological context constrains the use of the dependent variable [t], [ʔ] or [Ø], you need to know how many times each of these variants occurs out of *the total number of contexts* for each of the independent categories of phonological context, 'C', 'V' and 'Q'.

THE RIGHT WAY TO DO DISTRIBUTIONAL ANALYSIS

A distributional analysis, *aka* factor by factor analysis, is all about finding out how a context (independent factor) constrains the use of the (dependent) variant. In order to do this, the distribution must be calculated as shown in (2). The dependent variable variants are shown horizontally across the top of the table, 't', '0', and '?'. When you run the marginals, these variants should appear as the application values. The independent variables are listed group by group below. The factors within each group are listed vertically, in the leftmost column, i.e. Group 2 = 'V', 'C' and 'Q'. The numbers and percentages of each variant in each of these contexts (i.e. 'V', 'C' and 'Q') are shown in consecutive horizontal rows, divided into columns for the number and proportion (percentage) represented by each variant of the dependent variable.

```
(2)
    ● CELL CREATION ● 3/28/05 ● 12:27 PM
    ●●●●●●●●●●●●●●●●●●●●●●●●●●●●●●●●●●●●●●●●●●●●●●●●●
    Name of token file: YORK.t_d.Tkn
    Name of condition file: ch9_eg2_28-3-05.Cnd
    [condition file removed for illustration purposes]
    Number of cells: 3
    Application value(s): t0?
    Total no. of factors: 3
```

Group		t	0	?	Total	%
1 (new)						
V	N	456	44	20	520	45
	%	88	8	4		
C	N	227	240	31	498	43
	%	46	48	6		
Q	N	112	7	8	127	11
	%	88	6	6		
Total	N	795	291	59	1145	
	%	69	25	5		
TOTAL	N	795	291	59	1145	
	%	69	25	5		

Name of new cell file: ch9_eg2_28-3-05.Cel

The relevant observation is what proportion each variant represents out of the total number of contexts for each of the possible following phonological contexts in the data. Compare and contrast this proportion across contexts. For example, looking at the first row under the header '1 (new)', which is the set of contexts with a following vowel, 'V', you will see two rows. The first row has the Ns; the second, the proportion (%). There is a total of 520 tokens, which is 45 per cent of the total data. Do the same to examine following consonants, 'C' and following pause, 'Q'. Now, comparing across these three categories (factors), where does the [Ø] variant, 'O', occur most frequently? Unrealised forms can be seen to occur far more frequently with following consonants, 48 per cent, and much less frequently with following vowels, 8 per cent and following pause, 6 per cent, as indicated by the bolded numbers.

Notice how different the distributions in (1) are from the distributions in (2). Had you attempted to interpret our (t,d) data based on (1), you would have been reporting the wrong results. Any interpretation of such data would be false. Be careful not to make this mistake!

Note

The application values should reflect the variants of the dependent variable (not one of the independent variables!). These will be shown, horizontally, across the top of the marginal results in the results file produced by the variable rule program.

OVERALL DISTRIBUTION

Let us now proceed to a distributional analysis. This phase of your research can begin as soon as you have sufficient tokens in the data file that are coded for at least two factor groups. The most important question to ask is: What is the overall distribution of forms?

Anyone conducting an analysis of a linguistic variable should know the overall distribution of variants at every step of the way. I will often test my students with this question at the beginning of their research. The frequency of a variable process might seem like an obvious question, but students will often have no idea the first time I ask this question. But they always know *after* that!

So, to begin. What is the overall distribution of forms in the York (t,d) data? The proportion of each variant is evident in (2) above. Overall, you may report that unrealised variants represent 24 per cent of the data out of a total N of 1232. The overall rate of t/d deletion is 24 per cent.

SITUATING THE OVERALL RATE

Once the overall distribution of a variable is known, one of your first questions should be: How does this rate compare to other varieties of English? Is it more or less than what has been reported before? This immediately sets one's research in context, not only with other dialects, but also with earlier work. Being able to contextualise your findings, relevantly, in the prevailing literature is an extremely important part of conducting research. (I will return to the notion of 'relevant' later; see Chapter 11.)

Underlying forms?

Something to consider at the outset of an analysis involving phonology is what the underlying form(s) of your variable might be. As Labov (to appear) observes, 'One of the major tasks in the study of variation is the identification of underlying forms.' In the case of variable (t,d) you observe fluctuation between the presence and absence of a segment (i.e. the [t], [d] or [ʔ]). Where is this segment in the grammar? Is it present in the lexicon and variably deleted? Alternatively, is it variably inserted at some other level of grammar? Level of grammar is particularly germane to variables such as (t,d), which also functions as a suffixal inflection, thus implicating both phonology and morphology. The question then becomes: At what level of grammar does the variation exist? The phonological level or the morphological level?

A well-known indication of the presence of an underlying form comes from the existence of phonological conditioning (Labov to appear). A pattern that is readily visible in these marginal data is the sharp contrast between presence of realised forms in the context of vowels and absence in the presence of consonants. Universal tendencies toward CVCV structure might thus explain the elision of the [t,d] in the case of a CC or CCC cluster. If so, then this is a strong indication that [t,d] is present, then removed by a phonological simplification process. Such a hypothesis is bolstered by a number of other sociolinguistic tendencies, including 'hypercorrection, uniformity of use among community members, and/or moderate and systematic patterns of style-shifting' (Labov to appear). These show that [t,d] surfaces when speakers are more careful about the way they speak, also indicating the presence of an underlying segment. Generally speaking, patterns of variability often tell more about the variable than you might realise from simply looking at individual occurrences.

FACTOR BY FACTOR ANALYSIS

The overall rate of the variable is only the first step. It can only ever give you a broad understanding of the operation of your linguistic variable in your data. When the independent variables are examined, underlying trends and patterns emerge. The next step is to assess the overall distribution of variant forms by the individual factors which have been coded into the data. A good starting point is to check the overall distribution of forms by speaker, by sex, by age, etc. Then, turn to the internal factors. Since I have just shown you the overall distribution of variable (t,d) by following phonological context, let us look at it first.

Tip

When you run a set of marginals there will often be something awry with one code or another. In a data file that is thousands of tokens long, how will you ever find that particular datum and fix it? This is another way in which coding individual speakers separately is an advantage. Run the same set of marginals, but include the factor group for individual. Then cross-tabulate this factor group with the one that contains the problematic code. This will isolate its location to that speaker. Go into the token file and search for the speaker code. Then search for the problematic item code. Fix it. Save the token file. Go back to the analysis.

NOTICING TRENDS AND PATTERNS

Notice that the distributional analysis in (2) permits us to view two other important tendencies: 1) both following vowel and following pause have approximately the same effect on the use of [Ø], 4 per cent vs 6 per cent; and 2) while the use of [Ø] is phonologically conditioned, glottal stop is not. This can be inferred by the fact that both [Ø] patterns according to following phonological context: consonants 48 per cent vs vowels 8 per cent for [Ø], but consonants 6 per cent vs vowels 4 per cent for glottal stop. These are important observations, readily visible from the marginal data, which permit the analyst to make inferences about the variation in the grammar.

Tip

When you have coded your variable across one or more independent factors, run the marginals, print them, and start making observations about the trends and patterns you see. Note down everything you notice, including obvious errors in coding, and any other anomalies. Not only will this help you to fix the mistakes, it will also enable you to make decisions about continuing to extract and code your data. If you want to give yourself a lift, buy some highlighters in brilliant colours and use these to identify important trends.

Internal factors for variable (t,d) York

In Chapter 8 you were presented with a set of marginals for the *external* factors operating on variable (t,d) in York. I will not repeat this step here. Refer to example (30) for these results. I will now show the marginals for the overall distribution by all the *internal* factors for variable (t,d). (3) shows you the condition file. As is typical, the condition file begins with quite a number of important exclusions, all of which are annotated in the condition file. (For further discussion of annotation in condition files, see Chapter 8.) Note the extent to which we differentiated past tense forms. In the end, however, many of these were not sufficiently different and so many were collapsed together for the final runs.

```
(3)
(
;this condition file replicates GUY 1991
(2
; 'went'
  (NIL (col 5 W))
```

```
;takes out the dependent variable realised
;as phonetic[s]
  (NIL (COL 2 s))
;takes out tokens without underlying clusters
  (NIL (COL 9 R))
  (NIL (COL 9 1))
;these are all neutralisation contexts
  (NIL (COL 4 t))
  (NIL (COL 4 d))
  (NIL (COL 4 #))
  (NIL (COL 4 J))
  (NIL (COL 4 †))
;REMOVE comparatives
  (NIL (COL 5 C))
;zero-marked preterites
  (NIL (COL 5 o))
;zero-marked participles
  (NIL (COL 5 ø))
;single final consonants, categorical
  (NIL (COL 9 1))
;***exclude all PARTICIPIALS
;regular adjective
  (NIL (COL 5 J))
;semi-weak
  (NIL (COL 5 j))
;strong, suppletive
  (NIL (COL 5 Δ))
;strong active participles
  (NIL (COL 5 s))
;strong passive participles
  (NIL (COL 5 ß))
;replacive participles
  (NIL (COL 5 b))
;replacive passive participles
  (NIL (COL 5 ∫))
;replacive adjectives
  (NIL (COL 5 l))
;puts all closures as 'T' vs zero
  (T (COL 2 d))
  (0 (COL 2 0))
  (T (COL 2 t))
  (T (COL 2 #))
  (T (COL 2 N))
  (? (COL 2 ?))
  (T (COL 2 †))
  (T (COL 2 M)))
(5)
(3)
(4))
```

> **Tip**
>
> It is often the case that published works abstract way from the multitude of constructions that occurred in the data. New categories should be treated separately. They may pattern differently than the others. The only way to find out is to test it.

The results file in (4) shows you what the variable (t,d) data looks like before factor group 4 has been re-coded in any way. Here, the proportion of use of unrealised variants of (t,d), the applications, as opposed to realised variants of (t,d), the non-applications, can now be viewed for the internal factor following phonological segment (factor group 4). The number of cells is 257, the application value is '0' and the total number of factors is 44. How do you read the results?

```
(4)
    CELL CREATION ● 6/21/04 ● 3:22 PM
    ●●●●●●●●●●●●●●●●●●●●●●●●●●●●●●●●●●●●●●●●●●●●●●●●
        Name of token file: YORK.t_d.Tkn
    Name of condition file: ch9.egld.Cnd
    [condition file removed for illustration purposes ...]
        Number of cells: 257
        Application value(s): 0
        Total no. of factors: 44

Following phonological context
3 (4)
```

Group		Apps	Non-apps	Total	%	
V	N	44	476	520	45	VOWEL
	%	**8**	92			
k	N	22	9	31	3	/k/
	%	**71**	29			
w	N	33	41	74	6	/w/
	%	**45**	55			
Q	N	7	120	127	11	PAUSE
	%	**6**	94			
b	N	22	12	34	3	/b/
	%	**65**	35			
f	N	20	18	38	3	/f/
	%	**53**	47			
p	N	10	7	17	1	/p/
	%	**59**	41			
g	N	7	4	11	1	/dʒ/
	%	**64**	36			
m	N	48	22	70	6	/m/
	%	**69**	31			
j	N	8	25	33	3	/j/
	%	**24**	76			

n	N	5	3	8	1	/n/
	%	**63**	38			
s	N	37	17	54	5	/s/
	%	**69**	31			
l	N	6	19	25	2	/l/
	%	**24**	76			
h	N	7	56	63	6	/h/
	%	**11**	89			
r	N	8	21	29	3	/r/
	%	**28**	72			
Ø	N	1	0	1	0	/θ/
	%	100	0			* KnockOut *
S	N	3	3	6	1	/ʃ/
	%	50	50			
v	N	2	1	3	0	/v/
	%	67	33			
?	N	1	0	1	0	/ʔ/
	%	100	0			* KnockOut *
Total	N	291	854	1145		
	%	25	75			
TOTAL	N	291	854	1145		
	%	25	75			

Name of new cell file: ch9.eg1d.Cel

First, note that in (4) I have annotated the categories on the far right-hand side in order to make it more straightforward for you to read the results. I've also removed the condition file which you saw earlier in (3). Otherwise, the output in the results file is as it was produced by Goldvarb. The full results file, which also includes preceding phonological context and morphological category, can be found on the companion website as 'VRA results 1'.

It may be overwhelming at first to see the long list under the factor group. In fact, each of the internal factors has been coded for many different categories. This is typical of any coding schema at the outset of a distributional analysis. It is far better to code your data using an 'elaborated' coding schema, at least at the beginning. This gives you maximum flexibility in re-coding the data later on, whether it be by collapsing like categories together or removing categorical contexts. It is also an ideal way to treat certain lexical items separately to test whether they behave in the same way as the category they represent.

However, some of these distinctions may prove to have no real effect on the variable under investigation. As Guy (1988: 132) notes, 'You often start an analysis with an exhaustive list of finely discriminated environments that include every distinction you can think of that might possible be relevant.' As you shall see, the 'elaborated factors' strategy inevitably leads to small cells, sometimes even empty cells, when viewed interactively with other external factors. This will have ramifications later on when you turn to re-coding and dealing with interaction.

Following phonological context

Note the individual categories for following phonological segment and the distribution of the zero variant across them. A good way to do this is to highlight the proportion of unrealised variants and compare these across contexts. I have employed bold to make the relevant comparative data become more visible. Vowels (V) have a relatively low rate of unrealised variants, only 8 per cent (N = 520). This is comparable to the proportion of unrealised variants for following pause, 6 per cent (N = 127). Apparently, this is a variety where following vowels pattern with following pause. Next, start looking for other trends and patterns. Leaving aside the categories with very small Ns, the highest rates of unrealised (t,d) are with /k/, 71 per cent, /s/ 69 per cent, /m/ 69 per cent, /b/ 65 per cent, /dʒ/ 64 per cent and /n/ 63 per cent. The other consonants are not far behind: /p/ 59 per cent and /f/ 53 per cent. In fact the primary difference among the consonants come in the proportion observed for /r/ 28 per cent and /l/ 24 per cent. Thereafter, glides, /w/ 45 per cent and /j/ 24 per cent, are also relatively low. In sum, the major split in the data is between consonants and vowels, with glides and liquids intermediate.

What about /h/, which stands out amongst the consonants? This looks like a good candidate for what Labov refers to as an 'irrational constraint', i.e. one that runs counter to established linguistic findings (to appear). The question is: Why would the rate of unrealised variants be so low at only 11 per cent, setting this particular consonant apart from all others?

Coding, getting back to the data and re-coding

In order to find out, you need to be able to go back to the data and assess what is happening. In Goldvarb it is easy to search for a particular code in a specified factor group, e.g. 'h' in factor group 4. In Goldvarb 2001 and Goldvarb X you can even search for non-adjacent codes, i.e. a particular code in one factor group and another code in a different factor group, e.g. X in factor group A and Y in factor group B. Here, however I searched for 'h' in factor group 4. You find that typical tokens of following /h/ are as in (5).

(5)
a. My dad **_lost his_** temper. (YRK/b)
b. We nearly **_trashed her_** decorative plate. (YRK/N)
c. But it's really **_different here_**. (YRK/i)

The reason that following /h/ contexts are rarely deleted is because the [h] must not be present to inhibit elision of the final [t,d], i.e. in unstressed position they are reduced to zero. In other words, the following /h/ contexts are only 'h' in the orthography and in the phonology. This is the classic variable (h), *aka* h-dropping, which is part of the variable inventory of this variety of English. Why had we coded these contexts in this way? In our coding strategy for variable (t,d), we had based our coding schema on the assumption that (t,d) deletion is a phonological rule operating on underlying forms. Thus we coded the preceding and following phonological environments according to the *underlying* segments preceding and following the target /t,d/, whatever their surface realisation. However, with respect to following /h/, this is a case in which the elision of the [h] occurs *before* (t,d) deletion as observed by the distribution of forms in the data. This type of information can now be used to re-code this factor informatively. A re-code of the following phonological context is shown in (6), where following /h/ is now grouped with following vowels (bolded):

```
(6)
(0
;obstruent
(O (COL 4 n))
(O (COL 4 S))
(O (COL 4 t))
(O (COL 4 g))
(O (COL 4 k))
(O (COL 4 Ø))
(O (COL 4 b))
(O (COL 4 v))
(O (COL 4 z))
(O (COL 4 s))
(O (COL 4 d))
(O (COL 4 m))
(O (COL 4 f))
(O (COL 4 p))
(O (COL 4 ?))
; /l/
(L (COL 4 l))
; /r/
(R (COL 4 r))
```

```
; VOWELS
(V (COL 4 V) )
(V (COL 4 h) )
; GLIDES
(G (COL 4 j) )
(G (COL 4 w) )
; PAUSE
(Q (COL 4 Q) )
)
```

In addition, the re-code shows the major categories in the data as observed in the overall marginal data above. Consistent with their comparable frequencies of unrealised (t,d), obstruents are re-coded together. Vowels and /h/ are collapsed as both are glides. Lateral /l/ is left alone, as is /r/ and pause. These decisions are made based on a combination of two things: 1) the pattern visible in the marginals; and 2) the reports from earlier research in the literature. In this case, we followed Guy (1991a) in treating /l/ and /r/ separately because, although the hierarchy is different from that found by Guy, the proportions for the two categories are no closer than, for example, for /r/ versus glides. We do not know how Guy (or others) may have collapsed following /h/. While this may depend on the status of h-dropping in the dialects under investigation, it is also important to note that in running speech in any dialect, 'h' is often elided in certain function words, e.g. *him, his, her*, etc. In any case, consistent with its distributional status in our data, we may now group it with vowels. This demonstrates how coding decisions, distributional analysis and re-coding the data are intertwined in the process of variation analysis.

Note

In other cases, phonological variables may be coded not for underlying forms, but for surface forms. If so, then phonological features will be coded based on orthography, i.e. the way the word is spelled. Base your coding schema on what you actually hear in the data – unless, of course, there is an independent reason to do otherwise.

Preceding phonological context

The same basic procedure is followed in re-coding the other groups, preceding phonological context, as illustrated in (7), and functional category of the word, as in (8). Both factor groups are re-coded to reflect the categorisation schemas in previous analyses.

```
(7)
; PRECEDING SEGMENT
(0
;NASAL
(N (COL 3 n))
(N (COL 3 ©))
(N (COL 3 m))
; LIQUID
(L (COL 3 l))
; SIBILANT
(S (COL 3 Z))
(S (COL 3 S))
(S (COL 3 J))
(S (COL 3 †))
(S (COL 3 z))
(S (COL 3 s))
; STOP
(P (COL 3 t))
(P (COL 3 g))
(P (COL 3 k))
(P (COL 3 b))
(P (COL 3 d))
(P (COL 3 p))
(P (COL 3 ?))
; NON-SIBILANT FRICATIVE
(F (COL 3 Ø))
(F (COL 3 #))
(F (COL 3 v))
(F (COL 3 f))
)
```

```
(8)
; FUNCTIONAL CATEGORY OF THE WORD
(5
;REGULAR BI-MORPHEMIC PRETERITE
(P (COL 5 P))
(P (COL 5 p))
(P (COL 5 Z))
; SEMI-WEAK PRETERITES
(A (COL 5 A))
(A (COL 5 a))
(A (COL 5 ∩))
; STRONG PRETERITES
(M (COL 5 S))
; REPLACIVE PRETERITES
(M (COL 5 B))
;TRUE MONOMORPHEMES
(M (col 5 M))
```

```
;'went'
(M (col 5 W))
)
```

New marginals

These re-codes of the condition file produce the results in (9):

```
(9)
     ● CELL CREATION ● 6/23/04 ● 3:37 PM
     ●●●●●●●●●●●●●●●●●●●●●●●●●●●●●●●●●●●●●●●●●●●●●●●●●●●●●●●●
     Name of token file: YORK.t_d.Tkn
    Name of condition file: ch9.eg.9.Cnd
    [condition file removed for illustration purposes ...]
    Number of cells: 72
      Application value(s): 0
      Total no. of factors: 14
```

Group		Apps	Non-apps	Total	%
1 (new)					
N	N	76	363	439	36
	%	17	83		
L	N	27	103	130	11
	%	21	79		
F	N	15	112	127	10
	%	12	88		
S	N	146	221	367	30
	%	40	60		
P	N	27	142	169	14
	%	16	84		
Total	N	291	941	1232	
	%	24	76		
2 (new)					
V	N	52	584	636	52
	%	8	92		
O	N	177	114	291	24
	%	61	39		
G	N	41	70	111	9
	%	37	63		
Q	N	7	129	136	11
	%	5	95		
L	N	6	20	26	2
	%	23	77		
R	N	8	24	32	3
	%	25	75		
Total	N	291	941	1232	
	%	24	76		
3 (5)					
M	N	189	527	716	58
	%	26	74		

P	N	75	313	388	31
	%	19	81		
A	N	27	101	128	10
	%	21	79		
Total	N	291	941	1232	
	%	24	76		
TOTAL	N	291	941	1232	
	%	24	76		

The marginal data now show each of the internal factors categorised by divisions reported in much of the literature on variable (t,d). Following earlier research, preceding context is categorised into nasals ('N'), liquids ('L'), non-sibilant fricatives ('F'), sibilants ('S') and stops ('P'). Following context is categorised into vowels, ('V'), obstruents, ('O'), glides, ('G'), pause, ('Q'), and [l] ('L'), and [r] ('R'). Functional category is categorised into monomorphemes, 'M', past tense forms, 'P', and semi-weak past tense forms, 'A'. Numerous other possibilities for re-coding these factor groups exist. For example, I could have configured the preceding phonological context factor group so as to group sibilants against all other preceding contexts, as in (10), or I could have separated out [s], 's', from other sibilants, 'S', as in (11). The possibilities are innumerable. For example a categorisation schema of phonological segments might be based on point of articulation, voicing, sonority, etc. The important theme underlying this honing process is to arrive at the most logical configuration, the configuration that most adequately captures the trends and patterns in the data.

```
(10)
   ● CELL CREATION ● 11/20/05 ● 11:38:54
   ●●●●●●●●●●●●●●●●●●●●●●●●●●●●●●●●●●●●●●●●●●●●●●●●●●●
   Number of cells: 33
   Application value(s) : 0
   Total no. of factors: 11
```

Group		Apps	Non-apps	Total	%
1 (new)					
–	N	145	720	865	70
	%	17	83		
S	N	146	221	367	30
	%	40	60		
Total	N	291	941	1232	
	%	24	76		

```
(11)
   ● CELL CREATION ● 6/24/04 ● 3:56 PM
   ●●●●●●●●●●●●●●●●●●●●●●●●●●●●●●●●●●●●●●●●●●●●●●●●●●●●
     Name of token file: YORK.t_d.Tkn
   Name of condition file: ch9.eg10.Cnd
     Number of cells: 3
     Application value(s): 0
     Total no. of factors: 3
   Group          Apps    Non-apps    Total     %
   - - - - - - - - - - - - - - - - - - - - - - - - - - - - -
   1 (new)
     -       N     145       720       865      70
             %      17        83
     s       N     126       177       303      25
             %      42        58
     S       N      20        44        64       5
             %      31        69
   Total     N     291       941      1232
             %      24        76
```

Cross-tabulation of internal factor groups

Once you have completed a factor by factor distributional analysis, conduct a series of cross-tabulations. Goldvarb 2.1 and Goldvarb X 2001 offer easy explanations for how to conduct cross-tabulations of your marginal data. A cross-tabulation of two different external factors will produce a grid-line pattern in which each 'box' is called a 'cell'. When I refer to 'cell size', I am referring to the number of tokens in each of these cells. Here I discuss cross-tabulation with particular reference to cross-cutting internal factors. For additional discussion about cross-tabulation, see Chapter 8.

Cross-tabulation is extremely important for assessing the independence of factor groups (Labov to appear: fn. 11). Once the cells are loaded and the results file is displayed, it is a simple matter of finding the drop-down menu (under 'CELLS' for Goldvarb 2.1 and Goldvarb X; under 'Actions' for Goldvarb 2001). The program prompts you to indicate which groups to cross-tabulate. These numbers will relate directly back to the order of the factor groups in the condition file. The first one listed is always the dependent variable. Thereafter, the factor groups are given numbers from 2 onwards. In (4) above, where the three internal factor groups are included in the condition file, the grammatical category factor group, '5', is first in the condition file, then the preceding phonological factor group, '3', then the following phonological factor group, '4'. This means that when the results file is produced these three will be relabelled '1', '2' and '3' respectively. The original position in the token file will be retained in bracketed numbers alongside, i.e. 1 (5), 2 (3), 3 (4). In order to cross-tabulate the data in these factor groups, you must refer to them with their new numbers as produced in the results file – namely '1', '2' and '3'. So, a cross-tabulation of preceding phonological context and following phonological context is a cross-tabulation of factor group 1 and factor group 2, as in (12).

This is a classic example of what badly distributed natural speech data look like. Some cells have large amounts of data, e.g. words that end in /n/ followed by vowels, N = 232. Other cells are empty, e.g.

```
(12)
• CROSS-TABULATION • 6/23/04 • 3:37 PM •••••••••••••••••••••••••
• Cell file:  ch9.eg.9.Cel
• 6/23/04•3:37 PM
• Token file: YORK.t_d.Tkn
• Conditions: ch9.eg9.Cnd

Group #1 -- horizontally
Group #2 -- vertically
```

		N	%	L	%	F	%	S	%	P	%	Σ	%
V	0:	22	9:	5	8:	0	0:	24	16:	1	1|	52	8
	-:	210	91:	60	92:	81	100:	125	84:	108	99:	584	92
	Σ:	232	:	65	:	81	:	149	:	109	|	636	
O	0:	32	36:	19	53:	13	57:	88	81:	25	71|	177	61
	-:	56	64:	17	47:	10	43:	21	19:	10	29|	114	39
	Σ:	88	:	36	:	23	:	109	:	35	|	291	
G	0:	12	35:	3	27:	1	11:	24	48:	1	14|	41	37
	-:	22	65:	8	73:	8	89:	26	52:	6	86|	70	63
	Σ:	34	:	11	:	9	:	50	:	7	|	111	
Q	0:	6	9:	0	0:	0	0:	1	3:	0	0|	7	5
	-:	61	91:	10	100:	11	100:	33	97:	14	100|	129	95
	Σ:	67	:	10	:	11	:	34	:	14	|	136	

```
L  0:    1  20:    0    0:    0  --:    5  33:    0    0|     6  23
   -:    4  80:    5  100:    0  --:   10  67:    1  100|    20  77
   Σ:    5   :     5   :     0   :    15   :     1    |     26

   +  -  -  -  +  -  -  -  -  +  -  -  -  -  +  -  -  -  -  +  -  -  -  -  +  -  -  -  -

R  0:    3  23:    0    0:    1  33:    4   3:    0    0|     8  25
   -:   10  77:    3  100:    2  67:    6  97:    3  100|    24  75
   Σ:   13   :     3   :     3   :    10   :     3    |     32

   +---------+---------+---------+---------+---------+---------

Σ  0:   76  17:   27  21:   15  12:  146  40:   27  16|   291  24
   -:  363  83:  103  79:  112  88:  221  60:  142  84|   941  76
   Σ:  439   :   130   :   127   :   367   :   169    |  1232
```

words that end in /f/ followed by /l/ (N = 0), bolded in (12). A hypothetical example would be, *left late*, but for whatever reason such an example did not figure in the data. Notice, however, that following /l/ is very infrequent in the data overall – only 26 tokens. Following /r/ is also infrequent (N = 32).

The cross-tabulation also permits you to observe the extent of regularity in the application of preceding and following phonological influences on (t,d). In cells with sufficient data, the pattern of distribution of variants for preceding phonological context for following vowels and consonants is parallel (see bolded percentages). By this I mean that the relationship of more to less, i.e. bigger to smaller proportions, %s, stays constant across the board. For example, for every case of vowels, 'V', and following 'N', 'L', 'F', 'S' and 'P', there is less 'deletion' than with obstruents, 'O', for the same categories across the board. Notice that both vowels and consonants show precisely the same pattern for each one of the preceding contexts – following vowels have low rates of unrealised variants, following consonants have high rates, and this relationship is constant for each preceding context. The actual proportions differ, but the pattern is the same.

Now, let us consider the cross-tabulation of factor group 2 (following phonological context) with factor group 3 (morphological status), as in (13).

Here, too, despite marked differences in the Ns per cell (ranging from 339 for monomorphemes followed by a vowel to 3 tokens of semi-weak verbs followed by /l/), the regular effect of both following environment and morphological status is visible. In the first two columns (following vowels and obstruents), the effect of both factors is regular. Following

```
(13)
• CROSS-TABULATION • 6/23/04 • 3:42 PM ••••••••••••••••••••••••••••••••••
• Cell file:  ch9.eg.9.Cel
• 6/23/04•3:37 PM
• Token file: YORK.t_d.Tkn
• Conditions: ch9.eg9.Cnd

Group #2 -- horizontally
Group #3 -- vertically

          V   %    O   %    G   %    Q   %    L   %    R   %    Σ    %
      +  -  -  -  +  -  -  -  +  -  -  -  +  -  -  -  +  -  -  -  +  -  -  -  -
M 0:    43  13:  100  57:   30  42:    6   6:    5  26:    5  29|  189   26
  -:   296  87:   74  43:   41  58:   90  94:   14  74:   12  71|  527   74
  Σ:   339   :   174   :    71   :    96   :    19   :    17   |  716

      +  -  -  -  +  -  -  -  +  -  -  -  +  -  -  -  +  -  -  -  +  -  -  -  -
P 0:     7   3:   56  67:    7  26:    1   3:    1  25:    3  27|   75   19
  -:   223  97:   28  33:   20  74:   31  97:    3  75:    8  73|  313   81
  Σ:   230   :   84    :    27   :    32   :     4   :    11   |  388

      +  -  -  -  +  -  -  -  +  -  -  -  +  -  -  -  +  -  -  -  +  -  -  -  -
A 0:     2   3:   21  64:    4  31:    0   0:    0   0:    0   0|   27   21
  -:    65  97:   12  36:    9  69:    8 100:    3 100:    4 100|  101   79
  Σ:    67   :   33    :    13   :     8   :     3   :     4   |  128

      +---------+---------+---------+---------+---------+---------+----------
Σ 0:    52   8:  177  61:   41  37:    7   5:    6  23:    8  25|  291   24
  -:   584  92:  114  39:   70  63:  129  95:   20  77:   24  75|  941   76
  Σ:   636   :  291    :  111    :  136    :   26    :   32    | 1232
```

vowels have far fewer [Ø] than obstruents. Monomorphemes stand apart from past tense forms, either regular, 'P', or semi-weak, 'A'.

The regular patterns evident in the cross-tabulations of the internal factors in (12) and (13) highlight a consistent finding in variationist research: linguistic factors tend to be independent. However, it is not nearly as likely to have social factors that do not interact.

COMBINING FACTORS

Combining two factor groups is often necessary, either because some cells are empty and must be collapsed with others, or because the interface between two factors is the most explanatory distribution of the data. For illustration purposes, you could construct a test of the preceding and following phonological context combined. Such a re-code can be accomplished with the re-code function. Here is the logic of how it is done. The '0' in the condition file indicates that the factor group is new. The 'AND' function is used to combine the factors in one factor group with the factors in another factor group. A combined factor group for preceding and following context in the York (t,d) data set looks as in (14). At the beginning of the coding string, you must specify a new code to represent the combination of the two factors. Here, I have designated '1' for the re-code of preceding consonant with following vowel, 'q' for preceding consonant following pause, and '2' for preceding consonant following consonant (not shown).

```
(14)
; COMBINED FACTOR GROUP
(0
; PRECEDING CONSONANT ; FOLLOWING VOWEL [C..V]
(1 (AND (COL 3 Z) (COL 4 V) ))
(1 (AND (COL 3 S) (COL 4 V) ))
(1 (AND (COL 3 J) (COL 4 V) )) ...
; PRECEDING CONSONANT; FOLLOWING PAUSE
(q (AND (COL 3 Z) (COL 4 Q) ))
(q (AND (COL 3 J) (COL 4 Q) ))
(q (AND (COL 3 1) (COL 4 Q) )) ...
```

The marginal data as in (15) are produced.

```
(15)
    Number of cells: 190
    Application value(s): 0
    Total no. of factors: 40
```

Group		Apps	Non-apps	Total	%	
1 (new)						
1	N	52	585	637	52	[C..V]
	%	8	92			
2	N	233	228	461	37	[C..C]
	%	51	49			
q	N	7	129	136	11	[C..Q]
	%	5	95			
Total	N	292	942	1234		
	%	24	76			
TOTAL	N	292	942	1234		
	%	24	76			

Tip

If the distributions in the new combined factor group don't look quite right, run the marginals by including each of the combined factor groups separately and cross-tabulate them with the new factor group. This will show you precisely what is in each cell. You may have missed one of the factors somewhere.

In this case the combined factor groups does little to advance the analysis of variable (t,d) in the data. The relevant constraint is still a consonant cluster vs anything else. However, combined factor groups of this type are often useful in other situations. They are particularly invaluable in dealing with non-orthogonal external factor groups. For example, suppose there are no older speakers with education beyond 16 years of age, as in (16). A combined factor group of education/age will be able to handle this by creating three cells. Instead of two factor groups (Education; Age) with two categories each, you will have created one factor group with three categories, as in (17).

(16)

Two factor groups	Young	Old
+ Education	X	–
– Education	X	X

(17)

Combined factor group
Young; + Education
Young; – Education
Old; – Education

Note

The condition file permits substantial flexibility in re-coding factor groups. However, there are limits to everything. You cannot, for example, re-code the data from a re-code of the data. Keep this in mind when you devise the coding schema for internal factors. You need all the relevant factors coded in such a way as to be most useful to you later on.

FROM MARGINALS TO TABLES

The next step is to turn the marginal results into informative tables. From the marginal data shown in (2), the overall distribution of forms may be presented in table format as in (18) or, alternatively, as in (19):

(18)

Overall distribution of the realisation of tokens of final /t,d/ in York English c. 1996 ch9_eg2_28-3-05.Cnd 3/28/05 ● 12:27 PM					
Apical stop/affricate		Glottal stop/ glottalisation		Zero realisation	
%	N	%	N	%	N
69	795	5	59	25	291
Total N		1145			

(19)

Overall distribution of /t,d/ deletion in York English ch9_eg3_28-3-05.Cnd 3/28/05 ● 2:25 PM			
closure		zero realisation	
%	N	%	N
75	854	25	291
Total N	1145		

Here is a checklist for what a distributional analysis table should contain:

* title of the table
* application value
* name/type of data under investigation
* percentages
* number of contexts per cell (i.e. the denominator, the total number of contexts per cell – not the number of applications, the numerator!)
* total number of contexts in the data

Tip

In addition to the usual information, I insert the name and date of the condition file that was used to produce the results, usually beside the title of each table or figure. This is an invaluable practice as it links the results with the condition file that produced it and the data file it was based on. I cannot tell you how much time I have lost trying to reproduce a set of marginals because I cannot find the right condition file!

The factor by factor distributions can be presented in tables, as in (20)–(22):

(20)

Distribution of [t,d] deletion by *morphological class* in York English
6/24/04 ● 11:31 AM ch9.eg2.Cnd

Morphological class	%	N
Monomorphemes, *mist*	26	716
Semi-weak past tense, *kept*	21	128
Regular past tense, *missed*	19	388

(21)

Distribution of [t,d] deletion by *preceding phonological segment* in York English
6/24/04 ● 11:31 AM ch9.eg2.Cnd

Preceding phonological segment	%	N
Sibilant	40	367
Liquid	21	130
Nasal	17	439
Stop	16	169
Non-sibilant fricative	12	127

(22)

Distribution of [t,d] deletion by *following phonological segment* in York English
6/24/04 ● 11:31 AM ch9.eg2.Cnd

Following phonological segment	%	N
Obstruent	61	291
Glide	37	111
[l]	23	26

[r]	25	32
Vowel	8	636
Pause	5	136

Note

For each table, I have organised the factors hierarchically in terms of how frequently [t,d] is deleted. This facilitates the identification of patterns in the data.

SUMMARY

A distributional, factor by factor analysis of the type just presented offers numerous insights into the factors conditioning the occurrence of your linguistic variable. However tabulations of effects taken one at a time cannot reveal the combined impact of all the factors together. This is where variable rule analysis comes in as the right tool for the job. It can model the simultaneous operation of factor effects, reveal the relative importance of each one to the other, and select which ones are significant. In Chapter 10, I will show you how to analyse the same (t,d) data using the variable rule program.

Exercise 9: Performing a distributional analysis

At this point you should have a reasonable number of tokens of your variable extracted from your data divided equally among your speakers (Exercise 5). These should be coded according to the coding schema you have devised (Exercise 6).

In this exercise, you will conduct a factor by factor analysis of your data. Provide percentages of variant usage by each independent factor group you have coded (e.g. Where, specifically, does each variant occur? Where does it *not* occur?).

Include the following:

* The overall distribution of your linguistic variable
* The overall distribution by external linguistic factors, e.g. individual speaker, sex, age
* The overall distribution by internal linguistic factors
* These should be depicted in the form of tables, correctly labelled and containing both Ns, %s and Total Ns.
* An overall distribution table includes:
* How many of each variant *out of the total number of possible contexts* of occurrence for the variant.

Variant #1		Variant #2		
%	N	%	N	Total N

A factor by factor distribution table includes: how many of each variant out of the total number of each independent factor, where an independent factor can be extralinguistic (e.g. sex) or linguistic (e.g. main clause vs subordinate clause).

Female		Male		
Application value (choose one of the variants)		Application value (choose one of the variants)		
%	N	%	N	Total N

Make sure that each of these effects is known to you at this phase of your research. How do the factors manifest in the data? What are the trends? Are these effects attested previously in the literature? If so, how do the patterns you have found compare? Does the direction of effect (i.e. the relationship of more to less) corroborate previous research? Is it logical or illogical? Does it apply across all social factors?

What can you conclude from your findings? What causes the variation between variants? Make projections for further research. Write down your observations in detail, attempting to understand what is going on in the data.

Note

Label your tables informatively. For example, in your own tables 'Variant #1', 'X', etc. will be substituted for the actual form and number relevant to your study.

10   Multivariate analysis

> How do I work through a multivariate analysis?
> This chapter will illustrate the procedures for performing a
> multivariate analysis, particularly how to determine if the analysis is
> the 'best' one, how to look for and identify 'interaction', and what to
> do about it when you find it.

At this point, you are ready to move forward with a fully fledged
variable rule analysis of your data. Goldvarb 2.1, Goldvarb 2001 and
Goldvarb X permit variable rule analysis with binomial applications.
Only one or two values can be declared as application values (Rand and
Sankoff 1990: 24). The multinomial one level visible under the 'CELLS'
drop-down menu in Goldvarb 2.1 and Goldvarb X have never been
implemented. To my knowledge the only version of the variable rule
program which permits more than binomial application is Varbrul 3,
which permits the trinomial case. For further discussion, see Rousseau
and Sankoff (1978a, 1978b). However, very few analyses in the field have
used this type of analysis.

A further requirement for running the variable rule program is that
the condition file you use produces marginal results with no singletons
and no KnockOuts. Having worked through your analysis as described
in Chapter 8, you should already have a condition file, or series of
condition files, that meet this requirement. With one of these condition
files and the data file open, load the cells to memory, and save them.
Input the application value (one of the variants of the dependent variable or some combination thereof; see Chapter 8). Then, save the results
file that is produced. As detailed in Chapter 7, you have two choices for
analysis: 1) binomial, step-up/step-down and 2) binomial, one level.

BINOMIAL ONE-STEP ANALYSIS

First, consider an analysis for variable (t,d) in York as it was configured
in the condition file in example (9) in Chapter 9 (page 205). The
complete binomial one-step analysis is reproduced in (1):

(1)

● BINOMIAL VARBRUL, 1 step ● 6/25/04●11:16 AM
Name of cell file: ch10.eg.3.Cel
Using fast, less accurate method.
Averaging by weighting factors.
One-level binomial analysis ...

Run #1, 72 cells:
Iterations: 1 2 3 4 5 6 7
Convergence at Iteration 7
Input 0.162

Group	Factor	Weight	App/Total	Input/Weight
1:	N	0.424	0.17	0.12
	L	0.432	0.21	0.13
	F	0.340	0.12	0.09
	S	0.692	0.40	0.30
	P	0.439	0.16	0.13
2:	V	0.307	0.08	0.08
	O	0.884	0.61	0.60
	G	0.704	0.37	0.32
	Q	0.205	0.05	0.05
	L	0.491	0.23	0.16
	R	0.611	0.25	0.23
3:	M	0.521	0.26	0.17
	P	0.457	0.19	0.14
	A	0.513	0.22	0.17

Cell	Total	App'ns	Expected	Error
SVP	44	3	6.108	1.837
SVM	96	21	16.591	1.417
SVA	9	0	1.514	1.820
SRP	1	0	0.363	0.571
SRM	9	4	3.826	0.014
SQP	16	1	1.368	0.108
SQM	18	0	1.946	2.181
SOP	33	27	24.248	1.177
SOM	73	59	57.099	0.290
SOA	3	2	2.330	0.209
SLP	1	1	0.260	2.846
SLM	14	4	4.380	0.048
SGP	8	1	3.715	3.704
SGM	40	21	21.163	0.003
SGA	2	2	1.042	1.839
PVP	82	1	4.364	2.739
PVM	10	0	0.679	0.729
PVA	17	0	1.121	1.200
PRP	2	0	0.332	0.398

PRA	1	0	0.200	0.250
PQP	7	0	0.221	0.228
PQM	6	0	0.243	0.254
PQA	1	0	0.039	0.041
POP	22	14	10.811	1.849
POM	6	5	3.336	1.869
POA	7	6	3.836	2.701
PLP	1	0	0.109	0.123
PGP	5	1	1.161	0.029
PGM	1	0	0.282	0.392
PGA	1	0	0.275	0.379
NVP	24	1	1.208	0.038
NVM	205	21	13.178	4.961
NVA	4	0	0.250	0.266
NRP	5	2	0.790	2.202
NRM	8	1	1.565	0.254
NQP	2	0	0.060	0.061
NQM	63	6	2.414	5.540
NQA	2	0	0.074	0.077
NOP	11	5	5.244	0.022
NOM	**77**	**27**	**41.693**	**11.293**
NLP	1	0	0.104	0.116
NLM	4	1	0.521	0.507
NGP	6	4	1.331	6.878
NGM	28	8	7.554	0.036
LVP	27	2	1.399	0.272
LVM	18	1	1.190	0.033
LVA	20	2	1.284	0.427
LRP	1	0	0.162	0.193
LRA	2	0	0.391	0.485
LQP	2	0	0.061	0.063
LQM	8	0	0.316	0.329
LOP	8	5	3.874	0.634
LOM	18	9	9.881	0.174
LOA	11	6	5.950	0.001
LLP	1	0	0.106	0.119
LLM	1	0	0.134	0.154
LLA	3	0	0.390	0.448
LGP	2	1	0.454	0.849
LGM	2	1	0.552	0.503
LGA	7	1	1.886	0.569
FVP	54	0	1.926	1.997
FVM	10	0	0.457	0.479
FVA	17	0	0.754	0.789
FRP	2	1	0.231	2.886
FRA	1	0	0.141	0.164
FQP	5	0	0.105	0.107
FQM	1	0	0.027	0.028
FQA	5	0	0.131	0.135

FOP	10	5	3.886	0.523
FOA	13	8	5.768	1.553
FGP	6	0	0.995	1.193
FGA	3	1	0.599	0.335

Total Chi-square = 78.9376
Chi-square/cell = 1.0964
Log likelihood = −482.431

In this type of analysis, there is only one run of the data that includes all factor groups. In the first column, the numbers '1', '2' and '3' refer to the factor groups in the analysis. The symbols for each category within each factor group are listed thereafter, followed by the 'Weight', or probability of the dependent variable occurring in the context, the proportion of the dependent variable, or 'App/Total', and finally a value which combines the probability and the proportion, the 'Input/Weight'. This is followed by a listing of each cell (i.e. combinations of factors and factor groups) in the data. The results for each cell are detailed in the next set of four columns: first, how many tokens of this cell type are in the data, the 'Total'; second, how many times the application value of the dependent variable occurred within combinations of this type, the 'App'ns'; third, how many of these applications were expected given the model of the data; and finally the difference between the model and the actual data, the 'Error'.

The list of individual cells and their actual and expected values enables you to spot the places where there are anomalies in the data. Simply find the error values that are noticeably higher than the others. This is also the only Goldvarb analysis that provides a scattergram of how the data are distributed (see below). Another use of the one-step analysis is to compare analyses in which the frequency of the dependent variable differs substantially. In such a case, the 'Input/Weight' calculation permits analysis of the *combined* effect of corrected mean and factor weight. For example, if you were examining a variable process that differed dramatically in frequency from one variety to another this computation would enable you to determine the probability that the dependent variable will occur in a given context while at the same time controlling for its overall frequency of occurrence in that context. Further, this type of analysis permits the analyst to compare the probabilities for a given factor *across* independent runs, in addition to the more traditional comparison of factor weights *within* a single run. For further exemplification, see Poplack and Tagliamonte (1998).

Let us look in more detail at some of the useful features of the binomial one-step analysis.

WHAT TO DO WITH 'ERRORS'

Examination of the one-step results permits you to view the application values, 'App'ns', compared to the 'Expected' values. The 'Error' reports the difference between these two. Some researchers suggest that error values below 2.0 are good (Preston 1996: 11, Young and Bayley 1996: 272). But what about errors that are more? In my experience, such errors are very common. This may mean that there is interaction between factor groups or that 'a particular lexical item is exerting an undue influence' (Young and Bayley 1996: 272). When there is a large discrepancy, this should provoke the question: Why?

There is a rather large error produced for cells of the type, 'NOM', as in (2):

(2)

Cell	Total	App'ns	Expected	Error
NOM	77	27	41.693	**11.293**

Further, tokens of this type are fairly frequent, occurring 77 times in the data set. When this is the case, it is a good idea to return to your data file and find out what these anomalous cells are. In this case, you can do this by searching for tokens that are monomorphemes with preceding 'N' and following consonants that are 'O'. Of course, remember that there is no 'O' in factor group 4 of the data file. Instead, 'O' is the *re-coded* symbol for all consonants in the condition file. In other words, you will have to search for a number of different codes. Search the token file for contexts with preceding 'N' and any of the following categories that were re-coded as 'O'. In (3) you see the following consonants [f], [b] and [r].

```
(3)
(Σ?nfWNFΣ2S//nf      5.7    So we WENT for a spin
(#?nbWNFΣ2O//mB     32.2    at er, WENT back to Sam's
(%?nrWAFΣ2O//nR     31.7    And it WENT right up his bottom
```

The fact that many of these contexts involves the lexical item *went* should immediately set off warning bells. You know that exceptional items should be removed from the variable rule analysis, particularly those which are near categorical, i.e. KnockOuts, whether 100 per cent or 0 per cent. What happens if we take a closer look at this particular lexical item by separating it out for separate treatment in the marginal data? This involves a re-code of the condition file, which produces the marginal results in (4). The tokens of *went* are coded as 'W' (bolded).

(4)
```
● CELL CREATION ● 6/25/04 ● 11:21 AM ●●●●●●●●●●●●●●●●●●●●●●●●●●●●
    Name of token file: VA.YORK.t_d.Tkn
  Name of condition file: ch10.eg.4.went.Cnd

    Number of cells: 78
  Application value(s): 0
    Total no. of factors: 15
```

M	N	188	439	627	51
	%	30	70		
P	N	75	314	389	32
	%	19	81		
A	N	28	101	129	10
	%	22	78		
W	**N**	**1**	**88**	**89**	**7**
	%	**1**	**99**		
Total	N	292	942	1234	
	%	24	76		

Note

In order to separate out the lexical item *went*, it had to have been coded separately in the data file. *Went* had originally been grouped with monomorphemes in order to match this configuration of the data in Guy (1991a).

You can now see that the lexical item *went* has only 1 per cent deletion of the final consonant of its [nt] cluster. In other words, *went* is rarely pronounced [wɛn]. A linguistic explanation is plausible: some kind of two-way assimilation occurs whereby the final cluster is 'reduced' to a nasalised glottal, particularly in the environment of some following consonant. We may surmise from this evidence that, in York English at least, this lexical item in this contextual environment may be behaving exceptionally with respect to variable (t,d). This dictates re-running the data, this time excluding *went* due to its exceptional status.

Because *went* has been coded separately in the data file already, re-coding of the condition file to exclude it is simple. This is accomplished by using the NIL function of the LISP syntax in the condition file, by adding the code for *went* to the other re-codes for exclusions at the beginning of the condition file, as in (5). Note the annotation in the comment line. This serves to remind the analyst the reason for this re-code and to document this for future reference.

```
(5)
; 'went'
(NIL (col 5 W)))
;N = 89, 99% retained, exceptional
```

A binomial analysis with *went* removed produces a new error value and log likelihood as in (6). The full results file, VRA_results-2.doc, can be found on the companion website.

(6)
Binomial analysis, variable (t,d), *went* removed

Cell	Total	App'ns	Expected	Error
NOM	59	27	38.225	9.360

Log likelihood = −456.766

Notice that the error for the cell 'NOM' is now somewhat reduced. Comparison of the log likelihood across runs shows that when *went* is removed the log is closer to 0 at −456.766, thus somewhat improved from the earlier run at −482.431. This indicates that this run is a better fit of the model to the data. As such it can be construed as the better analysis. However, the error remains quite high. We may wonder if all nasal + alveolar clusters may be behaving uniquely in this way. Ongoing research may well take up exploration of this conjecture and analyse variable (t,d) in more detail, from the perspective of experimental phonetics (e.g. Temple 2003).

Tip

Notice how useful it was to have coded *went* separately. In virtually every analysis I do, I include a factor group for the lexical item. If the study is on verbs, each verb is coded separately. If the study is on adjectives, each adjective is coded separately (see Appendix D on the companion website). Of course there will always be highly infrequent lexical items; these may be collapsed into one group.

SCATTERGRAMS

Scattergrams represent the fit of the model to the data graphically. Points near the line have a good fit. Points near the diagonal corners have a bad fit. Further, 'the size of each point is proportional to the number of tokens in the corresponding cell(s), so that a large point far from the diagonal suggests interaction among its factors' (Rand and Sankoff 1990: 24). In (7) you see the scattergram associated with the binomial one-step analysis we saw earlier in (1), where *went* was included. The log likelihood is −482.431. The cells hover on or near the line of best fit, with the occasional out-lier. One of these is the problematic cell 'NOM'. It is the largest square to the left of the diagonal line.

(7)

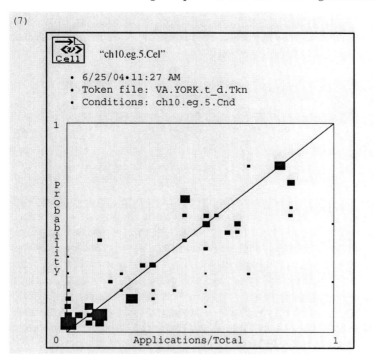

MORE ON LOG LIKELIHOOD

The log likelihood is a measure of the fit of the model to the data. A 'trick' that David Sankoff once showed me provides a good illustration of how the log likelihood measure works. Here is the method in a nutshell: 1) Run the data in a binomial one-step analysis; 2) find the cells with the highest error; 3) go to the cell file and remove the cells of this type (simply cut-and-paste that bit out of the cell file); 4) re-run the data. Watch the log likelihood improve. For example, in the analysis in (1) the log likelihood was −482.431. By removing the lexical item *went* the log likelihood improved to −456.766. If I now remove the same cell 'NOM', which now has applications = 22 and non-applications = 27, as in lines (8a–b) below, then save the cell file and re-run the data, an even better log likelihood is produced, −399.914 as in (8c). Examine the binomial one-step results once again. The greatest error you will find now, in the cell with the most data, is (9a). If I now go to the cell file and remove the cell again, lines (9a–b), and re-run the data, I end up with a run with a log likelihood improved again, at −390.319, as in (9c). Notice that, as we progressively improve the data (by removing the errors), the log likelihood gets closer and closer to 0.

```
(8)
a. NOM  49  22  32.229  9.485
b. 22  27
   NOM
c. Log likelihood = −399.914
```

```
(9)
a. NOP  11  5  7.792  3.431
b. 5  6
   NOP
c. Log likelihood = −390.319
```

Of course, this is silly. No one would ever doctor data like this. In fact, reviewers of this book admonished me not to even tell you how to do it. They said this knowledge was way too dangerous! Therefore, I emphasise that I include it here only as an exercise in helping you understand how the variable rule program functions. Indeed, I encourage you to play around with the program. It is quite informative to test out different analyses of your data like this in order to understand just how it all works. Run your data one way; run it another way. What happens if you exclude this? What happens if you exclude that? And so on. I could go on and on removing the problematic cells, but that would not advance the best explanation of variable (t,d) in these data. In other words, you should only pursue honing the data so far. In the end you must adhere to the cardinal rule of variation analysis: statistical analysis must be informed by linguistic insights.

Note

The more factor groups you put into an analysis, the bigger the log likelihood. A run with only two or three factor groups might produce a log likelihood of −456.24. A run with six factor groups might produce a log likelihood of −1456.24.

The one-step analysis does not assess statistical significance or relative strength of the factor groups. For this reason, most analyses use the step-up/step-down regression analysis. Indeed, this has become the 'gold standard' in variationist sociolinguistics.

STEP-UP/STEP-DOWN ANALYSIS

The same data can be run using the conditions as in (1), by selecting the binomial step-up/step-down option from the drop-down menu. The full results file is shown in (10). Attempt to understand each stage (level) of the analysis and what is going on with the combination of factor groups at each level to fully appreciate the analysis. Refer to Chapter 7 for a technical discussion. Then read through the regression as it steps up and down.

```
(10)
● BINOMIAL VARBRUL ● 6/25/04 ● 12:23 PM ●●●●●●●●●●●●●●●●●●●●●●●●
Name of cell file: ch10.eg.6.Cel

Using fast, less accurate method.
Averaging by weighting factors.
Threshold, step-up/down: 0.050001

Stepping Up ...
- - - - - - - Level #0 - - - - - - -

Run #1, 1 cells:
Iterations: 1 2
Convergence at Iteration 2
Input 0.254
Lo~ likelihood = −649.027

- - - - - - Level #1 - - - - - - -

Run #2, 5 cells:
Iterations: 1 2 3 4 5
Convergence at Iteration 5
Input 0.241
Group #1 -- N: 0.462, L: 0.462, F: 0.297, S: 0.676, P: 0.375
Log likelihood = −617.069 Significance = 0.000)

Run #3, 6 cells:
Iterations: 1 2 3 4 5
Convergence at Iteration 5
Input 0.189
```

Group #2 -- V: 0.291, O: 0.888, G: 0.727, Q: 0.200, L: 0.575, R: 0.620
Log likelihood = −479.576 Significance = 0.000

Run #4, 3 cells:
Iterations: 1 2 3 4
Convergence at Iteration 4
Input 0.251
Group #3 -- M: 0.561, P: 0.417, A: 0.453
Log likelihood = −641.120 Significance = 0.000
Add Group #2 with factors VOGQLR

− − − − − − −Level #2 − − − − − − −

Run #5, 29 cells:
Iterations: 1 2 3 4 5 6
Convergence at Iteration 6
Input 0.179
Group #1 – N: 0.492, L: 0.398, F: 0.294, S: 0.669, P: 0.382
Group #2 – V: 0.299, O: 0.891, G: 0.698, Q: 0.193, L: 0.499, R: 0.610
Log likelihood = −458.297 Significance = 0.000

Run #6, 18 cells:
Iterations: 1 2 3 4 5 6
Convergence at Iteration 6
Input 0.186
Group #2 -- V: 0.295, O: 0.891, G: 0.720, Q: 0.185, L: 0.549, R: 0.630
Group #3 -- M: 0.572, P: 0.418, A: 0.400
Log likelihood = −472.222 Significance = 0.001
Add Group #1 with factors NLFSP

− − − − − − −Level #3 − − − − − − −

Run #7, 72 cells:
Iterations: 1 2 3 4 5 6 7
Convergence at Iteration 7
Input 0.178
Group #1 -- N: 0.474, L: 0.398, F: 0.317, S: 0.662, P: 0.414
Group #2 -- V: 0.300, O: 0.891, G: 0.695, Q: 0.192, L: 0.486, R: 0.614
Group #3 -- M: 0.534, P: 0.443, A: 0.508
Log likelihood = −456.766 Significance = 0.219

No remaining groups significant

Groups selected while stepping up: 2 1
Best stepping-up run: #5
- -
Stepping Down ...
− − − − − − −Level #3 − − − − − − −

Run #8, 72 cells:
Iterations: 1 2 3 4 5 6 7
Convergence at Iteration 7
Input 0.178
Group #1 -- N: 0.474, L: 0.398, F: 0.317, S: 0.662, P: 0.414
Group #2 -- V: 0.300, O: 0.891, G: 0.695, Q: 0.192, L: 0.486, R: 0.614
Group #3 -- M: 0.534, P: 0.443, A: 0.508
Log likelihood = −456.766

```
- - - - - - - - - Level #2 - - - - - - -
Run #9, 18 cells:
Iterations: 1 2 3 4 5 6
Convergence at Iteration 6
Input 0.186
Group #2 -- V: 0.295, O: 0.891, G: 0.720, Q: 0.185, L: 0.549, R: 0.630
Group #3 -- M: 0.572, P: 0.418, A: 0.400
Log likelihood = -472.222 Significance = 0.000

Run #10, 15 cells:
Iterations: 1 2 3 4 5
Convergence at Iteration 5
Input 0.240
Group #1 -- N: 0.445, L: 0.459, F: 0.316, S: 0.672, P: 0.405
Group #3 -- M: 0.530, P: 0.441, A: 0.531
Log likelihood = -614.677 Significance = 0.000

Run #11, 29 cells:
Iterations: 1 2 3 4 5 6
Convergence at Iteration 6
Input 0.179
Group #1 -- N: 0.492, L: 0.398, F: 0.294, S: 0.669, P: 0.382
Group #2 -- V: 0.299, O: 0.891, G: 0.698, Q: 0.193, L: 0.499, R: 0.610
Log likelihood = -458.297 Significance = 0.219

Cut Group #3 with factors MPA
- - - - - - - - - Level #1 - - - - - - -

Run #12, 6 cells:
Iterations: 1 2 3 4 5
Convergence at Iteration 5
Input 0.189
Group #2 -- V: 0.291, O: 0.888, G: 0.727, Q: 0.200, L: 0.575, R: 0.620
Log likelihood = -479.576 Significance = 0.000

Run #13, 5 cells:
Iterations: 1 2 3 4 5
Convergence at Iteration 5
Input 0.241
Group #1 -- N: 0.462, L: 0.462, F: 0.297, S: 0.676, P: 0.375
Log likelihood = -617.069 Significance = 0.000

All remaining groups significant

Groups eliminated while stepping down: 3
Best stepping-up run: #5
Best stepping-down run: #11
Execution time: 0 min, 3.7 sec
```

The best fit of the model to the data is contained in the best stepping-up run, Run #5, bolded, while the best stepping-down run was, Run #11. This information is recorded at the end of the regression as well. The best stepping-up and the best stepping-down run should be identical.

According to Sankoff (1988c), if the factor groups are sufficiently non-orthogonal and any interaction or distributional problems are being handled by the program in an adequate manner, we should observe the following. As the regression progresses from the individual factor groups to the combinations of two, three, four and more, the factor weights associated with each factor should fluctuate only minimally as the regression steps up and steps down. This is exactly what the analysis reveals: the factor weights for each factor at each level fluctuate just a little. Convergence is reached for each run in fewer than twenty iterations – the maximum set by the program. The step-up and step-down analyses match. Ta-da! You have a good analysis of your data.

However, variable rule analyses are not always so straightforward. If factor groups are overlapping, interactive, or cells sizes across factor groups are widely diverging or even empty, the analysis will be compromised.

SPOTTING INTERACTION

When the model provided to the variable rule program is less than ideal, the step-up/step-down analysis will reveal these problematic overlaps in the data, thus providing a means to identify interaction.

Here is a checklist of things you should look for:

* What are the base-line factor weights for each factor group, i.e. the probability of each category of a factor group when it is considered on its own (Level 1)?
* How do the factor weights in each factor group compare to each other as the regression builds, testing first two, then three, then four and more factor groups together? In other words, how do the factor weights compare across levels of the analysis?
* If the factor weights for a factor fluctuate, ask yourself by how much. In other words, do they vary, but maintain the same constraint ranking? Does the constraint ranking between shift from one run to another? In what way?

These are the types of questions that will enable you to troubleshoot the analysis.

A example with interacting internal factors

The best example I know of for demonstrating problematic interaction comes from an analysis of variable (s) for plural marking in Nigerian Pidgin English (Tagliamonte et al. 1997), as in (11). In this variety plural nouns are sometimes marked with [s], as in (11a) and sometimes not, as in (11b):

(11)
a. Na de wey **got** de slip. (09/955)
  'That's where goats sleep.'
b. Wi gɛt **frɛns** wey wi de cɔmɔt ɔl di taim. (01/647)
  'We have friends that we go out with all the time.'

We tested a number of internal factors conditioning this variability, including preceding and following phonological segment, animacy, type of nominal reference and type of determiner. The problem was that two of the internal factors were highly interactive. Consider the cross-tabulation in (12), which shows you the intersection between type of nominal reference (generic, 'G', indefinite, 'I', and definite, 'D') and type of determiner (undetermined, 'U', demonstrative determiner, 'D', definite article, 'T', partitive determiner, 'P', numeric quantifier, 'N', other quantifier, 'Q').

```
(12)
 • CROSS-TABULATION • 6/26/04 • 11:38 AM ••••••••••••••••••••••••••••••
 • Cell file:  VA.ch10.NPEpl.Cel
 • 6/26/04•11:38 AM
 • Token file: NPEplu[10/12/93].Tkn
 • Conditions: VA.ch10.NPEpl.Cnd

Group #3 -- horizontally

Group #4 -- vertically
```

		U	%	D	%	P	%	T	%	N	%	Q	%	Σ	%
G	0:	165	46:	0	--:	0	--:	14	82:	0	--:	0	--|	179	48
	-:	194	54:	0	--:	0	--:	3	18:	0	--:	0	--|	197	52
	Σ:	359	:	0	:	0	:	17	:	0	:	0	|	376	
I	0:	74	55:	43	45:	23	50:	23	52:	53	24:	31	30|	247	38
	-:	61	45:	52	55:	23	50:	21	48:	165	76:	74	70|	396	62
	Σ:	135	:	95	:	46	:	44	:	218	:	105	|	643	
D	0:	10	63:	21	31:	16	38:	45	35:	1	6:	1	50|	94	34
	-:	6	38:	46	69:	26	62:	83	65:	17	94:	1	50|	179	66
	Σ:	16	:	67	:	42	:	128	:	18	:	2	|	273	
Σ	0:	249	49:	64	40:	39	44:	82	43:	54	23:	32	30|	520	40
	-:	261	51:	98	60:	49	56:	107	57:	182	77:	75	70|	772	60
	Σ:	510	:	162	:	88	:	189	:	236	:	107	|	1292	

The cross-tabulation shows that the categories of reference and determination are inextricably linked. Notice the pattern of empty cells (the zeros), small cells and badly distributed data. Most nouns with indefinite reference are delimited by a quantifier, as in (13a), those with definite reference are delimited with a definite article, demonstrative or possessive pronoun, as in (13b), and, most dramatic, virtually all nouns with generic reference are undetermined, as in (13c). The fact that the two categories are so highly correlated amongst themselves makes it particularly difficult to disentangle the effects of reference and determination.

(13)
  a. I no wes laik *tu mɔns*, di bɔi mari. (09/1788)
     'The boy didn't waste like two months, he got married.'
  b. *Doz wɔns* wey de kɔm klʌb na gutaimas. (01/610)
     'The ones who come to the club are goodtimers.'
  c. Yu no az *tɔilet* de dey. (13/263)
     'You know how toilets are.'

When these two factor groups are run together in a multivariate, step-up/step-down analysis, what happens? Follow through the regression in (14), following the factor weights associated with generic reference ('G'). These have been highlighted in the regression for illustration purposes.

```
(14)
● BINOMIAL VARBRUL ● 6/26/04 ● 11:58 AM ●●●●●●●●●●●●●●●●●●●●●●
Name of cell file: VA.ch10.NPEpl.5Cnd.Cel

Using fast, less accurate method.
Averaging by weighting factors.
Threshold, step-up/down: 0.050001

Stepping Up...
- - - - - - - - - -Level #0 - - - - - - - - -

Run #1, 1 cells:
Iterations: 1 2
Convergence at Iteration 2
Input 0.409
Log likelihood = −898.324

- - - - - - - - -Level #1 - - - - - - - - -

Run #2, 7 cells:
Iterations: 1 2 3 4 5
Convergence at Iteration 5
Input 0.400
Group #1 -- U: 0.588, D: 0.501, P: 0.545, T: 0.536, N: 0.312, Q: 0.426
Log likelihood = −873.056 Significance = 0.000
```

Run #3, 3 cells:
Iterations: 1 2 3 4
Convergence at Iteration 4
Input 0.402
Group #2 -- G: 0.574, -: 0.470
Log likelihood = −892.389 Significance = 0.001

Add Group #1 with factors UDPTNQ
- - - - - - - - - Level #2 - - - - - - - - -

Run #4, 15 cells:
Iterations: 1 2 3 4 5 6 7 8 9
Convergence at Iteration 9
Input 0.398
Group #1 -- U: 0.594, D: 0.497, P: 0.541, T: 0.533, N: 0.308, Q: 0.421
Group #2 - - G: 0.489, -: 0.505
Log likelihood = −872.796 Significance = 0.479

No remaining groups significant

Groups selected while stepping up: 1
Best stepping-up run: #2
- -
Stepping Down ...
- - - - - - - - - Level #2 - - - - - - - - -

Run #5, 15 cells:
Iterations: 1 2 3 4 5 6 7 8 9
Convergence at Iteration 9
Input 0.398
Group #1 -- U: 0.594, D: 0.497, P: 0.541, T: 0.533, N: 0.308, Q: 0.421
Group #2 -- G: 0.489, -: 0.505
Log likelihood = −872.796

- - - - - - - - - Level #1 - - - - - - - - -

Run #6, 3 cells:
Iterations: 1 2 3 4
Convergence at Iteration 4
Input 0.402
Group #2 - - G: 0.574, -: 0.470
Log likelihood = −892.389 Significance = 0.000

Run #7, 7 cells:
Iterations: 1 2 3 4 5
Convergence at Iteration 5
Input 0.400
Group #1 -- U: 0.588, D: 0.501, P: 0.545, T: 0.536, N: 0.312, Q: 0.426
Log likelihood = −873.056 Significance = 0.479

Cut Group #2 with factors G-
- - - - - - - - - Level #0 - - - - - - - - -

Run #8, 1 cells:
Iterations: 1 2
Convergence at Iteration 2

```
Input 0.409
Log likelihood = −898.324 Significance = 0.000
All remaining groups significant
Groups eliminated while stepping down: 2
Best stepping-up run: #2
Best stepping-down run: #7
Execution time: 0 min, 2.0 sec
```

Considered by itself, in Run #3, the nominal reference factor group shows that generic nouns favour zero plural marking at .57 and non-generics disfavour at .47. However, when this factor group is combined with the factor group of type of determination, the factor weights flip around. In runs #4 and #5, generics disfavour zero plural marking.

The interaction between these two groups is so severe that the effects of reference and determination cannot be unsnarled. The way we opted to handle this problem in the analysis was to test two different configurations of the same data set, each one differing only with respect to one thing. In one analysis we tested the syntactic structure of the NP (syntax). In the other, we tested the referential status of the noun (semantics). This eliminates the effects of interaction. Then, we compared the log likelihood of the two runs to see if this would give us any insight into which factor provided the better explanation. As it turned, neither one was immensely better than the other (Tagliamonte et al. 1997: 117). Both factors are implicated in plural marking in Nigerian Pidgin English. Of course, in natural language overlaps and interactions are to be expected. Thus, although it is often said in the literature than external factors interact with each other, it is also possible that internal factors of language will be intertwined as well.

Tip

Perhaps the most challenging question students ask is: How do I decide which is the best analysis of the data? This is not a black and white question. It depends on how you want to tell the story. However, the story must be methodologically sound and linguistically insightful. And you must keep in mind that there are many ways to tell a good story!

SUMMARY

At a certain point, you must balance the goal of finding the best fit of the quantitative model with the qualitative/interpretative goal of finding the best explanation. The latter is what enables you to make sense of it all. After possibly hundreds of runs of the data, configuring the condition files one way, and then another, and then another, you will finally get to the point where you are ready to interpret it. This moment comes when you think you have figured out what it all means. In Chapter 11, I will discuss what to do then.

Exercise 10: Spotting interaction

In this exercise you will learn how to do cross-tabs. This is an exercise in being aware of your data. In the process you may spot interaction.

Using your most up-to-date condition files, do cross–tabs of each of the factor groups. How are the factor groups distributed vis-à-vis each other? Are they well distributed? Are they unevenly distributed? How? Which ones?

Are any of the factor groups interactive to the point of possibly interfering with each other? Which ones? Why?

Try running the variable rule program on your data including two (or more) factor groups you think might be interacting. What happens? Is there any evidence of interaction? In particular, identify the points at which interaction can be identified in the regression.

If there is evidence of strong interaction between two factor groups, they should not be run in the same analysis. Instead, consider alternative solutions:

* Run two separate analyses
* Conduct additional re-configuring using the condition file.

In the case of the former, you might decide to run one analysis with factor group A and another analysis with factor group B. Then you may see which of the two provides the better analysis of the data. Compare the log likelihood for each run. Which is better?

Print the results files. Annotate each factor group with the factors it represents. Make observations and interpretations for each.

Your aim is to arrive at a condition file (or several condition files) for your data that provides the most linguistically and methodologically justified configuration.

Add all these results/findings to your lab book.

11   Interpreting your results

How do I report my results?
This chapter will outline the method for reporting the results of a multi-variate analysis, including Ns, %s and Total Ns, corrected mean, selected factors, etc.

The foundation of variation analysis is its attempt to discover not individual occurrences, not even overall rates of occurrence, but patterns of variability in the body (or bodies) of material under investigation. To aid in the interpretation of these patterns there are a number of different lines of evidence which arise from the statistical modelling techniques of multivariate analysis.

THREE LINES OF EVIDENCE

There are three levels of evidence (Poplack and Tagliamonte 2001: 92, Tagliamonte 2002: 731) available for interpreting the results of variation analysis as performed by the step-up/step-down method of multiple regression: 1) statistical significance, i.e. Which factors are statistically significant at the .05 level and which are not? 2) relative strength, i.e. Which factor group is most significant (largest range) or least (smallest range)? 3) What is the order (from more to less) of factors within a linguistic feature (constraint hierarchy)? Finally, bringing in the interpretative component of variation analysis, 4) Does this order reflect the direction predicted by one or the other of the hypotheses being tested? Each of these bits of information can, and should, be used to build your argumentation about the linguistic variable. Similarities and differences in the significance, ordering of constraints and strength of contextual factors provide a microscopic view of the grammar of the data under investigation, from which you may infer the structure of different grammars.

STATISTICAL SIGNIFICANCE

A first assessment comes from whether or not a factor group is statistically significant. Given a set of factor groups which are tested in your analysis, which ones are statistically significant? Which are not? Significant factors as well as non-significant factors are important for interpreting the results. Significance of one or a set of specific factor groups may lead to one interpretation. Significance of another factor group (or set) may lead to another. Which set of factor groups are significant will have a major bearing on making a decision about the underlying system (or grammar) in a given data set. Take the results in (1), extracted from Poplack et al. (2000a: 97), which model variable plural (s) in Early African American English (ANSE) compared to Nigerian Pidgin English (NPE). Are the underlying systems the same?

(1)

Variable rule analysis of factors contributing to the probability of zero plural

	ANSE	NPE
Corrected mean	.34	.40
Total N	1353	1316
Animacy of the noun		
[−animate, −human]	[ ]	.54
[+animate, +human]	[ ]	.38
Type of nominal reference		
Generic	**.44**	.57
Non-generic	**.52**	.47
Preceding phonological context		
Non-sibilant consonant	[ ]	[ ]
Sibilant consonant	[ ]	[ ]
Vowel	[ ]	[ ]
Following phonological context		
Consonant	**.71**	[ ]
Vowel	**.41**	[ ]
Pause	**.46**	[ ]

Consider the factors which are significant (shown in bold) vs those that are not significant (shown as square brackets). These results can be interpreted as follows. 1) Animacy conditions the use of plural -s in NPR, but not ANSE. 2) Type of nominal reference operates in both.

However, the pattern contrasts NPE where generics favour zero and ANSE where zero is favoured for non-generics. Finally, 3) following phonological context operates in ANSE, but not in NPE. The conditioning of plural -*s* is visibly not the same in these two varieties and the contrast with respect to following phonological conditioning is telling. Therefore, although the form is the same, the underlying system that produces the variation is different.

Notice that we opted to report the non-significance of certain factors by using square brackets. This practice is sometimes adopted in the presentation of variable rule analysis results when the factor weights of non-significant factors are not relevant to the argumentation. More recently, researchers tend to display all the factor weights, regardless of significance, so that readers can use all the available information to interpret and understand the analysis.

Tip

Sometimes a student will tell me that he or she has removed a factor group because it was not significant. This is not the point. Its non-significance may be a key bit of evidence for your argumentation!

A note of caution is necessary. In some situations, statistical significance does not provide the best evidence for interpreting results. A data set with a larger number of tokens will tend to detect more factors to be statistically significant than one with fewer tokens. This means you should not compare the results of parallel analyses in two or more communities on the basis of significance alone (Poplack and Tagliamonte 2001: 93). In such cases, the more revealing measure is the constraint ranking.

CONSTRAINT RANKING

Constraint ranking is the hierarchy from more to less of the categories within a factor group. This provides a detailed model of the structure of the relationship between variant and linguistic context, or the 'grammar' underlying the variable surface manifestations (Poplack and Tagliamonte 2001: 94). Consider the factor weights for the factor group 'Grammatical category' for variable (ing), in (2). I have abstracted the information in the tables somewhat for illustration purposes. What does the constraint ranking tell you?

(2)
Variable (ing) York English

Probability of [n] for grammatical category

Grammatical category	Factor weight
Participle	.61
Gerund	.58
Adjective	.26
Noun	.19
Range	42

In (2) the ranking of constraints shows that verbal categories such as participles and gerunds favour the [n] variant while adjectives and nouns disfavour it, i.e. they favour the standard variant [ŋ]. Further, the two groups pattern with a notable divide between them. Given these results, variable (ing) in York has a linguistic explanation – it distinguishes major categories of the grammar.

The results from constraint ranking may also reveal the social relationship between variant and context. Consider the factor weights for the factor group 'Occupation' in (3), for variable (ing), and in (4) for variable (t,d). In both cases, the factor group is significant, but the patterns differ. What do the constraint rankings tell you?

(3)
Variable (ing) York English

Probability of [n] for occupation

Occupation	Factor weight
Blue collar	.60
Student	.57
White collar	.44
Professional/managerial	.44
Range	28
Ch_11.eg2.Cnd 9/17/04	

(4)
Variable (t,d) York English

Probability of [ø] for occupation

Occupation	Factor weight
Blue collar	.42
Student	.55

White collar	.54
Professional/managerial	.53
Range	*13*
t,d.ch 12.social class.Cnd	

In (3) the ranking of constraints shows students and blue-collar workers favour the [n] variant, while white-collar and professional/managerial workers favour the standard variant [ŋ]. Moreover, there is a visible divide between these two groups. The factor weights are higher and close together for the former, and low and identical for the latter. Given these results, variable (ing) in York can be interpreted as a sociolinguistic marker. The results for variable (t,d) in (4) show a slightly different picture. Here blue-collar workers are distinguished from all other categories in favouring the non-standard variant, [Ø]. The others pattern similarly, favouring the realised variant with approximately the same probability. This suggests that variable (ing) is not only a working-class marker, because it is favoured among the younger college-educated population. On the other hand, variable (t,d) does appear to mark social class because in this case the break in the population is between blue-collar workers and all others. This comparison of the constraint ranking of the same factor group *across* variables reveals additional evidence to explain the individual variables.

The constraint ranking of factors within a factor group, as well as the direction of their effects, are predicted to remain constant regardless of extralinguistic circumstances (Poplack and Tagliamonte 2001: 92). Thus, in a situation of stable variability you can expect parallel constraint rankings of internal factors across external factors. Such a hypothesis is confirmed in (5), where the results for one of the linguistic factor groups, following phonological segment, has been run separately for blue- and white-collar workers. Notice that, although the actual values for the factor weights are slightly different, the constraint rankings are parallel.

(5)

Variable (t,d) in York

Probability of [t,d] by following phonological segment and occupation		
Factor group	Blue collar	White collar
Input	.87	.76
Following phonological segment	Factor weight	Factor weight
Pause	.78	.85
Vowel	.77	.70

Liquids, glides	.25	.33
Obstruent	.11	.10
Range	67	75
ch12.white_2.Cnd; ch12.blue_2.Cnd		

(6)
Variable (ing) in York

Probability of [ŋ] for grammatical category and education

Factor group	More educated	Less educated
Input	.35	.33
Grammatical category	Factor weight	Factor weight
Noun	.77	.82
Adjective	.73	.78
Participle	.43	.38
Gerund	.38	.43
Range	39	39
ch12.−edu.Cnd; ch12.+edu.Cnd		

In (6), there is little to distinguish speakers of different education levels as far as their use of variable (ing) is concerned. While the ranking of participles and gerunds shifts, the major division between disfavouring factors remains. Moreover, participles and gerunds pattern similarly in both groups in contrast to nouns and adjectives.

Even when contrasting data sets of different sizes, with varying frequencies of forms, the patterns of use, even in the smaller data set, will tend to be relatively stable. Indeed, the hierarchy of constraints constituting each factor is taken to represent the variable grammar (Poplack and Tagliamonte 2001: 93). This is why this evidence is so important.

CONSTRAINT HIERARCHY AND UNIVERSALS

The constraint hierarchy serves as an important check in controlling for language universals. Universals entail constancy across language varieties. Parallels across form, frequency and constraints would lead to such an interpretation. Conversely, if two varieties do *not* share the same constraint hierarchies, then universals have effectively been ruled out. Consider again the results presented in (1), but now look at the constraint ranking of the factor group 'Type of nominal reference', repeated below in (7).

(7)		
Variable(s) in ANSE and NPE		
Probability of zero plural		
	ANSE	NPE
Type of nominal reference		
Generic	.44	.57
Non-generic	.52	.47

Notice that, although the same factor group is selected as significant in both varieties, the constraint hierarchy is different. This suggests that the underlying mechanism producing the surface form is different in ANSE and NPE, at least with respect to this factor. But what about if a variable rule analysis contains several different factor groups?

The results for each factor group in an analysis contribute information that can be used to interpret the results. For example, if a number of factor groups exhibit dissimilarities across varieties, then their variable grammars are more likely to be distinct. Each element of dissimilarity increases the chances that the results could not have arisen coincidentally. This is another reason why you should use all the bits of information in your analysis to interpret and explain your results.

Note

What is the difference between frequency and pattern? Frequency is simply the rate of variant occurrence. 'Pattern' refers to the hierarchy of the factors which make up a factor group, i.e. how they are ordered by factor weight from more to less. Frequency may fluctuate due to any number of (non-linguistic) factors; however, patterns are expected to stay constant. This is why proportional analysis must be used with caution when inferring differences among data sets, particularly those already disparate in terms of collection procedures, interviewer technique and a host of other factors.

CONSTRAINT RANKING AND ORIGINS

The constraint hierarchy can also be used to assess the relationship and provenance of forms. Patterns can serve to identify varieties. Parallels in such patterns across varieties reveal the similarities of their grammars. Conversely, if two varieties do *not* share the same constraint hierarchies, then such kinship may been ruled out, at least for the linguistic variable under analysis. This is why, based in part on the results in (1), we concluded that, although ANSE and NPE share the same plural markers (in this case the variants -s and zero), their unique functions are evidence for the distinctness of the two varieties' grammars. In NPE, the tendency for the -s suffix to appear on generic nouns probably derives from Igbo, the L1 of most of our informants, where these types of nouns are singled out for plural marking. In this way, the evidence from constraint ranking is particularly important for identifying the nature (origins and provenance) of varieties (e.g. Poplack 2000, Poplack and Tagliamonte 2001).

RELATIVE STRENGTH

The last line of evidence comes from the relative strength exerted by a factor group in an analysis of variation. Strength is measured by the 'range', which is then compared with the ranges of the other significant factor groups. The range is calculated by subtracting the lowest factor weight from the highest factor weight. When these numbers are compared for each of the factor groups in an analysis, the highest number (i.e. range) identifies the strongest constraint. The lowest number identifies the weakest constraint, and so forth. The range (or magnitude of effect) enables you to situate factor groups with respect to each other. It can also be used to compare the variable grammar of linguistic features across analyses.

Relative strength across varieties

The magnitude of factors is particularly important when you are comparing the variable grammar of a linguistic feature across a number of varieties. If the relative strength of factors is parallel across comparative data sets, then this adds to the interpretation of similarity. If the relative strength is different, then this adds to the interpretation of difference.

For example, in a study of variable (t,d) across five varieties (Poplack and Tagliamonte 2001) – 'SE' (Samana English), 'ESR' (Ex-Slave Recordings), 'NPR' (North Preston), 'GYE' (Guysborough Enclave) and 'GYV' (Guysborough Village) – we demonstrated that phonological factors were the very strongest constraints. For illustration purposes, the table in (8) displays the range values only abstracted from Poplack and Tagliamonte (2001: 124, table 6.2). The 'n/s' means that the factor group was not significant.

(8)

Relative strength of factors to the probability of stem weak verbs; range values only

	SE	ESR	NPR	GYE	GYV
Preceding phonological segment	55	41	38	27	65
Following phonological segment	36	49	60	43	51
Temporal disambiguation	23	n/s	29	21	37
Verbal aspect	16	n/s	16	17	6
Stativity/anteriority	n/s	n/s	n/s	n/s	n/s

Notice that the strength of the phonological factors far exceeds either temporal disambiguation or verbal aspect. This bit of evidence from the relative strength of factors was one of the many 'bits' of evidence we used to support our contention that these varieties had an underlying system in which the suffix (t,d) of the English past tense was part of the grammar. In other words, comparison of the relative magnitude of these effects motivates the claim that zero realisations result primarily from the phonological process of consonant cluster simplification (in contrast to creoles, where aspectual factors would be predicted to prevail). In both cases, the factor is part of the variable grammar, but it is much stronger in one than the other.

You may have noticed that the ranking of the two phonological factors vis-à-vis each other differs across varieties. In SE and GYV preceding phonological environment is strongest, but in ESR, NPR and GYE following phonological segment is strongest. We did not explore this finding. However, in other analyses such differences may be critical to the explanation. In some cases, for example, a factor group may operate at varying strengths across varieties. Why? Such a result can sometimes be used to argue that the varieties under investigation represent different stages in the development of the particular system of grammar under investigation. For example, in a study of variable (gonna) (Poplack and Tagliamonte 2001), we demonstrated the widely divergent strengths of the same set of factors across varieties. Why would this happen? Each variety represented a different stage in ongoing grammatical change, in this case toward increasing use of *going to* to mark future temporal reference.

The study was based on five varieties which could be differentiated, in part, by their degree of participation in mainstream developments. In the table in (9), these varieties are ordered by degree of isolation, from those with enclave status ('SE', 'NPR' and 'GYE'); to the rural variety ('GYV'), to the mainstream variety, Ottawa English 'OTT'. We interpreted the results in terms of the progress of each variety along the developmental path of *going to*. Where a factor group incorporates early constraints, as in the case of animacy, we can assess whether these have been neutralised or continue to be reflected in the variety in question. Other measures (e.g. grammatical person) reveal further developments, and we can also determine which varieties participate in these.

The table in (9) displays the range values of factors abstracted from Poplack and Tagliamonte (2001). What does the strength of each factor, in each variety, tell us? (ESR was not included here, due to small Ns.)

(9)

Relative strength of factors to the probability of *going to*; Range values only				
Early African American English			Rural	Mainstream
SE	NPR	GYE	GYV	OTT
Point of reference				
Range 41	46	43	22	52
Type of clause				
Range 10	22	24	12	7
Animacy of subject				
Range 1	2	3	2	11
Grammatical person				
Range 0	2	15	8	23
Lexical content				
Range 22	21	19	29	1
Proximity in the future				
Range 4	3	5	21	16

First, point of reference contributes a strong (if not the strongest) statistically significant effect across the board. Second, the importance of type of clause is minimal in mainstream OTT. This suggests that this factor is weakening. Third, the animacy distinction, once thought to constrain the use of *going to*, is neutralised in each of the African-origin varieties as well as in rural GYV. The range values are very low. In mainstream OTT, on the other hand, this factor is comparatively strong. This innovation is not shared by the other communities. Fourth, the grammatical person constraint, weak in the enclave communities, is much strengthened in OTT. Fifth, with regard to lexical verb, the opposite trend is observed. The effect weakens. In OTT, its strength is negligible. Finally, with regard to proximity in the future, you observe strengthening of the constraint in the more mainstream communities,

GYV and OTT. In sum, the range values indicate contrasting 'waves' of development – as indicated by the shifting weights of the constraints operating on the use of *going to* in these varieties. In other words, the range helps to determine the location of each variety along a trajectory of change that is ongoing in the language.

In summary, the three lines of evidence (statistical significance, constraint ranking and relative strength of factors) combine to give the analyst a remarkably rich set of findings from which to build his or her argumentation. The relevant questions to ask are:

1. Which factors are statistically significant?
2. What is the relative contribution of the linguistic features selected, i.e. which factor group is most significant (largest range) or least (smallest range)?
3. What is the order (from more to less) of factors within a linguistic feature (constraint hierarchy)?
4. Crucially, does this order reflect the direction predicted by one or the other of the hypotheses being tested?

THE COMPARATIVE METHOD

One of the interesting aspects of variation analysis is its utility for making comparisons and reconstructing origins using 'the comparative method' (Poplack and Tagliamonte 2001). In historical linguistics it is widely held that earlier stages of a language can be observed through comparative analysis of cognate forms in later, related varieties (e.g. Hoenigswald 1960: 119, Meillet 1967). The comparative method is 'the procedure whereby morphs of two or more sister languages are matched in order to reconstruct the ancestor language' (Hoenigswald 1960: 119). In comparative sociolinguistics, the means by which the sister varieties are compared is the detailed information arising from the lines of evidence from variation analysis. In fact, the quantitative paradigm provides the kind of 'precise information on the states of the language' called for by Meillet (1967: 138). Doing comparative sociolinguistics means making a consistent comparison of each of the lines of evidence, but with the addition of two or more relevant bodies of material to compare and/or contrast. The target of investigation will typically be varieties of a language, e.g. dialects, but the comparison might also involve different age groups in a single community, different speakers interviewed at different points in time or even different stages of acquisition.

ORIGINS

Variation analysis is also useful for tracing the history and origins of varieties. However, an important question is: What type of evidence is relevant? Simple presence of the same surface form in two varieties is not enough, because the form may function differently from one to the other. The overall frequency of a feature across varieties is not enough because the rates of presence or absence of variants will vary according to features of the situation (Poplack and Tagliamonte 1991: 318). However, the pattern of variants within factor groups provide the right type of evidence. This is because precisely where a variant occurs in the language, as determined by the relative frequency of the feature across its different contexts of use – the constraint ranking – is something endemic to the variety and should stay constant regardless of the external situation. The environmental constraints (i.e. the factor effects) on variation are thought to be the fundamental units of linguistic change (Labov 1982: 75). Through the evidence from the various statistical techniques of the variable rule program, we can 'trace the path of linguistic development through a multidimensional space'. Indeed, the systematic patterned use of variants is taken to represent the underlying grammatical structure.

According to Poplack and Tagliamonte (1991: 318), determining the precise historical origins of a linguistic feature requires at least two bits of evidence: 1) existence of similar or identical features in the putative source dialect; and 2) the same hierarchy of constraints conditioning its appearance.

INTERPRETING SIMILARITIES AND DIFFERENCES

Similarities and differences across two or more data sets can be assessed by comparing the patterning of variability in each one. If the direction of effects of a factor group is shared by the varieties under investigation, this can be evidence that the variant under study does the same grammatical work in each variety. Further, if the direction of effect of a factor group is shared by varieties, and the effect is not universal, this can be evidence that the varieties have inherited that constraint from a common source. On the other hand, where there are dissimilarities, this can be grounds for concluding that the phenomena in question belong to different linguistic systems.

The next step is to present your findings informatively.

REPORTING YOUR RESULTS

In the last few chapters I have reviewed distributional analysis and variable rule analysis. The next question is how to report them. Your audience must be able to tell if the findings for the factor groups being presented were the significant ones, the strongest ones, or the only ones that had been included in the analysis. Further, how significant were they? What were the Ns per cell? What was the total number of contexts considered? One of the most important axioms of variationist analysis is to provide sufficient information to ensure replicability.

I will now itemise precisely how to get from a variable rule analysis to the types of tables you see in *Language Variation and Change*, the leading journal of the field.

VARIABLE RULE ANALYSIS IN TABLE FORMAT

Variable rule analyses are typically reported in table format, as in (10), which illustrates the components necessary for optimal interpretation of the findings.

(10)

Multivariate analyses of the contribution of internal and external factors selected as significant to the probability of [t,d] deletion; factor groups not selected as significant in square brackets

		Contemporary British English	
Corrected mean			.17
Log likelihood			−430.787
Total N			1232
	Factor weight	%	N
Following phonological segment			
Obstruent	.83	52	357
Glide	.70	37	111
/r/	.60	25	32
/l/	.50	23	26
Vowel	.30	8	570
Pause	.20	5	136
Range	63		
Preceding phonological segment			
Sibilant	.69	40	367
Nasal	.45	17	439
Liquid	.43	21	130
Stop	.43	16	169

Non-sibilant fricative	.29	12	127
Range	*40*		
Morphological class			
Monomorpheme, e.g. *mist*	[.53]	26	716
Irregular past, e.g. *kept*	[.50]	21	128
Regular past, e.g. *missed*	[.45]	19	388
Speaker sex			
Male	.59	30	484
Female	.44	22	634
Range	*15*		
Speaker age			
14–24	[.45]	24	375
35–44	[.54]	24	272
55–64	[.55]	27	262
75–84	[.48]	27	209

First, label the table with a title that describes the data being analysed and, importantly, the application value – in this case, [Ø], the absence of a final consonant in a word-final cluster. Second, make sure that readers can interpret from the table which factor groups have been included. This is the essence of variable rule analysis, modelling the simultaneous effects of cross-cutting factors. Third, provide a clear indication of which of these factor groups have been selected as significant and which have not. Ideally the factor groups should appear in the table with the strongest factor group at the top of the table, and thereafter the factor groups should be listed in decreasing order of strength. Within each factor group, the factor with the highest contribution to the rule should appear first, and thereafter the factors ordered in decreasing order of strength. Fourth, record for each factor: 1) the value of the probability rounded to two decimal places, 2) the proportion, i.e. the per cent, and 3) the number of contexts per cell, i.e. the Ns per cell. Finally, provide the total number of contexts treated in the analysis, i.e. the total number or total N and the corrected mean, or input. Other features may be included as well, as long as they form part of the discussion: the value measuring the strength of each factor group, i.e. the range, the log likelihood, etc.

You may be wondering where all this information came from. To produce a variable rule analysis table you need to refer to the marginal results as well as the output of the multiple regression. Example (11) below contains the marginal results. Example (10) in Chapter 10 (page 226) has the regression. Refer to both of these in order to understand where the information in the variable rule analysis table in (10) has come from. I have labelled the locations of the relevant information in (11) below in angled brackets, numerically ordered.

(11)
    ● CELL CREATION ● 6/26/04 ● 9:01 AM
    Name of token file:
    VA.YORK.t_d.Tkn
    Name of condition file:
    ch10.eg.11.Cnd
    [condition file removed for illustration]
      Number of cells: 534
    <1> Application value(s) : 0
    Total no. of factors: 27
    <2>

Group		Apps	Non-apps	Total	%
1 (new)					
L	N	27	100	**127**	11
	%	**21**	79	**<5>**	
		<4>			
F	N	15	112	127	11
	%	12	88		
N	N	68	262	330	29
	%	21	79		
S	N	146	221	367	33
	%	40	60		
P	N	27	142	169	15
	%	16	84		
Total	N	283	837	1120	
	%	25	75		
2 (new)					
O	N	173	91	264	24
	%	66	34		
V	N	49	521	570	51
	%	9	91		
G	N	40	66	106	9
	%	38	62		
Q	N	7	120	127	11
	%	6	94		
L	N	6	18	24	2
	%	25	75		
R	N	8	21	29	3
	%	28	72		
Total	N	283	837	1120	
	%	25	75		
3 (5)					
M	N	180	422	602	54
	%	30	70		
P	N	75	314	389	35
	%	19	81		

A	N	28	101	129	12
	%	22	78		
Total	N	283	837	1120	
	%	25	75		

4 (new)

F	N	138	497	635	57
	%	22	78		
M	N	145	340	485	43
	%	30	70		
Total	N	283	837	1120	
	%	25	75		

5 (new)

5	N	71	191	262	23
	%	27	73		
1	N	90	285	375	33
	%	24	76		
3	N	65	208	273	24
	%	24	76		
7	N	57	153	210	19
	%	27	73		
Total	N	283	837	1120	
	%	25	75		

6 (new)

−	N	192	537	729	69
	%	26	74		
+	N	84	249	333	31
	%	25	75		
Total	N	276	786	1062	
	%	26	74		

7 (new)

L	N	82	191	273	27
	%	30	70		
M	N	112	393	505	50
	%	22	78		
S	N	14	53	67	7
	%	21	79		
P	N	24	88	112	11
	%	21	79		
W	N	23	29	52	5
	%	44	56		
Total	N	255	754	1009	
	%	25	75		

TOTAL	N	283	837	**1120**	
	%	25	75	**<3>**	

Application value

The application value is found at < 1 > at the top of the marginals. Thereafter, applications and non-applications appear in the header for the tables, at < 2 >. The total number of contexts in the analysis appears at the end of marginal data, as total N, 1120, at < 3 >. For the proportion of each factor in each factor group, select the percentage under the applications column, at < 4 >, where '21' appears just above it. 21 per cent is the proportion of use of /l/ out of the total number of contexts of /l/, which is 127, just above < 5 >. In other words, 27/127. Continue in this way through the proportion results for each of the factors, for each of the factor groups, in the marginal data.

Factor weights, log likelihood, range

The groups selected while stepping up are the significant factors. The groups eliminated while stepping down are the non-significant factors. The former is listed at the end of the stepping-up part of the regression, while the latter is listed at the end of the stepping down, as in (12). These two should match.

```
(12)
Groups selected while stepping up: 2 1 7 4
Best stepping-up run: #21
Groups eliminated while stepping down: 3 6 5
Best stepping-up run: #21
Best stepping-down run: #44
```

The factor weights for significant factors presented in the variable rule analysis table are obtained from the best stepping-up run. The best stepping-up run for the binomial step-up/step-down analysis for the marginals produced in (11) is Run #21, reproduced here as (13). The input, or corrected mean, is listed as .167. This value is often rounded to two decimal places, i.e. .17. The factor weights for each factor group are listed for each factor according to its code. The log likelihood appears just below, along with the significance. The range values for each factor group are obtained by subtracting the lowest factor weight from the highest factor weight.

Note

The range value is not a factor weight. It is simply a number and should not appear with a decimal.

```
(13)
Run #21, 206 cells:
Iterations: 1 2 3 4 5 6 7
Convergence at Iteration 7
Input 0.167
Group #1 - - L: 0.386, F: 0.285, N: 0.491, S: 0.675, P: 0.383
Group #2 - - O: 0.901, V: 0.300, G: 0.684, Q: 0.174, L: 0.508,
            R: 0.631
Group #4 - - F: 0.455, M: 0.559
Group #7 - - L: 0.591, M: 0.441, S: 0.413, P: 0.493, W: 0.706
Log likelihood = −430.787 Significance = 0.024
```

Non-significant factors

If you wish to include the factor weights for the non-significant factors in your table, these can be obtained from the first iteration of the step-down analysis where all the factors are forced into the regression. This is Run #27, as reproduced in (14).

```
(14)
Stepping Down ...
- - - - - - - - - - - - Level #7 - - - - - - - - -
Run #27, 534 cells:
Iterations: 1 2 3 4 5 6 7 8 9 10 11 12 13 14 15 16 17 18 19 20
No Convergence at Iteration 20
Input 0.164
Group #1 - - L: 0.378, F: 0.302, N: 0.479, S: 0.668, P: 0.414
Group #2 - - O: 0.904, V: 0.298, G: 0.677, Q: 0.172, L: 0.510,
            R: 0.637
Group #3 - - M: 0.529, P: 0.447, A: 0.528
Group #4 - - F: 0.454, M: 0.560
Group #5 - - 5: 0.478, 1: 0.463, 3: 0.569, 7: 0.503
Group #6 - - -: 0.506, +: 0.487
Group #7 - - L: 0.588, M: 0.435, S: 0.444, P: 0.505, W: 0.714
Log likelihood = −427.215
```

The three factor groups which were not selected as significant are groups 3, 5 and 6, bolded in (14). Notice that the factor weights for these factors hover near .50, indicating that there is little tendency either way for these factors.

Turning back to the table, it now becomes evident what factor(s) explain variable (t,d) in York English. The factors which exert the strongest conditioning effect are preceding and following phonological segment, with the preceding context exerting nearly double the strength of the following segment. Further, a small, but significant effect is exerted by speaker sex: males favour the [Ø] form.

SUMMARY

There are many important 'bits' of information in a variation analysis. Each bit is like a nugget of gold for building a story about your linguistic variable. The bits relevant in one analysis may not be the same bits relevant in another, because this will depend on the nature of the linguistic variable and the data set(s) under investigation. However, every single bit that is useful should be deployed to support your argumentation. Indeed, the story of your variable should be discernible in your variable rule analysis tables; you have only to interpret it. This is the topic for the final chapter, Chapter 12.

Note

Experts in the field can simply gaze at the variable rule output of an analysis and know the story of the variable without ever having to listen to the presentation or read the paper. Make sure you get all the bits! If not, one of those experts is likely to point the missing ones out to you.

Exercise 11: Putting variable rule results into a table

Using the variable rule results from the analysis of your data that provides (one of) the best explanation(s) of your data, 'translate' the marginal data and multivariate analysis results into table format.
Use the following checklist:

* title of table, with application value clearly stated
* factor groups run in the analysis, selected as significant and not selected as significant indicated
* total number of tokens in the analysis (Total N)
* corrected mean/input
* listing of each factor, with factor weight (probability) to at least two decimal points
* listing of each factor's proportion and number in cell (Ns)
* range for each significant factor group

Once your results are in this format, gaze at them and try to understand what is going on. Are there ways you could improve the analysis? Are there anomalies that should be checked, fixed or redone another way? Make sure your table contains everything needed to understand your findings. If more is needed, pursue your analysis further. Remember to use every bit of relevant evidence in your tables to interpret the results.

12　Finding the story

What does it all mean?
　This chapter will discuss the relevant results for interpreting a variation analysis. What it all boils down to is 'finding the story'.

There comes a time when the analyses must stop. The marginal data has been honed to perfection. The multivariate analyses have been run enough. The results are as they are. Now it is time to pause and reflect, to interpret them.

The essential task is to understand and explain the nature of variability in a data set. What constrains it? What underlying mechanism produced it? What grammatical work is the variable doing in the grammar? If two (or more) data sets are being compared, do they share an underlying grammar? To what extent is their grammar shared and, if only to a certain extent, how far? Is the variable stable or is it implicated in linguistic change? Can the path of its linguistic development be traced through the variable grammar? Is it an innovation, a re-analysis or a retention?

By the time you have reached this point, and if you have completed each of the exercises in this book, most of the work is already done. You have articulated the issues and posed the questions. You have collected the data, constructed the corpus, discovered the variable, and circumscribed, extracted and coded it. You have gone through the many-layered procedures of analysis, re-analysis, honing and refining. You know your data inside out, every cross-tabulated cell of it. You have put your results into tables and pondered all the bits of information in them. You know what the patterns are, you know what the trends are, you know which factors are strong and which are weak. You have some ideas about why. But the hardest part of all is the point when you have to 'bite the bullet' and defend an explanation of how it all fits together.

I wish I could give you a checklist at this point which would tell you how to do this neatly and easily. But this part of the process is seldom straightforward and hardly ever easy. The next best thing is to tell you how to synthesise what you have already done and to provide you with a model with some examples from my own research.

WHAT IT ALL MEANS

Most variation analysis papers end with a discussion and/or a conclusion. The discussion section of a paper is the place where you pull the strings together, i.e. all the bits of information. The conclusion is where you extrapolate from the many strands of evidence and make a statement, not simply for the analysis at hand, but how it fits in with the rest, and where it takes off for the future. This important part of a variation analysis requires you to answer the question: What does it all mean?

WHAT DID YOU FIND?

Begin the discussion of your results by summarising what you have found. Part of this synopsis may involve reviewing the available evidence and the premises on which the arguments in the literature have been based, as in (1).

(1)
a. We begin by reviewing the available evidence . . . (Poplack and Tagliamonte 1989: 77)
b. In a number of independent analyses of three distinct variables . . . we have found . . . (Poplack and Tagliamonte 1991: 331)

Directly address whether previous arguments have been convincing. Do your findings negate them or bolster them? Identify which of your findings are particularly noteworthy. Your review of the findings should start with the overarching findings, and then move on to the details.

TIE UP LOSE ENDS

Go back to the beginning. Make sure you address every issue you raised at the beginning of your research (Exercise 2). In some cases, the issues raised at the outset of your analysis can simply be repeated in the conclusions, but with all the answers inserted, as in (2).

(2)
a. We now return to the question of the origin of these rules ... (Poplack and Tagliamonte 1994)
b. The hypothesis informing this project is that ... (Poplack and Tagliamonte 1991: 331)

WHAT IS THE EXPLANATION?

The next step is to offer a plausible explanation for the results that you have reported. What can account for the facts and what can be ruled out, as in (3)?

(3)
... raises the question of the type of sociolinguistic scenario that may have led to the current state of affairs. (Poplack and Tagliamonte 1991: 332)

Your explanation should establish the link between the (socio)linguistic issue and the social, historical, economical or other external context.

ADDRESS OBJECTIONS

Address objections that could be raised by your interpretations. It is often the case that these are the very questions that could be (or were!) asked at presentation of your research, either at a conference, to a department or to a class. Remember to record such questions. Build these directly into the argumentation in your discussion section, as in (4).

(4)
a. It may be objected that at least one of the shared patterns is universal ... (Poplack and Tagliamonte 1991: 331)
b. How can these results be interpreted in terms of the objections raised by X ... ? (Poplack and Tagliamonte 2005: 218)

Readers of your paper will undoubtedly think of the same question(s) and you will have answered them, providing a step-by-step argumentation that can make your case effectively.

THE WEAKEST LINK?

Every argument, every explanation, will have some components that are stronger than others. Be upfront about the bits that are weaker. If one part of your explanation is based on relatively little evidence, mitigate your suggestions about it. If an explanation is speculative, say so, as in (5).

(5)
Given the difficulty of reconstructing the conditioning of a variable process which has now basically gone to completion, this suggestion remains speculative. (Poplack and Tagliamonte 1989: 77)

Readers hate it when your language is overly confident. A good way to make sure your wording has the ideal tone is to write your discussion and conclusions freely, then go back and remove all the intensifiers, adverbs and adjectives.

Tip

Every one of us will tend toward a set of favourite words when describing their findings. My students once had a T-shirt made for me with this written on it: 'Striking, yet vanishingly rare'. It was a hilarious inside joke ... at my expense! If you catch yourself overusing certain words, make it a practice to search for them in your writing and use a thesaurus to find suitable new ones. Nowadays, I try not to rely on the same overused words; I even try to use a few new words every once in a while.

METHODOLOGICAL DEVELOPMENTS

Papers written in the tradition of variation analysis often contain detailed methodological techniques, which at times innovate beyond what has gone before. Numerous papers in the field are entirely methodological, whether in their in-depth exploration of particular aspects of the methodology, e.g. interaction (Sigley 2003), constraints (Horvath and Horvath 2003), circumscribing the variable context (Blake 1994), or even developing new techniques (Sankoff and Rousseau 1989, Guy 1991b). When the particular methodological twists of an analysis hold intrinsic interest, it is fitting to state the relevance of the method in addition to the research findings. This adds to the ongoing evolution and development of the field itself.

CONTEXTUALISE YOUR RESULTS

Perhaps the most important component of integrating your findings and your explanation is to contextualise them. How do they fit in (or not) with research that has gone before? In other words, you should strive to embed your research within the prevailing research on the same topic. Discuss the relevance of your research within the literature where its implications lie. This is perhaps the most meaningful aspect of the research enterprise – making it relevant.

The first step in synthesis is to be able to situate your research vis-à-vis other research on the same topic. To do this you have to have read and digested everything you can find on your topic so that you can cite the *relevant* findings. Do not simply cite a research paper because the topic is the same as your own or targets the same variety. Instead, cite the specific and singular *findings* of that paper which impinge on your own. Find the bits that matter. Make the link. Record the exact page numbers, figure or table. Your ability to situate and interpret beyond the analysis itself is an emblem of excellence.

Tip

After you read a paper, write down what its implications are for your own research. Put them in a spot where you can go back and understand how that analysis fits with your own when you are writing your conclusions.

PROJECTING INTO THE FUTURE

No piece of research can do it all, and few analyses are ever done without the analyst realising that there is still something else that could be done. This is the perfect opportunity to assess where the research could most profitably be taken next, as in (6).

(6)
a. ... the findings of this study suggest that further research on *be like* ... will be a good place to look for, and 'catch', the burgeoning global 'mega trends' of language change. (Tagliamonte and Hudson 1999: 168)
b. How many more similarities to be found, both within Britain and elsewhere, will be profitable areas to explore in future research. Indeed, the nuances of community differences revealed in these data may provide important evidence in further broad cross-community comparisons. (Tagliamonte et al. 2005: 106)

Whether or not you are the one to take these steps is not important. In framing your research like this, you position it usefully in ongoing developments to come.

PULLING IT ALL TOGETHER

Finally, you get to the denouement. This is the time for the broad perspective, the forest. It is the stage when you abstract away from the trees, the individual findings, the numbers, the different analyses and all the bits. It is the time to see the vista. It is now incumbent on you to digest the material and tell a story. Of course, there is a delicate balance between the story and the evidence. Some papers in the literature tell a great story, but where is the evidence? Similarly, some papers have loads of evidence, but not much of a story. A good research paper should have it all: cogent argumentation, solid evidence and a chronologically ordered, unfolding narrative, which may even contain conflict, climax and resolution. In your conclusions, your evidence should be woven into the argumentation like gold filament on a tapestry.

Every good story should end with the most important point. Conclude with this general statement. Make it succinct and comprehensible. You want your audience to remember it. The ideal strategy for developing your story is to tell it. This is one of the reasons why researchers make oral presentations – to get feedback. In the next section, I review some pointers about how to present your research to an audience.

MAKING AN ORAL PRESENTATION

Perhaps the most judicious decision in presenting your research is deciding what is important and what is not. In other words, what encapsulates your research and what can be left for the written document? Most talks are approximately twenty minutes, with ten minutes for questions. Some talks are shorter, usually fifteen minutes, although ten is not unusual, and few talks are more than twenty. How do you fit everything in? The simple answer is, you cannot. You will only have time to introduce enough information to enable your audience to understand the issue(s) and to highlight the major findings. Think of an oral presentation as an advertisement for your research.

The first step is to organise your material. A presentation, *aka* talk, should be comprehensible, accessible and well structured. This requires that you do not try to cover too many points. Hone the findings down to one or two major ones. Eliminate detail. Keep moving forward along a well-developed plan. One of the worst pitfalls of presenting research is never getting to the results. My own rule of thumb is to take approximately three minutes to set up the argument. Summarise the main points. Be concrete and specific. Another way to conceive of your presentation is that it is a story, but it must be a story with a point. However, because it is a narrative of sorts, you can (and should) create suspense and, if you can, humour. Conclude by providing a sense of completion. Round up the results with a finale.

Of course, no talk should be without a foundation of originality. The results and your interpretation of them must be novel and interesting. However, this is the thing that should already be in place *before* the talk. Ask yourself this question: If I had to summarise the relevance of my talk in two sentences, what would I say? Be sure these important sentences make it into the talk.

Academic prowess is not required to ensure effectiveness of your technical presentation. This is just a matter of attention to detail and practice. Decide in advance whether you will use transparencies (overheads), handouts, audio-tapes, PowerPoint, etc. Make sure that your audience can see your visual aids. By this, I mean big fontsizes. Go to the back of a room, and check to make sure you can read what is projected on to the screen. Keep your handouts, transparencies (overheads), slides and other aids as legible and simple as possible. A lot of different sizes and colours of fonts is too distracting and cluttered. Remember that white space is just as important as writing, tables, figures, etc. Finally – and perhaps most important – timing! Practise and make sure your talk fits into the allotted time.

Tip

Make sure your handout and your transparencies (overheads, slides) contain comprehensible information, i.e. no short forms or acronyms. No one in the audience will understand them!

Finally, finally – communication skills. Your demeanour, voice quality and ability to field questions are vital components of a good presentation. In fact, research suggests that this may be all your audience remembers. Impressions are everything. Good communicators know that eye contact, facial expressions, body language, intonation, etc. make the difference. A number of things to attend to are the following: How loud is your voice? Adjust the level to the situation. Control the rate and pitch of your voice, enunciate, emphasise and pause wherever this fits with your message. Remember to breathe.

Many people find it scary to talk in public. The only way around this is by systematic desensitisation. However, there are a number of good ways to reduce stage fright. Employ the age-old strategy of peer review. Enlist help from your friends and colleagues. Get them to tell you what they think. Another possibility is to video-tape yourself, or to talk in front of a mirror. At the very least, rehearse. I have spent many early mornings locked in the bathroom of the conference hotel talking to myself in the mirror!

Responding to your audience is also an important component of research presentation. Questions from your audience may take many different forms, but most call for elaboration and explanation. When you reply, your answer should be specific, succinct and courteous: 1) rephrase the question, 2) give a brief historical review, then 3) provide the information or explanation that was called for. If you don't know the answer, say so, and thank the person for a provocative question.

Tip

Whenever anyone asks you a question or makes a comment about your research, write down: 1) the question/comment; and 2) the person who asked/commented. You will need this information later on to incorporate into the written version of your paper.

Finally, finally, finally – make sure you avoid what I refer to as the 'so what' factor – in the audience's opinion, not yours! When it comes to your conclusions, take another opportunity to make a memorable statement. Issue a challenge or an appeal to your listeners. Summarise your major points or ideas. Cite a choice quotation. Epitomise the point with an illustration. Express your own intention or endorsement. When you are finished, nod, say, 'Thank you', or end with a flourish. Your audience needs to know conclusively that you have finished your talk and that they can now ask questions.

FINALE

In conclusion, this book records the scholarly traditions and methods of variation analysis as I know and practise them. You have all the tools you need to do it yourself now. In the process I wish you the thrill of discovery, the satisfaction of taking on a problem and figuring it out, and all the fun I know you can have along the way. The data are waiting.

Exercise 12: Writing a research paper

The purpose of this exercise is to write a variation analysis paper. Your written paper should contain some or all of the following sections. Use it as a model.

1.0 Introduction (follow format in Exercise 2)
1.1 The (socio)linguistic issue(s)
1.2 The data and its relevance to 1.1

2.0 Data and method
2.1 Data
    2.1.1 Description of the corpus (Exercise 2)
    2.1.2 Sample design with justification
    2.1.3 Overview of linguistic features in the data (possibly some inclusion of Exercises 3 and 4)
2.2 Circumscribing the variable context (Exercise 5)
    2.2.1 Introduce your linguistic variable
    2.2.2 Definition of the variable context
    2.2.3 Exceptional distributions

3.0 Situating the linguistic variable (follow format in Exercises 5 and 6)
    3.1.1 Previous analyses
    3.1.2 Synchronic and/or diachronic perspective
    3.1.3 Discussion and critical commentary of previous research
    3.1.4 Formulation of hypotheses

4.0 Coding and analysis
4.1 Describe and justify your coding schema (follow format in Exercise 6)
4.2 Lay out the claims in the literature
4.3 State your own hypotheses

5.0 Results (from Exercises 7, 8, 9 and 10)
5.1 Distributional analysis (Exercise 9)
    5.1.1 An overall distribution of the linguistic feature
    5.1.2 A factor by factor distributional analysis
    5.1.3 Cross-tabulation of factors where relevant
5.2 Multivariate analysis (Exercises 10 and 11)
    5.2.1 Multivariate analysis tables
    5.2.2 Any additional analysis
5.3 Summarise your findings

6.0 Discussion
    6.1.1 Interpret your findings and explain them
    6.1.2 What are the implications?
    6.1.3 Make projections for further research

7.0 Conclusions
7.1 Synthesise your findings and embed them meaningfully in the field

Glossary of terms

application	occurrence of a variable rule
application value	variant defined as the outcome of the variable rule
binomial one step	type of variable rule analysis in which all groups and all cells are treated at the same time
binomial step-up/step-down	type of variable rule analysis in which computations are done one step at a time with different configurations of factor groups
cell file	input to the variable rule program; contains the factor groups and factors in each group and how many of each cell occurred in the data
chi-square	test statistic, the sum of the squares of observed values minus expected values divided by the expected values
circumscribe (or define) the variable context	the process of determining which forms may be considered variants of each other (i.e. a variable) and in which contexts
coding schema, coding instructions, coding system	a set of hypotheses about a factor group constraining a linguistic variable, and their relevant categories
coding string	the alphabetic and numeric codes corresponding to the factor groups and factors coded into the token file
collapse factors	the process of combining two or more factors into one factor
collocation	a strong tendency for two separate items to occur side by side
concordance	an alphabetical listing of words in the context in which they occurred
condition file	the list of instructions (in a LISP list) to the variable rule program as to how the data are to be configured

263

consent form	document that contains an interviewee's written consent to be audio-recorded and/or participate in a research project
convergence	when a certain degree of accuracy is reached in one of the iterations of a step-up/step-down variable rule analysis
cross-tabulate	analysis which shows how two factors are related
cross-variety comparison	comparison that involves more than one variety
degrees of freedom	number of adjustable parameters of a model
dependent variable	feature that alternates (i.e. varies) when some independent variable changes
disfavour	in probabilistic terms this means 'it is not likely to occur'
distribution analysis	frequency, as a proportion, of each variant of the dependent variable
exceptional distributions	contexts of the dependent variable that are exceptional in one way or another
factor	independent variable (i.e. factor group) or a category within an independent variable
factor by factor analysis	analysis that considers each independent variable one at a time
factor group (FG)	independent variable
factor weight	values assigned by the variable rule program indicating the probability of rule application
favoured	in probabilistic terms, this means 'it is likely to occur'
friend of a friend	in social network analysis, a second-order contact, a person who plays an intermediary role in a community
independent variables	features that influence the dependent variable; independent variables can be external (e.g. sex, socioeconomic class, age) or internal (e.g. lexical item, clause type, semantic or syntactic features)
index	alphabetical listing of words
input, corrected mean	an overall measure of rule application
interaction	non-orthogonality, overlap in the intersection of factor groups
interview schedule	series of questions, ordered hierarchically by topic, used for conducting a sociolinguistic interview

iteration	one of the steps in the step-up/step-down analysis of the variable rule program; in each step the program finds the 'maximum likelihood' estimation of a set of factor weights to a certain degree of accuracy
KnockOut (KO)	value of 0 or 100 per cent in a cell
linguistic variable	feature of language that varies; simply stated, different ways of saying the same thing
LISP	high-level computer programming language in which statements and data are in the form of lists enclosed in parentheses
log likelihood	measure of the goodness of fit of an analysis; figures closer to zero represent better models than those further removed from zero
logit, logit of the percentage	mathematical feature underlying the variable rule program
marginals, comparison of marginals	frequencies and percentages of the variant forms in the data, according to independent variable(s)
maximum likelihood	as estimation of the probability that the model matches the observed distribution of the data
multiple regression	type of statistical model that addresses the relationship among multiple variables
networks	group of individuals that are socially linked
no-re-code	condition file that configures all factor groups as is, without modification
non-application	context in which a variable rule does not apply
non-orthogonal	non-independent factor groups; this means that they may be subgroups or super-categories of each other
Ns	number of tokens in a cell
orthogonal (factor groups)	independent factor groups; this means they should not be subgroups of each other or super-categories of each other
orthographic transcription	transcription that employs standard orthography for words
overall distribution	frequency of each variant of the dependent variable with no other consideration
principle of accountability	a methodological axiom; all contexts of a variable must be taken into account, including all contexts in which the variants occurred, as well as those in which they could have occurred but did not

probability (in language)	idea of choice, or options, in language use
probability (in variable rule analysis)	factor weights assigned by the variable rule analysis
proportion	frequency of a variant expressed in terms of percentage, i.e. how many occurrences out of a total number of relevant contexts
re-code	configuration of a condition file which modifies it from a no-re-code and leads to a different 'view' of the data
results file	file that contains the results of the comparison of marginals and variable rule analysis
run (re-run) the data	computation performed by the variable rule program, i.e. a comparison of marginals or variable rule analysis of a dataset
singleton	single instance
statistical significance	results were not produced by chance; the variable program assesses statistical significance at the .05 level
step-up/step-down analysis	type of variable rule analysis in which computations are done one step at a time with different configurations of factor groups
token	instance of a linguistic variable, an example
token file	file containing the data for a variable rule analysis, including the coding strings, reference markers and contexts
transcription protocol	record of how conversational data has been transcribed
variable, see linguistic variable	
variable rule analysis	type of multivariate analysis which uses the logit additive model in which many independent factors can be treated simultaneously
variable rules	mathematical construct mirroring the systematic choice mechanism of language

References

Tri-council policy statement: ethical conduct for research involving humans, 1998 (with 2000, 2002 updates). http://www.pre.ethics.gc.ca/english/policystatement/policystatement.cfm

Ball, Catherine. (1996). A diachronic study of relative markers in spoken and written English. *Language Variation and Change*. 8(2): 227–58.

Baugh, John. (1980). *Black street speech: its history, structure and survival*. Austin: University of Texas Press.

Bayley, Robert. (2002). The quantitative paradigm. In *The handbook of language variation and change*. J. K. Chambers, Peter Trudgill and Natalie Schilling-Estes (eds), Malden and Oxford: Blackwell Publishers. 117–41.

Beal, Joan, Corrigan, Karen and Moisl, Hermann (eds). (to appear a). *Using unconventional digital language corpora*, vol. I, *Synchronic corpora*. Basingstoke: Palgrave Macmillan.

(to appear b). *Using unconventional digital language corpora*, vol. II, *Diachronic corpora*. Basingstoke, Hampshire: Palgrave Macmillan.

Beals, Katharine, Denton, Jeannette, Knippen, Robert, et al. (eds). (1994). *CLS 30: Papers from the 30th regional meeting of the Chicago Linguistic Society: the parasession on variation in linguistic theory*. Chicago: Chicago Linguistic Society.

Bell, Allan. (1999). Styling the other to define the self: a study in New Zealand identity making. *Journal of Sociolinguistics*. 3(4): 523–41.

Bickerton, Derek. (1975). *Dynamics of a creole system*. New York: Cambridge University Press.

Blake, Renée. (1994). Resolving the don't count cases in the quantitative analysis of the copula in African American Vernacular English. Paper presented at Stanford University.

Boas, David, Meyerhoff, Miriam and Nagy, Naomi. (2002). *Goldsearch*. Durham, NH: English Department, University of New Hampshire.

Cameron, Deborah. (1990). Demythologizing sociolinguistics: why language does not reflect society. In *Ideologies of language*. John E. Joseph and Talbot J. Taylor (eds), London and New York: Routledge. 79–93.

Cedergren, Henrietta J. and Sankoff, David. (1974). Variable rules: performance as a statistical reflection of competence. *Language*. 50(2): 333–55.

Chambers, J. K. (2003). *Sociolinguistic theory: linguistic variation and its social significance*. Malden and Oxford: Blackwell Publishers.

Chomsky, Noam. (1957). *Syntactic structures*. The Hague: Mouton.

Cornips, Leonie and Corrigan, Karen (eds). (2005). *Syntax and variation: reconciling the biological and the social*. Amsterdam: John Benjamins.

Coupland, Nikolas and Jaworski, Adam. (1997). Introduction. In *Sociolinguistics: a reader*. Nikolas Coupland and Adam Jaworski (eds), New York: St Martin's Press. 1–3.

Cukor-Avila, Patricia. (1995). The evolution of AAVE in a rural Texas community: an ethnolinguistic study. Ph.D. dissertation, University of Michigan.

Cukor-Avila, Patricia and Bailey, Guy. (2001). The effects of the race of the interviewer on sociolinguistic fieldwork. *Journal of Sociolinguistics*. 5: 254–70.

Curme, George O. (1947). *English grammar*. New York: Barnes and Noble.

D'Arcy, Alexandra. (2005). Like: syntax and development. Ph.D. dissertation, University of Toronto.

Denison, David. (1998). Syntax. In *The Cambridge history of the English language, 1776–present day* vol. IV. Suzanne Romaine (ed.), Cambridge: Cambridge University Press. 92–329.

Eckert, Penelope. (2000). *Language variation as social practice*. Oxford and Malden: Blackwell Publishers.

Fasold, Ralph. (1972). *Tense marking in Black English: a linguistic and social analysis*. Washington, DC: Center for Applied Linguistics.

Feagin, Crawford. (2002). Entering the community: fieldwork. In *The handbook of language variation and change*. J. K. Chambers, Peter Trudgill and Natalie Schilling-Estes (eds), Malden and Oxford: Blackwell Publishers. 20–39.

Godfrey, Elisabeth and Tagliamonte, Sali A. (1999). Another piece for the verbal -s story: evidence from Devon in southwest England. *Language Variation and Change*. 11(1): 87–121.

Guy, Gregory R. (1988). Advanced varbrul analysis. In *Linguistic change and contact*. Kathleen Ferrara, Becky Brown, Keith Walters and John Baugh (eds), Austin, TX: Department of Linguistics, University of Texas at Austin. 124–36.

(1991a). Contextual conditioning in variable lexical phonology. *Language Variation and Change*. 3(2): 223–39.

(1991b). Explanation in variable phonology: an exponential model of morphological constraints. *Language Variation and Change*. 3(1): 1–22.

(1993). The quantitative analysis of linguistic variation. In *American dialect research*. Dennis Preston (ed.), Amsterdam and Philadelphia: John Benjamins. 223–49.

Hoenigswald, Henry M. (1960). *Language change and linguistic reconstruction*. Chicago: University of Chicago Press.

Hopper, Paul J. and Traugott, Elizabeth Closs. (1993). *Grammaticalization.* Cambridge: Cambridge University Press.

Horvath, Barbara M. and Horvath, Ronald J. (2003). A closer look at the constraint hierarchy: order, contrast, and geographical scale. *Language Variation and Change.* 15(2): 143–70.

Ito, Rika and Tagliamonte, Sali A. (2003). *Well weird, right dodgy, very strange, really cool:* layering and recycling in English intensifiers. *Language in Society.* 32(2): 257–79.

Jespersen, Otto H. (1909/1949). *A modern English grammar on historical principles: part vi: morphology.* London: George Allen and Unwin Ltd.

Jones, Megan and Tagliamonte, Sali A. (2004). From Somerset to Samaná: Pre-verbal *did* in the voyage of English. *Language Variation and Change.* 16(2): 93–126.

Kroch, Anthony S. (1989). Reflexes of grammar in patterns of language change. *Language Variation and Change.* 1(3): 199–244.

Krug, Manfred. (1998). *Gotta* – the tenth central modal in English? Social, stylistic and regional variation in the British national corpus as evidence of ongoing grammaticalization. In *The major varieties of English,* vol. I. Hans Lindquist, Staffan Klintborg, Magnus Levin and Maria Estling (eds), Växjö: Växjö University. 177–91.

Laberge, Suzanne. (1980). The changing distribution of indefinite pronouns in discourse. In *Language use and the uses of language.* Roger W. Shuy and Anna Shnukal (eds), Washington, DC: Georgetown University Press. 76–87.

Labov, William. (1963). The social motivation of a sound change. *Word.* 19: 273–309.

(1966/1982). *The social stratification of English in New York City.* Washington, DC: Center for Applied Linguistics.

(1969a). Contraction, deletion, and inherent variability of the English copula. *Language.* 45(4): 715–62.

(1969b). The logic of non-standard English. In *Georgetown monographs on languages and linguistics 22.* John Alatis (ed.), Washington, DC: Georgetown University Press. 1–44.

(1970). The study of language in its social context. *Studium Generale.* 23(1): 30–87.

(1971). Some principles of linguistic methodology. *Language in Society.* 1(1): 97–120.

(1972a). *The design of a sociolinguistic research project.* Report of the Sociolinguistics Workshop, Central Institute of Indian Languages.

(1972b). *Language in the inner city.* Philadelphia: University of Pennsylvania Press.

(1972c). *Sociolinguistic patterns.* Philadelphia: University of Pennsylvania Press.

(1973). *Sample questionnaire used by the project on linguistic change and variation.* University of Pennsylvania, 1 March 1973.

(1982). Building on empirical foundations. In *Perspectives on historical linguistics*. Winfred P. Lehmann and Yakov Malkiel (eds), Amsterdam and Philadelphia: John Benjamins. 17–92.

(1984). Field methods of the project on linguistic change and variation. In *Language in use: readings in sociolinguistics*. John Baugh and Joel Sherzer (eds), Englewood Cliffs, NJ: Prentice-Hall. 28–54.

(1994). *Principles of linguistic change*, vol. I, *Internal factors*. Cambridge and Oxford: Blackwell Publishers.

(2001). *Principles of linguistic change*, vol. II, *Social factors*. Malden and Oxford: Blackwell Publishers.

(to appear). Quantitative reasoning in linguistics. In *Sociolinguistics/ Soziolinguistik*. U. Ammon, N. Dittmar, K. Mattheier and Peter Trudgill (eds), Berlin: Mouton De Gruyter. http://www.ling.upenn.edu/~wlabor/ home.html

Labov, William, Cohen, Paul, Robins, Clarence, et al. (1968). *A study of the non-standard English of Negro and Puerto Rican speakers in New York City*. Final report, Co-operative Research Report 3288, vol. I. US Regional Survey.

Labov, William and Waletzky, Joshua. (1967). Narrative analysis: oral versions of personal experience. In *Essays on the verbal and visual arts*. June Helm (ed.), Seattle: University of Washington Press. 12–44.

Lavandera, Beatriz R. (1978). Where does the sociolinguistic variable stop? *Language in Society*. 7(2): 171–83.

(1982). Le principe de réinterprétation dans la théorie de la variation. In *Die soziolinguistik in romanischsprachigen Ländern/La sociolinguistique dans les pays de langue romane*. Norbert Dittmar and Brigitte Schlieben-Lange (eds), Tübingen: Gunter Narr Verlag. 87–95.

Macaulay, Ronald K. S. (1976). Social class and language in Glasgow. *Language in Society*. 5: 173–88.

(1991). 'Coz it izny spelt when they say it': displaying dialect in writing. *American Speech*. 66(3): 280–91.

Martin, Stefan and Wolfram, Walt. (1998). The sentence in African-American Vernacular English. In *African-American English*. Salikoko Mufwene, John Rickford, Guy Bailey and John Baugh (eds), London and New York: Routledge. 11–36.

Meechan, Marjory and Foley, Michele. (1994). On resolving disagreement: linguistic theory and variation – there's bridges. *Language Variation and Change*. 6(1): 63–85.

Meillet, Antoine. (1967). *The comparative method in historical linguistics*. Paris: Librairie Honoré Champion.

Milroy, James. (1992). *Linguistic variation and change*. Oxford: Blackwell Publishers.

Milroy, Lesley. (1980). *Language and social networks*. Baltimore, MD: University Park Press.

(1987). *Observing and analysing natural language*. Oxford: Blackwell Publishers.

Milroy, Lesley and Gordon, Matthew. (2003). *Sociolinguistics: method and interpretation*. Malden and Oxford: Blackwell Publishers.

Murray, James A. H. (1873). *The dialect of the southern counties of Scotland: its pronunciation, grammar and historical relations*. London: Philological Society.

Nevalainen, Terttu. (1997). The processes of adverb derivation in late middle and early modern English. In *Grammaticalization at work: studies of long term developments in English*. Matti Rissanen, Merja Kytö and Kirsi Heikkonen (eds), Berlin and New York: Mouton de Gruyter. 145–89.

Nevalainen, Terttu and Raumolin-Brunberg, Helena. (2003). *Historical sociolinguistics: language change in Tudor and Stuart England*. Harlow, Essex: Pearson Education Limited.

Paolillo, John. (2002). *Analyzing linguistic variation: statistical models and methods*. Stanford, CA: CSLI Publications.

Paradis, Claude. (1996). Interactional conditioning of linguistic heterogeneity. In *Towards a social science of language*, vol. II, *Social interaction and discourse structures*. Gregory R. Guy, Crawford Feagin, Deborah Schiffrin and John Baugh (eds), Amsterdam and Philadelphia: John Benjamins. 115–33.

Payne, Arvilla. (1976). The acquisition of the phonological system of a second dialect. Ph.D. dissertation, University of Pennsylvania.

Pintzuk, Susan. (1995). Variation and change in old English clause structure. *Language Variation and Change*. 7(2): 229–60.

Poplack, Shana. (1979). Function and process in a variable phonology. Ph.D. dissertation, University of Pennsylvania.

(1989). The care and handling of a megacorpus: the Ottawa-Hull French project. In *Language change and variation*. Ralph Fasold and Deborah Schiffrin (eds), Amsterdam and Philadelphia: John Benjamins. 411–44.

(1993). Variation theory and language contact. In *Variation theory and language contact: American dialect research*. Dennis Preston (ed.), Amsterdam and Philadelphia: John Benjamins. 251–86.

(ed.). (2000). *The English history of African American English*. Malden and Oxford: Blackwell Publishers.

Poplack, Shana and Meechan, Marjory. (1998). Introduction: how languages fit together in codemixing: instant loans, easy conditions: the productivity of bilingual borrowing. *Journal of Bilingualism*. 2(2) (special issue): 127–38.

Poplack, Shana and Tagliamonte, Sali A. (1989). There's no tense like the present: verbal -s inflection in Early Black English. *Language Variation and Change*. 1(1): 47–84.

(1991). African American English in the diaspora: evidence from old-line Nova Scotians. *Language Variation and Change*. 3(3): 301–39.

(1993). African American English in the diaspora: evidence from old-line Nova Scotians. In *Focus on Canada*. Sandra Clarke (ed.), Amsterdam: John Benjamins. 109–50.

(1994). *-S* or nothing: marking the plural in the African American diaspora. *American Speech.* 69(3): 227–59.

(1998). Nothing in context: variation, grammaticization and past time marking in Nigerian Pidgin English. In *Changing meanings, changing functions: papers relating to grammaticalization in contact languages.* Philip Baker and Anand Syea (eds), Westminster: University of Westminster Press. 71–94.

(2001). *African American English in the diaspora: tense and aspect.* Malden: Blackwell Publishers.

(2005). Back to the present: verbal *-s* in the (African American) diaspora. In *Transported dialects: the legacies of non-standard colonial English.* Raymond Hickey (ed.), Cambridge: Cambridge University Press. 203–23.

Poplack, Shana, Tagliamonte, Sali A. and Eze, Ejike. (2000a). Reconstructing the source of early African American English plural marking: a comparative study of English and creole. In *The English history of African American English.* Shana Poplack (ed.), Malden and Oxford: Blackwell Publishers. 73–98.

Poplack, Shana, Van Herk, Gerard and Harvie, Dawn. (2000b). Ottawa historical grammar resource on English: unpublished documentation and user's manual. University of Ottawa.

Preston, Dennis. (1985). The li'l abner syndrome: written representations of speech. *American Speech.* 60(4): 328–36.

(1996). Variationist perspectives on second language acquisition. In *Second language acquisition and linguistic variation.* Robert Bayley and Dennis Preston (eds), Amsterdam and Philadelphia: John Benjamins. 1–45.

(2000). Mowr and mowr bayud spellin': confessions of a sociolinguist. *Journal of Sociolinguistics.* 4(4): 614–21.

Quirk, Randolph. (1957). Relative clauses in educated spoken English. *English Studies.* 38: 97–109.

Rand, David and Patera, Tatiana. (1992). Concorder. Computer program. Montreal: Centre de Recherches Mathématiques, University of Montreal. Version 1.1S.

Rand, David and Sankoff, David. (1990). Goldvarb 2.1: a variable rule application for the Macintosh. Montreal: Centre de Recherches Mathématiques, University of Montreal. Version 2. http://www.crm.umontreal.ca/~sankoff/GoldVarb_Eng.html

Rickford, John R. (1999). *African American Vernacular English.* Malden and Oxford: Blackwell Publishers.

Roberts, Ian and Rousseau, Anna. (2003). *Syntactic change: a minimalist approach to grammaticalization.* Cambridge: Cambridge University Press.

Robinson, John, Lawrence, Helen and Tagliamonte, Sali. (2001). Goldvarb 2001. Department of Language and Linguistic Science, University of York. http://www.york.ac.uk/depts/lang/webstuff/goldvarb/.

Rousseau, Pascale and Sankoff, David. (1978a). A solution to the problem of grouping speakers. In *Linguistic variation: models and methods.* David Sankoff (ed.), New York: Academic Press. 97–117.

(1978b). Advances in variable rule methodology. In *Linguistic variation: models and methods.* David Sankoff (ed.), New York: Academic Press. 57–69.

Sankoff, David. (1975). Varbrul 2. Unpublished program and documentation.

(1978). Probability and linguistic variation. *Synthèse.* 37: 217–38.

(1982). Sociolinguistic method and linguistic theory. In *Logic, methodology, philosophy of science.* L. Jonathan Cohen, Jerzy Los, Helmut Pfeiffer and Klaus Peter Podewski (eds), Amsterdam: North Holland/Warsaw: Polish Scientific. 677–89.

(1988a). Problems of representativeness. In *Sociolinguistics: an international handbook of the science of language and society.* Ulrich Ammon, Norbert Dittmar and Klaus J. Mattheier (eds), Berlin: Walter de Gruyter. 899–903.

(1988b). Sociolinguistics and syntactic variation. In *Linguistics: the Cambridge survey.* Frederick J. Newmeyer (ed.), Cambridge: Cambridge University Press. 140–61.

(1988c). Variable rules. In *Sociolinguistics: an international handbook of the science of language and society.* Ulrich Ammon, Norbert Dittmar and Klaus J. Mattheier (eds), Berlin: Walter de Gruyter. 984–97.

Sankoff, David and Labov, William. (1979). On the uses of variable rules. *Language in Society.* 8(2): 189–222.

Sankoff, David and Rousseau, Pascale. (1979). Categorical contexts and variable rules. In *Papers from the Scandinavian symposium on syntactic variation, Stockholm, May 18–19, 1979.* Sven Jacobson (ed.), Stockholm: Almqvist and Wiksell. 7–22.

(1989). Statistical evidence for rule ordering. *Language Variation and Change.* 1(1): 1–18.

Sankoff, David and Sankoff, Gillian. (1973). Sample survey methods and computer-assisted analysis in the study of grammatical variation. In *Canadian languages in their social context.* Regna Darnell (ed.), Edmonton: Linguistic Research Inc. 7–63.

Sankoff, David, Tagliamonte, Sali and Smith, Eric. (2005). Goldvarb X. Computer program. Department of Linguistics, University of Toronto, Canada. http://individual.utoronto.ca/tagliamonte/Goldvarb/GV_index.htm

Sankoff, David and Thibault, Pierrette. (1981). Weak complementarity: tense and aspect in Montreal French. In *Syntactic change,* vol. 25. B. B. Johns and D. R. Strong (eds), Ann Arbor: University of Michigan. 205–16.

Sankoff, Gillian. (1973). Above and beyond phonology in variable rules. In *New ways of analyzing variation in English.* Charles-James N. Bailey and Roger W. Shuy (eds), Washington, DC: Georgetown University Press. 44–62.

(1974). A quantitative paradigm for the study of communicative competence. In *Explorations in the ethnography of speaking.* Richard Bauman and Joel Sherzer (eds), Cambridge: Cambridge University Press. 18–49.

(ed.). (1980). *The social life of language*. Philadelphia: University of Pennsylvania Press.

Sankoff, Gillian and Cedergren, Henrietta. (1972). Some results of a sociolinguistic study of Montreal French. In *Linguistic diversity in Canadian society*. Regna Darnell (ed.), Edmonton: Linguistic Research Inc. 61–87.

Sankoff, Gillian and Thibault, Pierrette. (1980). The alternation between the auxiliaries *avoir* and *être* in Montréal French. In *The social life of language*. Gillian Sankoff (ed.), Philadelphia: University of Philadelphia Press. 311–45.

Shuy, Roger. (1983). Unexpected by-products of fieldwork. *American Speech*. 58(4): 345–58.

Shuy, Roger, Wolfram, Walt and Riley, William. (1968). *Field techniques in an urban language study*. Washington, DC: Center for Applied Linguistics.

Sigley, Robert. (2003). The importance of interaction effects. *Language Variation and Change*. 15(2): 227–53.

Smith, Jennifer. (2001). Ye ø na hear that kind o' things: negative *do* in Buckie. *English World-Wide* 21(2): 231–59.

Swan, Michael. (1995). *Practical English usage*. Oxford: Oxford University Press.

Tagliamonte, Sali A. (1997). 'The', [?], or t'other: uncovering the patterns of York English definite articles. Unpublished manuscript.

(1998). Was/were variation across the generations: view from the city of York. *Language Variation and Change*. 10(2): 153–91.

(2002). Comparative sociolinguistics. In *Handbook of language variation and change*. Jack Chambers, Peter Trudgill and Natalie Schilling-Estes (eds), Malden and Oxford: Blackwell Publishers. 729–63.

(2004). Someth[in]'s go[ing] on!: variable *ing* at ground zero. In *Language variation in Europe: papers from the second international conference on language variation in Europe, ICLAVE 2*. Britt-Louise Gunnarsson, Lena Bergström, Gerd Eklund, Staffan Fidell, Lise H. Hansen, Angela Karstadt, Bengt Nordberg, Eva Sundergren and Mats Thelander (eds), Uppsala, Sweden, 12–14 June 2003.

(2005). *So who? Like how? Just what?* Discourse markers in the conversations of young Canadians. *Journal of pragmatics* (special issue). 37(11): 1896–915.

(to appear a). Representing real language: consistency, trade-offs and thinking ahead! In *Using unconventional digital language corpora*, vol. I, *Synchronic corpora*. Joan Beal, Karen Corrigan and Hermann Moisl (eds), Basingstoke: Palgrave Macmillan.

(to appear b). 'So cool, right?': Canadian English entering the 21st century. *Canadian Journal of Linguistics* (special issue).

Tagliamonte, Sali A. and Hudson, Rachel. (1999). *Be like* et al. Beyond America: the quotative system in British and Canadian youth. *Journal of Sociolinguistics*. 3(2): 147–72.

Tagliamonte, Sali A. and Ito, Rika. (2002). Think *really* different: continuity and specialization in the English adverbs. *Journal of Sociolinguistics*. 6(2): 236–66.

Tagliamonte, Sali A. and Molfenter, Sonja. (2005). Kids in new contexts: acquiring a second dialect of the same language. Paper presented at Methods XII: the 12th international conference on methods in dialectology, Moncton, NB, 1–5 August 2005.

Tagliamonte, Sali A., Molfenter, Sonja and King, Matthew. (2004). Taking it to the streets! A sociolinguistic survey of old-line Toronto. Paper presented at New Ways of Analysing Variation 33, Ann Arbor, 1 Oct 2004.

Tagliamonte, Sali A. and Poplack, Shana. (1988). How Black English *past* got to the present: evidence from Samaná. *Language in Society*. 17(4): 513–33.

(1993). The zero-marked verb: testing the creole hypothesis. *Journal of Pidgin and Creole Languages*. 8(2): 171–206.

Tagliamonte, Sali A., Poplack, Shana and Eze, Ejike. (1997). Pluralization patterns in Nigerian Pidgin English. *Journal of Pidgin and Creole Languages*. 12(1): 103–29.

Tagliamonte, Sali A. and Roberts, Chris. (2005). So cool, so weird, so innovative! The use of intensifiers in the television series *Friends*. *American Speech*. 80(3): 280–300.

Tagliamonte, Sali A. and Smith, Jennifer. (2000). Old *was*; new ecology: viewing English through the sociolinguistic filter. In *The English history of African American English*. Shana Poplack (ed.), Oxford and Malden: Blackwell Publishers. 141–71.

(2005). No momentary fancy! The zero 'complementizer' in English dialects. *English Language and Linguistics*. 9(2): 1–21.

Tagliamonte, Sali A., Smith, Jennifer and Lawrence, Helen. (2005). No taming the vernacular! Insights from the relatives in northern Britain. *Language Variation and Change*. 17(2): 75–112.

(to appear). English dialects in the British isles in cross-variety perspective: a base-line for future research. In *Dialects across borders: selected papers from the 11th international conference on methods in dialectology, Joensuu, August 2002*. Markku Filppula, Juhani Klemola, Marjatta Palander and Esa Penttilä (eds), Amsterdam and Philadelphia: John Benjamins.

Tagliamonte, Sali A. and Temple, Rosalind. (2005). New perspectives on an ol' variable: (t,d) in British English. *Language Variation and Change*. 17(3): 281–302.

Taylor, Ann. (1994). The change from SOV to SVO in Ancient Greek. *Language Variation and Change*. 6(1): 1–37.

(to appear). The York–Toronto–Helsinki parsed corpus of Old English Prose. In *Using unconventional digital language corpora*, Vol. II, *Diachronic corpora*. Joan Beal, Karen Corrigan and Hermann Moisl (eds), Basingstoke: Palgrave Macmillan.

Temple, Rosalind. (2003). What is '-t,d deletion'? A new look at an old sociolinguistic variable. *Proceedings of the 15th International Congress of Phonetic Sciences*, Barcelona, 3–9 August 2003. 1835–8.

Trudgill, Peter. (1974). *The Social Differentiation of English in Norwich.* Cambridge: University of Cambridge Press.

(ed.). (1978). *Sociolinguistic patterns in British English.* London: Edward Arnold.

(1999). New-dialect formation and dedialectalisation: embryonic and vestigial variants. *Journal of English Linguistics.* 27(4): 319–27.

(2000). *Sociolinguistics: an introduction to language in society.* London: Penguin.

Warner, Anthony. (1993). *English auxiliaries: structure and history.* Cambridge: Cambridge University Press.

Weiner, Judith and Labov, William. (1983). Constraints on the agentless passive. *Journal of Linguistics.* 19(1): 29–58.

Weinreich, Uriel, Labov, William and Herzog, Marvin. (1968). Empirical foundations for a theory of language change. In *Directions for historical linguistics.* Winfred P. Lehmann and Yakov Malkiel (eds), Austin: University of Texas Press. 95–188.

Wolfram, Walt. (1969). *A sociolinguistic description of Detroit Negro speech.* Washington, DC: Center for Applied Linguistics.

(1991). The linguistic variable: fact and fantasy. *American Speech.* 66(1): 22–32.

(1993). Identifying and interpreting variables. In *American dialect research.* Dennis Preston (ed.), Amsterdam and Philadelphia: John Benjamins. 193–221.

Wolfram, Walt and Schilling-Estes, Natalie. (1995). Moribund dialects and the endangerment canon: the case of the Ocracoke brogue. *Language.* 71(4): 696–721.

Young, Robert and Bayley, Robert. (1996). Varbrul analysis for second language acquisition research. In *Second language acquisition and linguistic variation.* Robert Bayley and Dennis R. Preston (eds), Amsterdam: John Benjamins. 253–306.

Index

CPSIA information can be obtained at www.ICGtesting.com
Printed in the USA
LVOW11s2135101214

418209LV00001B/15/P

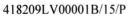